# Children of the French Empire

*Miscegenation and Colonial
Society in French West Africa
1895–1960*

OWEN WHITE

CLARENDON PRESS · OXFORD

# OXFORD
UNIVERSITY PRESS

Great Clarendon Street, Oxford OX2 6DP
Oxford University Press is a department of the University of Oxford.
It furthers the University's objective of excellence in research, scholarship,
and education by publishing worldwide in

Oxford New York

Athens Auckland Bangkok Bogotá Buenos Aires Calcutta
Cape Town Chennai Dar es Salaam Delhi Florence Hong Kong Istanbul
Karachi Kuala Lumpur Madrid Melbourne Mexico City Mumbai
Nairobi Paris São Paulo Singapore Taipei Tokyo Toronto Warsaw

and associated companies in Berlin Ibadan

Oxford is a registered trade mark of Oxford University Press
in the UK and certain other countries

Published in the United States
by Oxford University Press Inc., New York

British Library Cataloguing in Publication Data

Data available

Library of Congress Cataloging in Publication Data
White, Owen, Dr.
Children of the French empire : miscegenation and colonial society
in French West Africa, 1895–1960 / Owen White.
— (Oxford historical monographs)
Includes bibliographical references and index.
1. Racially mixed children—Africa, French-speaking West—
History—20th century. 2. Miscegenation—Africa, French-speaking
West—History—20th century. 3. Africa, French-speaking West—Race
relations. I. Title. II. Series.
HQ777.9.W53 2000 306.84'6—dc21 99–38791
ISBN 0 19 820819 7

1 3 5 7 9 10 8 6 4 2

Typeset by Graphicraft Limited, Hong Kong
Printed in Great Britain
on acid-free paper by
Bookcraft Ltd,
Midsomer Norton, Somerset

# ACKNOWLEDGEMENTS

Over a period of several years Robert Gildea has been unfailingly support-ive and helpful, first as supervisor of the Oxford D.Phil. thesis on which this book is based, and then as my sub-editor. Of the other friends and colleagues who read and commented on my work, I am especially grateful for the advice and encouragement of Megan Vaughan, Tony Kirk-Greene, Ruth Dickens, Amanda Sackur, and in particular my thesis examiners, John Hargreaves and Ruth Harris. In France I particularly appreciated the assistance of the staff of the Centre des Archives d'Outre-Mer in Aix-en-Provence, while in Senegal I was similarly grateful to the staff of the Archives Nationales du Sénégal, and to Babacar Sow and Lisa Washington Sow for their generous hospitality. This book would not have been written without the financial support of the British Academy. My final and most personal debt of thanks is to Patricia Sloane White, who throughout my time in Oxford has improved the quality both of my work and, more importantly, my life generally. Latterly she made sure I did not linger too long over the manuscript for this book; our wedding day turned out to be my final and happiest deadline.

# CONTENTS

# ABBREVIATIONS

| | |
|---|---|
| AEF | Afrique Équatoriale Française (French Equatorial Africa) |
| AMI | Assistance Médicale Indigène |
| ANS | Archives Nationales du Sénégal, Dakar |
| AOF | Afrique Occidentale Française (French West Africa) |
| AP | Affaires Politiques |
| CAOM | Centre des Archives d'Outre-Mer, Aix-en-Provence |
| CSC | Conseil Supérieur des Colonies |
| ENFOM | École Nationale de la France d'Outre-Mer |
| FM | Fonds Moderne |
| GG | Governor-General (of French West Africa unless stated) |
| HC | High Commissioner |
| IF | Institut de France, Paris |
| Lt.-G. | Lieutenant-Governor |
| RDA | Rassemblement Démocratique Africain |
| SG | Série Géographique |

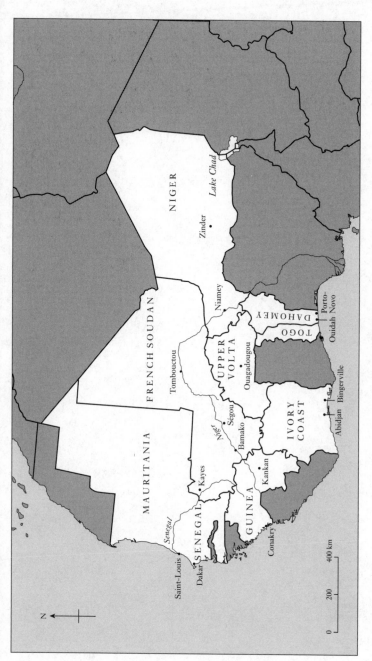

Map of French West Africa and Togo, c.1930

# Introduction

In 1902 a doctor from Bordeaux named Louis Joseph Barot published a guide for Europeans in West Africa. In many ways it was the *Lonely Planet* guide of its day, intended not just for tourists but also for colonial administrators, traders, soldiers, and settlers. Dr Barot was a practical man who had plied his profession on military expeditions in Guinea and the Ivory Coast, and his book was similarly down-to-earth: a 'survival kit', composed to a large degree of medical advice, along with such less apparently crucial information as the price of hammocks. But some of Barot's recommendations were more intimate. Certain European men, he knew, suffering the lack of European women in West Africa, would equally lack 'the moral strength necessary to endure two years of absolute continence'. In such cases, Barot could offer only one prescription: 'a temporary union with a well-chosen native woman.' For Barot, however, such unions were potentially useful to the French as they went about securing their influence in the region. 'It is by creating mulatto races', he concluded, 'that we most easily Gallicize West Africa.'[1]

When I first read Barot's remarks, what struck me most was how little his ideas seemed to have in common with what people in *fin-de-siècle* France itself were saying about sexual contact between the different peoples of the world. In metropolitan France the tendency was to associate *métissage*, meaning miscegenation or the interbreeding of people classified as belonging to different races, with cultural decline or 'racial degeneration'. I knew that other historians had already established that the notion of *métissage* was of great interest to the French.[2] However, the human, 'real-life' dimension to *métissage* remained largely absent in such histories. After all, it was clear that Barot was writing about something which was already taking place

[1] Dr Louis Joseph Barot, *Guide pratique de l'européen dans l'Afrique occidentale* (Paris, 1902), 328–31. The passage also appears in translation in John D. Hargreaves, *France and West Africa: An Anthology of Historical Documents* (London, 1969), 206–9; this was the source which first interested me in this subject.

[2] See e.g. Pierre-André Taguieff, 'Doctrines de la race et hantise du métissage: fragments d'une histoire de la mixophobie savante', *Nouvelle Revue d'Ethnopsychiatrie*, 17 (1991), 53–100; William B. Cohen, *The French Encounter with Africans: White Responses to Blacks, 1530–1880* (Bloomington, Ind., 1980); Robert Nye, 'Degeneration and the Medical Model of Cultural Crisis in the French Belle Epoque', in S. Drescher, D. Sabean, and A. Sharlin (eds.), *Political Symbolism in Modern Europe* (New Brunswick, NJ, 1982), 19–41.

—to the extent, indeed, that in 1902 two state-funded homes for *métis*, the children of *métissage*, already existed, one at Kita, one at Dinguira, in what is now Mali. 'Here for a modest sum,' wrote Barot, 'children of Europeans are brought up and taught manual trades, according to their aptitudes.'[3]

The main aim of this book, therefore, is to reconstruct the lives of the children mentioned in Barot's account during the period of French rule in West Africa. I have not paid much attention to the mixed-race communities first founded in the pre-colonial trading-posts of Senegal, especially Saint-Louis and Gorée, though from time to time these communities do form part of the story. Instead, I have chosen to focus on the offspring of 'temporary unions' between French men and African women from the period of French expansion across West Africa in the late nineteenth century until independence in 1960.

In doing this I have benefited from the fact that the 'métis problem', as it was often described, was regularly discussed by officials at all levels, leaving a trail of correspondence and reports through the archives of the federal government of French West Africa and the colonial ministry. Likewise, non-governmental organizations such as the Société d'Anthropologie de Paris had their own reasons for finding métis of interest, while many memoir-writers and individual travellers to French West Africa also saw fit to devote a few pages to the 'métis problem'. Given the origin of these sources, this book has much to say about French attitudes to métis and miscegenation, and attempts to locate these attitudes in a historical context. But the views of black Africans and métis themselves, though more difficult to discover in the written sources, particularly before the 1930s, also feature here.

Though the colonial authorities in West Africa were greatly preoccupied with the practical effects of *métissage*, some contemporary observers felt that these concerns were out of proportion to the numbers of métis involved. In 1944, for example, the head of the judiciary in French West Africa suggested that 'the métis problem, if one considers their tiny number in relation to the native mass in black Africa, has greater moral or sentimental significance than social significance'.[4] The 1938 census counted 3,437 'métis of European descent' in French West Africa among a population of approximately 14.5 million.[5] An upper figure of between 3,500 and 4,000 métis

---

[3] Barot, *Guide pratique*, 330–1. These institutions both feature in Ch. 2.

[4] Archives Nationales du Sénégal, Dakar (ANS), Fonds Moderne (FM): 17G 187, report for the Brazzaville Conference by Robert Attuly, 10 Jan. 1944.

[5] The figure 3,437 is composed of 2,752 métis with a French parent and 685 with a parent from some other European nation. See the supplement to *Le Monde Colonial Illustré*, 184 (Oct. 1938), p. xxix. French demographic knowledge of West Africa remained incomplete throughout the colonial period, making this perhaps not the most reliable of documents.

'of European descent' in French West Africa should serve as a rough guide for what follows. Explaining the French preoccupation with such a small section of the population in West Africa is one of the main objectives of this book.

Though small in overall number, métis could be found scattered across West Africa to the farthest limits of the French presence there. Though there had been a continuous French presence in coastal regions of West Africa since the seventeenth century, expansion into the interior did not generate significant momentum until the late 1870s, and even then progressed haphazardly.[6] Nevertheless, by the turn of the century France had taken control—despite areas of continued resistance—of a huge swathe of territory in West Africa. In broad outline, this included (or was soon to include) the modern states of Senegal, Guinea, the Ivory Coast, Benin, Burkina Faso, Mali, and Niger; in addition, French control over Mauritania was asserted over the next two decades.

Even as the process of what the French termed 'pacification' progressed, a federal structure was, in 1895, set up for the administration of France's acquisitions in West Africa. Local administrations in each colony were answerable to a governor-general, based from 1902 in Dakar. The structure evolved until, in 1904, French West Africa consisted of six colonies: Senegal, the Ivory Coast, Guinea, Dahomey (modern-day Benin), Upper Senegal and Niger (a huge territory, equating roughly to the modern states of Mali, Burkina Faso, and Niger), and Mauritania.[7] The greater part of the former German colony of Togo was acquired as a League of Nations mandate after the First World War.[8] In 1919 the colony of Upper Volta (now Burkina Faso) was created; in a further reorganization the following year, Upper Senegal and Niger was renamed the French Soudan,

[6] Innumerable studies have, of course, been written on the so-called 'scramble for Africa'. For a succinct introduction to the specific case of West Africa which also includes a useful bibliography, see John D. Hargreaves, 'The European partition of West Africa', in J. F. A. Ajayi and Michael Crowder (eds.), *History of West Africa*, ii (2nd edn., Harlow, 1987), 403–28; for more on the areas occupied by the French, see Catherine Coquery-Vidrovitch (ed.), *L'Afrique occidentale au temps des français* (Paris, 1992).

[7] On these developments see Alice Conklin, *A Mission to Civilize: The Republican Idea of Empire in France and West Africa, 1895–1930* (Stanford, 1997), in particular 11–51; also C. W. Newbury, 'The Formation of the Government General of French West Africa', *Journal of African History*, 1 (1960), 111–28; C. Harrison, T. B. Ingawa, and S. M. Martin, 'The Establishment of Colonial Rule in West Africa, c.1900–1914', in Ajayi and Crowder (eds.), *History of West Africa*, in particular 487–9.

[8] Togo was administered as part of French West Africa only between 1936 and 1945. Its mandate status, moreover, meant that the French did not have a wholly free hand in the administration of the territory. See J. F. A. Ajayi and Michael Crowder, 'West Africa 1919–1939: The Colonial situation', in id. (eds.), *History of West Africa*, 584.

while the military territory of Niger (administered separately since 1911) became a civil territory.[9]

Despite this centralized federal structure, French West Africa was in reality a rather ramshackle edifice. With the metropolitan government reluctant to offer much financial support to the federation, the administration had little financial room for manoeuvre, forced to rely on taxes levied from what were, by and large, already poor areas. The turnover of personnel was high, both in West Africa and in the colonial ministry in Paris; it has been stated that it is impossible to speak of the latter as representing 'a collective official mind'.[10] Moreover, it has been shown that, at least until the 1920s, the better students from the École Coloniale, which trained colonial administrators, tended to gravitate towards French Indochina, which promised better pay and more rapid promotion, in preference to black Africa.[11] With these problems of finance and manpower, and with little French settlement in West Africa,[12] local auxiliaries were constantly needed to assist in the administration of the federation. For this reason, as implied by Barot's remarks cited above, and as will be shown in detail later, there was considerable interest in métis for the services they were thought potentially able to provide the French.

Before breaking down the contents of the book, a few words are needed on some of the terminology used. Throughout the colonial period a number of different terms were applied to people born of unions between Europeans and Africans. The most common of these were *métis*, *mulâtre*, and *eurafricain*. I have finally chosen to use the word 'métis' as my main term of reference for such people (plural: métis; feminine form: métisse/s).[13] On occasion I use the term 'person of mixed race' to denote the same thing.[14] The word *mulâtre*, or mulatto, though it remained in use throughout the

---

[9] Upper Volta was dissolved in 1932, its territory divided between the Ivory Coast, the French Soudan, and Niger, but was re-established in 1947. I have preferred the term 'French Soudan' instead of 'Upper Senegal and Niger' in cases where both might have been applicable.

[10] Christopher M. Andrew and A. S. Kanya-Forstner, *France Overseas: The Great War and the Climax of French Imperial Expansion* (London, 1981), 21.

[11] William B. Cohen, *Rulers of Empire: The French Colonial Service in Africa* (Stanford, 1971), 46. The École Coloniale was renamed the École Nationale de la France d'Outre-Mer in 1934.

[12] The 1938 census revealed 16,396 French people in West Africa among a population of 14,713,748. See *Le Monde Colonial Illustré*, 184 (Oct. 1938), p. xxix.

[13] I have left this word unitalicized in the text. For an interesting etymological discussion, see Sylviane Albertan-Coppola, 'La Notion de métissage à travers les dictionnaires du XVIIIème siècle', in Jean-Claude Carpanin Marimoutou and Jean-Michel Racault (eds.), *Métissages*, i (Saint-Denis de la Réunion, 1992), 35–50.

[14] As Ian Goldin points out with reference to the specific case of South Africa in his excellent *Making Race: The Politics and Economics of Coloured Identity in South Africa* (London, 1987), p. xxvii, ' "Mixed race" implies the prior existence of "pure" race-groups and gives credence to apartheid notions of racial purity. No race exists which is not mixed.' While

colonial period, particularly in Senegal, is derived from the word 'mule' and carries connotations of sterility—something which métis were often thought to be among themselves. 'Métis' was the term most commonly used in French West Africa in the colonial period, by the subjects themselves as much as by other Africans or the French. In French Indochina there was some objection to the word. One administrator in Tonkin in 1938 stated that it was demeaning, as it was applied also to hybrids of different species of animal or types of material. He listed cases in which *eurasiens* —as they preferred to be called—had reacted violently to being called 'métis'.[15] Although some West African métis, as will be shown, began to use the term *eurafricain* from the 1940s, there does not appear to have been the same hostility to the word 'métis', and they continued to use the term to describe themselves. In any case, many métis, as will be shown, would not have chosen to describe themselves as *eurafricains*. In the end, it would have been historically misleading not to apply the term 'métis' to the people whose lives are described in this book.

Most West African métis were inauspiciously born of the temporary unions of convenience described by Dr Barot. Chapter 1 sketches a history of the contact between French men and African women which created a métis population in West Africa, comparing French attitudes and practices with those of other Europeans, and giving some idea of how such relationships were conducted across the federation and changed over time.

Chapters 2 and 3 shift the focus to the children born of such unions, describing how the French addressed the problem of what was to be done with them. Chapter 2 examines the thinking which led to the creation of special homes for métis children deemed to have been abandoned by their parents, set up first by missionaries and then, when the Third Republic's programme of laicization of education came to French West Africa, by the colonial administration itself. Chapter 3 focuses on the education offered to métis children in these so-called 'orphanages', and the types of employment they were encouraged to follow, presenting case studies of two such institutions to help illuminate the lives of the children brought up there.

The aim of Chapter 4 is to show how a widespread but essentially abstract interest in miscegenation in metropolitan France found a concrete expression in the treatment of métis in West Africa. Through an analysis

agreeing with Goldin's point, I found it necessary here on occasion to use some English alternative to the word 'métis'; though clumsy, I preferred 'person of mixed race' to the equally objectionable 'mulatto' or 'coloured'.

[15] Centre des Archives d'Outre-Mer, Aix-en-Provence (CAOM), Commission Guernut 97, 'Le Problème eurasien au Tonkin', 102–3.

of the work of a variety of writers and social scientists in the *métropole* from the mid-nineteenth century on, it suggests that the characteristics ascribed to métis often reflected French fears of cultural and racial decline. These stereotyped 'mixed-race characteristics', however, proved to be remarkably tenacious. I attempt to show how such ideas manifested themselves in French West Africa, and assess their practical impact.

The problem of identity is central to Chapter 5, which deals with the thorny question of the legal status of métis. It analyses the various debates which assessed the wisdom of allowing métis to seek confirmation of their 'Frenchness' through paternity suits or by facilitating their accession to French citizenship. The problem of citizenship for métis offers a chance to assess how far the French idea of 'assimilation', which held that France's colonial subjects could be fully integrated into French civilization, could ever be put into practice in a system which depended on maintaining distinctions between 'the rulers' and 'the ruled'.

While Chapters 1 to 5 are concerned primarily with French actions and attitudes, Chapter 6 offers a different perspective. The first section deals with black African attitudes to métis. The remainder of the chapter focuses on the point of view of métis themselves. Through case studies of a handful of individuals, and by describing the activities of voluntary associations set up by métis in French West Africa from the 1930s, it analyses the quest of métis for some viable sense of identity in a racially divided colonial society. In the Union des Eurafricains de l'AOF, an association which claimed to represent the interests of métis across French West Africa, it finds evidence of an educated, urbanized social grouping which was attempting—with a measure of success—to escape from the margins of colonial society to which many métis felt confined, and to play a fuller and more active social role during what proved to be the final years of French rule in West Africa.

# I

# Miscegenation in French West Africa

Sexual relations represented an important point of interracial contact between French and Africans from the seventeenth century, when French traders first established a permanent base on the coast of Senegal, right through the period of France's full-scale colonization of much of West Africa. This chapter will sketch a history of what the French called *métissage*: its practice, attitudes towards it, and its effects in the areas of West Africa under French control. In the process, it will draw attention to some of the complexities involved in writing about the subject, suggesting that interracial sexual relations in the colonies cannot be written about simply in terms of French strength and African powerlessness. The chapter serves as a backdrop to the rest of the book, which will concentrate on the most visible, if circumstantial, evidence for the extent of such relations: the children they produced. We begin, however, with the first arrival of Europeans in West Africa.

## MÉTISSAGE IN PRE-COLONIAL WEST AFRICA

European men sought out West African women as companions from the earliest days of their presence there. Portuguese settlers in coastal areas of Senegambia and Upper Guinea lived with African women from as early as the fifteenth century. The women who engaged in such relationships, it has been argued, tended to be well placed in local society, and used their links with the Portuguese traders to secure commercial privileges. The Portuguese influence in the region is testified by the term the French later applied to such women—*signares*, from the Portuguese word *senhoras*.[1]

In 1659 a permanent French trading post or *comptoir* was founded on the island of N'Dar, renamed Saint-Louis. The Compagnie du Sénégal,

---

[1] See George E. Brooks, Jr., 'The *Signares* of Saint-Louis and Gorée: Women Entrepreneurs in Eighteenth-Century Senegal', in Nancy J. Hafkin and Edna G. Bay (eds.), *Women in Africa: Studies in Social and Economic Change* (Stanford, 1976), 19–20. Malyn Newitt states that the Portuguese 'often claimed to make a positive virtue of miscegenation', in *Portugal in Africa: The Last Hundred Years* (London, 1981), 143.

which operated this post, recruited employees on three-year contracts. Around 80 per cent were men aged between 18 and 30. Links were rapidly formed with the local female population, despite frequent efforts by the Company to prevent them. In 1695, for example, the Company fenced off the Europeans' living quarters, instigated communal eating and obligatory prayer with the chaplain, and used guards to check that everyone was sleeping where they were supposed to be.[2]

These sanctions do not appear to have been successful. In fact, it soon became evident to all but the most dedicated moralists that interracial unions brought certain practical advantages. The *signares* could check that the young Frenchmen, often unused to taking care of themselves, maintained decent living standards: ensuring that they ate appropriate food, kept alcohol consumption to a minimum, wore well-aerated clothes covering the whole body, and lived in ventilated lodgings. They could also give access to and administer local medicines. In this way they stabilized the French community, and may have lessened the high mortality rates it suffered. *Métissage* could therefore be said to have been responsible for the survival not just of individuals, but also of the business interests these individuals represented. This stability may also have dissuaded Company employees from deserting and going into competition as private traders.[3]

In the 1720s the Governor of Senegal himself, Julien Dubellay, proposed that marriage between Company employees and local women should be permitted, but the scheme was rejected by the directors of the Compagnie du Sénégal in Paris.[4] Despite official disapproval, however, long-term unions with cohabitation remained common. By the mid-eighteenth century, writes George E. Brooks, '*signares* had attained considerable economic consequence and had contributed to creating a Senegalese life-style so attractive to Europeans that they refused to obey Company directives against cohabitation and commerce with African women'.[5]

[2] See Nathalie Reyss, 'Saint-Louis du Sénégal à l'époque précoloniale. L'émergence d'une société métisse originale, 1658–1854', Ph.D. thesis (Univ. of Paris I, 1983), 52; James F. Searing, *West African Slavery and Atlantic Commerce: The Senegal River Valley, 1700–1860* (Cambridge, 1993), 98–9.

[3] See John D. Hargreaves, 'Assimilation in Eighteenth-Century Senegal', *Journal of African History*, 6 (1965), 178–9; Amanda Sackur, 'The French Revolution and Race Relations in Senegal, 1780–1810', in J. F. Ade Ajayi and J. D. Y. Peel (eds.), *People and Empires in African History* (Harlow, 1992), 71; Brooks, 'The *Signares*', 41; Searing, *West African Slavery*, 96–8; Reyss, 'Saint-Louis du Sénégal', 52–4.

[4] Brooks, 'The *Signares*', 22.

[5] Ibid. 23. For more on the *signares*, see Searing, *West African Slavery*, 93–128; Yvonne Knibiehler and Regine Goutalier, *La Femme au temps des colonies* (Paris, 1985), 53–67.

Catholic marriages recognized by French law between French men and West African women were rare. More usual were 'mariages à la mode du pays' (marriages according to the customs of the country), marked with local rites and lasting for the duration of the European's stay in Africa.[6] High-ranking French officials sometimes engaged in such unions. François Blanchot, for example, during his second term of office as Governor of Senegal from 1802 to 1807, was legally married to a woman in France, yet still took an African woman as his wife in a *mariage à la mode du pays*. This union produced three daughters who took their father's surname; two of them went on to marry rich métis.[7] These types of relationship were embraced just as readily by the English during their occupations of Saint-Louis and the island of Gorée, as is testified by the establishment of long-surviving mixed-race families with names like Dodds, O'Hara, Patterson, and Armstrong.[8]

As this last fact implies, children resulting from these unions were often recognized as legitimate by their fathers. Many were baptized and given European names, and by inheriting their fathers' wealth virtual dynasties were often founded.[9] The departing European—who, as in Blanchot's case, may have been returning to a family in France—would often bequeath business interests to his sometime consort or children. In this way some *signares* came to acquire large fortunes and high prestige, becoming important slave-owners, and a métis society was created with economic power that continued at least until the mid-nineteenth century, and with political influence lasting beyond then.[10]

While it would be wrong to paint too rosy a picture of race relations in pre-colonial Senegal,[11] it would be equally unwise to ignore the possibility that *métissage* was mutually beneficial to French and Africans alike. A similar reciprocal relationship has been noted in the Canadian fur trade in the eighteenth and nineteenth centuries.[12] Brooks concludes that signareship was 'so advantageous and attractive to all involved, at least in Senegal, that it became self-perpetuating'.[13]

[6] Brooks, 'The *Signares*', 34–5.     [7] Reyss, 'Saint-Louis du Sénégal', 125.
[8] Saint-Louis was occupied by the English from 1758 to 1779 and again from 1809 to 1814. Gorée, which the French acquired from the Dutch in 1677, was under English control in 1693, 1758–63, 1779–83, and 1800–17.
[9] Reyss, 'Saint-Louis du Sénégal', 57.
[10] See ibid., and Brooks, 'The *Signares*', 38. The best account is Searing, *West African Slavery*, 93–128, which properly emphasizes the role of the *signares* in the slave trade. Other accounts, as Searing points out, have preferred to present overly picturesque portraits of pre-colonial Saint-Louis and Gorée; e.g. Jean-Pierre Biondi, *Saint-Louis du Sénégal* (Paris, 1987).
[11] For evidence of racial inequalities, see Sackur, 'The French Revolution and Race Relations'.
[12] See Ronald Hyam, *Empire and Sexuality: The British Experience* (Manchester, 1990), 95–8.
[13] Brooks, 'The *Signares*', 44.

In the nineteenth century, however, there were significant changes in the nature of the relationship between Europeans and Africans in Senegal. Following the French repossession of Senegal in 1817, local traders or *traitants*, many of whom were métis, began to lose out to commercial houses from Bordeaux in intensifying competition for the lucrative gum trade. Furthermore, the abolition of slavery in the French empire in 1848, as Madina Ly-Tall and David Robinson have observed, 'dramatically reduced the wealth, status and power of many of the larger *traitants* and thereby opened the way for more direct control of trade by the Bordelese'.[14] The end of the slave trade was, indeed, an economic disaster for the métis community of Senegal.[15] Though métis were prominent in local politics in Senegal at least until the First World War, new economic opportunities, for instance in the rapid growth in groundnut production, largely passed them by.[16]

This sense of economic and social transition is reflected in *Esquisses Sénégalaises*, a description published in 1853 of the peoples of Senegal by Abbé Boilat, a métis priest. In his section on 'les mulâtres', Boilat harked back to a Golden Age for the métis community, when, 'without much effort', the gum trade had yielded 'colossal fortunes', and 'all the families lived comfortably: gold glittered on the neck, ears, and arms of their wives, their daughters, their numerous servants; joy and happiness reigned everywhere.'[17] Excessive competition and declining gum prices in France, however, were financially ruining the métis community. Boilat now recommended young people to follow other careers: 'Let arts and crafts be more highly valued, and above all let us concern ourselves with culture.'[18]

The changes noted by Boilat became more obvious when Captain Louis Léon César Faidherbe became Governor of Senegal in 1854. Faidherbe's

---

[14] Madina Ly-Tall and David Robinson, 'The Western Sudan and the Coming of the French', in Ajayi and Crowder (eds.), *History of West Africa*, 353–4.

[15] Searing, *West African Slavery*, 163–7; also 185–6, detailing the compensation paid to slave-owners.

[16] Reyss, 'Saint-Louis du Sénégal', 188–9. For a study of the political influence of métis families in Senegal, see François Manchuelle, 'Métis et colons: la famille Devès et l'émergence politique des Africains au Sénégal, 1881–1897', *Cahiers d'Études Africaines*, 24 (1984), 477–504; also G. Wesley Johnson, *The Emergence of Black Politics in Senegal: The Struggle for Power in the Four Communes, 1900–1920* (Stanford, 1971).

[17] Abbé P.-D. Boilat, *Esquisses Sénégalaises* (Paris, 1853), 210. Searing locates Boilat's 'golden age' in the period 1763 to 1790; *West African Slavery*, 114. A similarly nostalgic tone pervades Frédéric Carrère and Paul Holle, *De la Sénégambie Française* (Paris, 1855), 16–17.

[18] Boilat, *Esquisses Sénégalaises*, 211; see also Carrère and Holle, *De la Sénégambie Française*, 353. On the gum trade in nineteenth-century Senegal see Searing, *West African Slavery*, 163–93.

rise to this position had much to do with the alliances he built with Bordelese merchants, whose economic ascendancy was confirmed during his two spells as Governor, from 1854 to 1861, and again from 1863 to 1865. Faidherbe followed a successful policy of military, diplomatic, and commercial expansion into mainland West Africa, was promoted to the rank of general, and merits his description as 'more than any other single individual, the architect of colonial Senegal'.[19]

Faidherbe likewise occupies a position of importance in the history of *métissage* in French West Africa, as he contracted a *mariage à la mode du pays* with a 15-year-old Khassonké girl, Dioucounda Sidibe. She was to be the last African wife to be kept openly in the Governor's palace. In February 1857 she gave birth to a son, baptized Louis Léon Faidherbe.[20]

The religious reformer Boilat wrote in 1853 that *mariages à la mode du pays* were immoral. He claimed they had fallen, in Saint-Louis at least, into 'contempt and dishonour'.[21] Unsurprisingly, Faidherbe encountered clerical opposition for his encouragement of such relationships. He vigorously defended his beliefs, and argued in 1855 that 'it is deplorable that we distance the native population from us'.[22] On the other hand, a leading member of the Saint-Louisian clergy claimed that Faidherbe had refused to allow a French officer legally to marry an African woman, on the grounds that this would bring dishonour to the officer's French family.[23]

The case of Faidherbe suggests that social relations in Senegal were changing in line with the expansion and increasing formalization of French power in West Africa. From Faidherbe's time onwards, with the slave trade abolished, people of mixed race appear mainly in the service of whites. Some became interpreters, or were used as intermediaries in Faidherbe's dealings with the kingdoms of the interior. Others, such as Paul Holle, who successfully commanded the defence of the French fort at Medine when it was besieged by al-Hajj Umar's army in 1857, made their careers in the military. Indeed, Faidherbe's own métis son was a sub-lieutenant in the marines when he died of yellow fever aged 24.[24]

[19] Ly-Tall and Robinson, 'The Western Sudan', 355.

[20] In 1858, Faidherbe married his 18-year-old niece; Louis Léon was brought up with the three children resulting from this marriage. See Alain Coursier, *Faidherbe 1818–1889: Du Sénégal à l'Armée du Nord* (Paris, 1989) 47–8, 101–2. For more on Faidherbe, see Leland C. Barrows, 'Louis Léon César Faidherbe (1818–1889)', in L. H. Gann and P. Duignan (eds.), *African Proconsuls: European Governors in Africa* (New York, 1978), 51–79.

[21] Boilat, *Esquisses Sénégalaises*, 209. Boilat was part of a missionary assault on customary marriage; see Searing, *West African Slavery*, 126, 164.

[22] Coursier, *Faidherbe*, 101–2.   [23] Ibid.

[24] Reyss, 'Saint-Louis du Sénégal', 188–9; Coursier, *Faidherbe*, 101.

Though Faidherbe was prepared to defend interracial unions, his hostility to the commercial privileges of the métis community of Saint-Louis suggests that race relations in Senegal were entering a new phase. It was one thing to keep a 15-year-old wife, quite another to compete economically with Africans on equal terms. Under Faidherbe, we can begin to see more clearly the assertion of imperial authority with its attendant unequal power relations. *Métissage* continued to play an integral part in colonial life, but henceforth its practice was enframed by the fact of French power.

MÉTISSAGE IN COLONIAL WEST AFRICA:
FUELLING THE FANTASY, RECOGNIZING THE REALITY

In his book *Empire and Sexuality*, Ronald Hyam documents in some detail the extent of sexual activity and the sense of excitement felt by young British men at the sexual opportunities open to them in Britain's overseas possessions.[25] French sources reveal a similar excitement and willingness to exploit such perceived possibilities. A good example of this is *L'Art d'aimer aux colonies*, written in the 1890s by Dr Jacobus X . . . (*sic*), a specialist in genito-urinary disorders who spent twenty-eight years in the colonies after graduation from medical school in the 1860s. Jacobus claimed his motives in writing the book to be purely scientific, but its content suggests less lofty aims. Page after page offers detailed descriptions of the genitals of the peoples of the French Empire, interspersed with plates depicting women from French territories in poses less than usual in a medical textbook.

At times it reads like a guidebook for the sexual tourist. In the section on the French West Indies, for example, Jacobus writes that: 'The connoisseur has a varied choice of exotic flowers, from the Negress to the *Misti*, who is almost white.'[26] He then assesses in intimate detail their respective advantages and disadvantages as lovers for white men. The book implies that the fulfilment of every sexual desire is within reach, without reference to the women involved. Men who preferred to have intercourse with virgins, for instance, were apparently readily satisfied in Senegal. For the 'modest sum' of between ten and twenty francs, a price affordable to all colonials, there were 'women of ill repute' in Saint-Louis who could procure young girls, guaranteed virgins, referred to as 'pas percées' (unpierced). There

[25] Hyam, *Empire and Sexuality*; see also Kenneth Ballhatchet, *Race, Sex and Class under the Raj: Imperial Attitudes and Policies and their Critics, 1793–1905* (London, 1980).

[26] Le Docteur Jacobus X . . . , *L'Art d'aimer aux colonies* (Paris, 1927), 142–3. The content of the book suggests that it was written in the early 1890s.

was the added attraction that such girls were thought not to be able to pass on venereal disease, or become pregnant, although it is difficult to imagine the latter contingency troubling many clients. These girls, who were taken from the class of domestic slaves, could be as young as 8. (The age of consent in France itself was 13.)

Jacobus confidently asserted that there were no adverse effects in such unions because the black woman's vagina was larger than that of the white woman, just as the white man's penis could not compare in size with that of the black man. Both these 'facts', which echo certain beliefs held by late-nineteenth-century French physical anthropologists,[27] are regularly stated throughout the book.[28] Likewise, Jacobus claimed that the nervous system of black people was less developed, thereby explaining the inability of white men to arouse black women sexually. Conversely, he described mixed-race women, particularly those born themselves of métis parents, as 'naturally lascivious'.[29]

The reign of the *signares* had already helped to establish the cult of mixed-race beauty in French Senegal, as rich, well-connected métisses were sought out by newly arrived French men.[30] Jacobus never stops to consider whether the alleged unresponsiveness of African women may have stemmed from a lack of desire to have sexual intercourse with a French man. Mixed-race women, on the other hand, belonged to a class that generally aspired to acceptance into the French community, which may well have influenced their sexual relations.

By no means did everyone share Jacobus's positive vision of the colonies as an arena of sexual promise. Another experienced colonial doctor, Dr Armand Corre, wrote of colonial vice in 1894 in *L'Ethnographie criminelle*. Corre hinted darkly that the rape of indigenous women was not uncommon, and spoke of the 'survivors' of the colonial 'test' returning to France as moral wrecks, joining an army of degenerate delinquents led astray by vice.[31]

Despite the unease expressed by Corre, one section of a practical guide for the European living in West Africa published in 1902 suggests that in some quarters there was a desire to integrate *métissage* into a broader vision of colonial rule. Dr Barot's *Guide pratique de l'européen dans l'Afrique*

---

[27] See e.g. Paul Broca, *On the Phenomena of Hybridity in the Genus Homo*, ed. C. Carter Blake (London, 1864), 28.

[28] Jacobus, *L'Art d'aimer*, 248–9.

[29] Ibid. 243–5, 262. For more on this idea, see Chs. 4 and 6 below.

[30] See Searing, *West African Slavery*, 113.

[31] Dr Armand Corre, *L'Ethnographie criminelle* (Paris, 1894), esp. 34–5. See also Marcel Desbiefs, *Le Vice en Algérie* (Paris, 1900). The supposed dangers of degeneracy to French people in the colonies will be covered more fully in Ch. 4.

*occidentale* was not an official handbook, and it cannot therefore be assumed that there was official approval for all of his ideas.[32] Nevertheless, a preface by Louis Gustave Binger, a former governor of the Ivory Coast and director of the Africa section at the Colonial Ministry, does give the enterprise a semi-official tone. Though the guide is largely filled with medical advice, there are four pages on relations between Europeans and African women which are of great interest.

Though listed later on as one of the six great enemies of the European in the colonies—the others being the sun, the water, the soil, mosquitoes, and alcohol[33]—African women, despite their tendency to spread venereal diseases (never spread by men in this kind of account), still have a role to play in Barot's conception of colonial rule. He advocates 'a temporary union with a well-chosen native woman', to last throughout a tour of duty.[34] What this entailed, in fact, was the diffusion throughout West Africa of the tradition of *mariage à la mode du pays* which had been embraced in the pre-colonial trading posts of Senegal. Barot's justifications for this course of action likewise resemble in many ways the reasons that made *métissage* unofficially permissible, if only on pragmatic grounds, in the *comptoirs*. He writes that a woman chosen as a temporary wife is less likely to be infected with venereal disease than a black prostitute. But she is more than a kind of human prophylactic against the medical dangers of promiscuity; she may ensure the man's general well-being, and even serve as a moral protector, a guard against colonial excess:

The European who has a native wife, if she is not too unintelligent, finally becomes a little attached to her; she diverts him, cares for him, dispels boredom and some-times prevents him from indulging in alcoholism or sexual debauchery, which are unfortunately so common in hot countries.[35]

The man may also find such a relationship useful if he wishes to learn the woman's language. She would be, to use a phrase coined by the British but which was also understood and used by French administrators, a 'sleeping dictionary'. Finally, there are possible political benefits to such unions. Barot writes that they may be used to 'tighten the bonds of sympathy which bind the Negro to the European', and strategically deployed in treaties to aid the process of 'pacification'.

[32] Hyam incorrectly makes this assumption in *Empire and Sexuality*, 157.

[33] Barot, *Guide pratique*, 336–7.

[34] Ibid. 328–31. Translations of Barot taken from John D. Hargreaves, *France and West Africa*, 206–9.

[35] Barot, *Guide pratique*, 329.

   This document raises at least two important points. First, the way in which such unions were sanctioned by Barot as part of a specifically colonial moral code lifted them clear of the opposition to miscegenation which continued to predominate, at least in academic circles, in metropolitan France at the time. In 1896, for example, Georges Vacher de Lapouge used excessive racial intermixture to explain the depressed French birth rate, by supposedly increasing sterility.[36] In 1899 Léopold de Saussure equated the colonial policy of assimilation (which, theoretically at least, viewed conquered peoples as having the potential to be fully integrated into French civilization) with 'disorganization, financial deficit, and a *lowering of morality*'.[37] But Barot, while acknowledging that temporary unions were to be condemned in terms of 'strict morality', could excuse them as 'a necessary evil' on the basis that 'one must take account of the differences of civilization and environment of the country and of the conditions of life in which one finds oneself in the colonies'.[38] (This, of course, neatly sidestepped the fact that temporary unions did not exist in many areas before the French arrived.) This separation of colonial and metropolitan or 'absolute' mores, as will be shown, was achieved with increasing difficulty in Britain.
   The second and intrinsically related point to note here concerns the French conception of male sexuality. One of Barot's basic premisses for the advocacy of temporary unions was that it was too much to expect 'the moral strength necessary to endure two years of absolute continence'.[39] Even in a relatively morally censorious work such as Dr Corre's *L'Ethnographie criminelle*, the idea of expecting 'the restraint and chastity of a monk' from a young man was not considered worth taking seriously.[40] The sexual urge, among men at least, was accepted as natural, its expression inevitable. However, the practical implications of this acceptance were not neglected. If the French were to rule well, sexual debauchery was something worth avoiding. Therefore, it was sensible not to allow sexual activity to become divorced from its wider social context, and to channel it instead into an invented—or at least borrowed—'tradition', which could even have some political benefit.

---

[36] See Joseph J. Spengler, *France Faces Depopulation: Postlude Edition, 1936–1976* (Durham, NC, 1979), 138. For more on metropolitan views on miscegenation, see Ch. 4.
[37] My italics. Léopold de Saussure, *La Psychologie de la colonisation française dans ses rapports avec les sociétés indigènes* (Paris, 1899), 108. See also Raymond F. Betts, *Assimilation and Association in French Colonial Theory, 1890–1914* (New York, 1961), 73.
[38] Barot, *Guide pratique*, 330.       [39] Ibid. 328.
[40] Corre, *L'Ethnographie criminelle*, 34.

There are sharp comparisons to be drawn here with the approach of other colonial powers, particularly Great Britain. Hyam has shown that sexual activity in the British colonies, however widespread, could not by this time be accepted in the same way. It was increasingly frowned upon in the face of a well-organized 'Purity Campaign' glorifying sexual restraint, and also fell foul of a growing desire in the late nineteenth and early twentieth centuries to make the empire more 'respectable'. Finally, prompted by public and parliamentary censure following various colonial sexual scandals, the Secretary of State for the Colonies, Lord Crewe, in 1909 issued a circular threatening punishment for British administrators engaging in 'arrangements of concubinage with girls or women belonging to the native populations'.[41] Concubinage—a term which may well not have reflected the African view of these 'arrangements'—did not suddenly disappear, but it did decrease significantly, and in the instances where it still occurred it had to operate even more discreetly than before.[42] Henceforth, the elite Sudanese political service, with its whiter-than-white reputation, was the model to follow, though the temptations and fantasies remained. The administrator K. D. D. Henderson, for example, reveals how he was once told he could have his choice of any Missiri girl, to which his initial response was to think 'how wonderful it would be to say, "Rightho, parade them on Tuesday" '.[43]

The French view of the Crewe Circular can perhaps be deduced from an apocryphal story related by Louis Vignon, a teacher at the École Coloniale in 1919. He wrote that some years previously the Lieutenant-Governor of Burma had issued a circular attacking concubinage. (Such an attack, though in Hyam's words 'half-hearted', did take place in the 1890s.[44]) The Englishman, continued Vignon, respects the commands of his superiors, so the Governor's orders were obeyed, at least outwardly. Three months later, however, at a sports day in Rangoon, a race was contested by two horses, Governor's Circular and Physical Necessity, won by the latter. While Vignon expressed doubts about the truth of the story, the image it created still resonated for him.[45]

[41] Hyam, *Empire and Sexuality*, 157–81; id., 'Concubinage and the Colonial Service: The Crewe Circular (1909)', *Journal of Imperial and Commonwealth History*, 14 (1986), 170–86. Missionaries played a prominent role in the British attack on interracial unions; the position of French missionaries on this question will be considered in Ch. 2.

[42] See Helen Callaway, *Gender, Culture and Empire: European Women in Colonial Nigeria* (Basingstoke, 1987), 48–50.

[43] Francis M. Deng and M. W. Daly, *'Bonds of Silk': The Human Factor in the British Administration of the Sudan* (East Lansing, Mich. 1989), 46.

[44] Hyam, *Empire and Sexuality*, 120.

[45] Louis Vignon, *Un Programme de politique coloniale. Les Questions indigènes* (Paris, 1919), 372.

Similar scepticism was expressed in the 1930s when the Italians attempted to outlaw miscegenation in Ethiopia. Absolute racial separation and 'collaboration without contact' were enumerated by the Italian Minister for the Colonies, Lessona, as two of the fundamental principles of Italian colonial policy. The Italian newspaper *Azione Coloniale* noted that this was the opposite of French policy.[46] An administrator in Dahomey in 1938 doubted, however, that the Italian initiative would be successful, an attitude perhaps justified by the massive growth in prostitution in Addis Ababa after 1938:[47]

We all know from having been soldiers the inherent needs of our nature in the flush of youth. Are 20-year-old Italians likely to be immune to these fiery passions? Clandestine relations will inevitably become common practice. Human nature, hot blood, solitude, and privations will all do their work.[48]

No directive comparable to the Crewe Circular was ever issued for the French colonies. Moreover, evidence suggests that French administrators engaged in interracial unions well into the 1930s and beyond, as will be shown later. However, it was in the early years of French expansion in West Africa, particularly before the First World War, that such unions were most common. After all, it is clear that Dr Barot was attempting to formalize something which was already taking place on a considerable scale. The following section will attempt to shed more light on the types of relationship he described.

### THE 'TEMPORARY MARRIAGE' IN PRACTICE

That sexual relations between French men and West African women were widespread is not in doubt; the growing number of métis across West Africa in the late nineteenth and early twentieth centuries provides proof enough on its own. The nature of such relationships, however, tends to remain obscure. Most written sources available on this subject are fragmented or

---

[46] CAOM, AP 900; *Azione Coloniale*, 22 July 1937, translated in CAOM, Commission Guernut 20/AXXIII. See also Alberto Sbacchi, *Ethiopia under Mussolini: Fascism and the Colonial Experience* (London, 1985).
[47] Hyam, *Empire and Sexuality*, 139–40.
[48] CAOM, Commission Guernut 101. The Germans also outlawed mixed marriages in South West Africa (Namibia) in 1905. See Helmut Bley, *South-West Africa under German Rule, 1894–1914* (Evanston, Ill, 1971), 212–19; Michel Polényk, 'Race pure et "bâtardisation": l'exemple du sud-ouest Africain Allemand', in Jean-Luc Alber, Claudine Bavoux, and Michel Watin (eds.), *Métissages*, ii (Saint-Dénis de la Réunion, 1991), 241–52.

anecdotal. For example, Georges Hardy, sometime Inspector-General of Education in French West Africa, wrote of the surprise on the face of a clothes-seller when a colonial asked him for four outfits for four 10-year-old children: 'Do you have four twins, Monsieur?'—'No, Monsieur, but I have four wives.'[49] More substantial evidence does exist, however, in which the African women involved appear as more than passive objects.

The experiences of Maurice Delafosse, a distinguished ethnologist and colonial administrator who went on to play an influential role at the École Coloniale, are of particular interest in this regard. In 1899 Delafosse noticed a girl in the court of his friend Aoussou, the chief of Abli in Baoulé country in the Ivory Coast. Delafosse discovered that she was the chief's niece. Her name was Amoïn Kré, and she became Delafosse's wife in a *mariage à la mode du pays*. She remained with him until 1907; excluding various absences, they lived together for a total of five years. After the death at birth of one child, the union produced two sons, Henri in 1903 and Jean in 1906. Delafosse took what was by this time the relatively unusual step of recognizing these children as his own, just before his marriage to Alice Houdas, his old Arabic teacher's daughter, in November 1907. He was never to see Henri and Jean again after his final stay in the Ivory Coast in 1908. Educated by Catholic missionaries, both went on to successful careers, Jean rising to political prominence by independence in 1960, two years before his death.[50]

Amoïn was extremely unhappy about the departure of her husband, who in the new year of 1909 was transferred to the colony of Upper Senegal and Niger. In February she went to see Governor Angoulvant, no friend of Delafosse, in Bingerville, then the Ivorian capital. There, she complained that Delafosse had threatened her and her parents over the question of what was to be done with their children. It appears that she was reluctant to concur with Delafosse's wish that Jean should, like his brother, be handed over to the mission in Dabou, although this was eventually done and she received a sum of money from Delafosse. She went on to further temporary marriages with at least two French men, by both of whom she had children.[51]

[49] Georges Hardy, *Une Conquête morale: L'Enseignement en A.O.F.* (Paris, 1917), 70. Hardy opposed interracial unions, writing that 'whenever possible, one must avoid racial mixture' (p. 74).

[50] Louise Delafosse, *Maurice Delafosse: le berrichon conquis par l'Afrique* (Paris, 1976), 163–4. See also Christopher Harrison, *France and Islam in West Africa, 1860–1960* (Cambridge, 1988), 102–5. Maurice Delafosse himself died in 1926.

[51] Louise Delafosse, *Maurice Delafosse*, 271–2. Jacques Donatien, one of Amoïn Kré's sons by another French man, was recognized as a French citizen in 1933; see ANS, FM: 23G 23.

Some idea of the extent to which the experience of Amoïn Kré and Maurice Delafosse was typical can be derived from the findings of a survey commissioned by the Société Antiesclavagiste de France in 1910. The survey enquired into a range of issues concerning marriage and the organization of the family in French West Africa and French Equatorial Africa. Its aim, as stated in the preface to the published findings, was to draw attention to the 'lamentable exploitation of women and children' in French Africa.[52]

The survey was conducted by means of a questionnaire sent to local administrators in French West Africa via the Governor-General, William Ponty. The questionnaire contained two questions of particular relevance here. First, it asked whether temporary marriages were permitted with 'outsiders', such as traders from other parts of Africa, soldiers, or administrators. Secondly, information was sought on the conditions under which such unions were allowed, and their subsequent effects. Unfortunately, the number of responses to the questionnaire varied greatly from colony to colony. The society received forty-two replies from the Ivory Coast, for example, but just two from Senegal.[53] However, the survey does suggest certain common features in the practice of temporary unions.

The survey seems to confirm the vital point that such unions were in many instances introduced by the French. In the regions of Bougoumi, Bobo Dioulasso, and Bandiagara (Upper Senegal and Niger), the survey claimed, marriage was seen as intrinsically permanent in pre-colonial custom. At the time of the French conquest, however,

temporary marriages were contracted between local women and native soldiers or camp-followers. It was at that time agreed that the union would be broken upon the departure of the husband from the wife's locality. Little by little the custom spread. Hardly anyone except the elderly opposed it in any way. After the dissolution [of the union], any children are considered to be illegitimate and

---

[52] Preface by Mgr. A. Le Roy (author of the questionnaire on the family and marriage, anti-slavery society member, and superior of the Congrégation des Pères du Saint-Esprit) in *Enquête coloniale dans l'Afrique française occidentale et équatoriale sur l'organisation de la famille indigène, les fiançailles, le mariage avec une esquisse générale des langues de l'Afrique et une esquisse ethnologique des principales populations de l'Afrique française équatoriale par le Dr Poutrin* (Paris, 1930), p. vi. Some library catalogues credit Maurice Delafosse with editing this publication, but his only apparent contribution is a monograph on the languages of French Africa. For more on this survey, including the tortuous history of its publication, see Emmanuelle Sibeud, 'Du questionnaire à la pratique: l'enquête de la Société Antiesclavagiste de France sur la famille africaine en 1910', in Claude Blanckaert (ed.), *Le Terrain des sciences humaines. Instructions et enquêtes (XVIIIᵉ–XXᵉ siècle)* (Paris, 1997), 329–55.

[53] There were thirty-two replies from Upper Senegal and Niger, twenty-eight from Guinea, five from Mauritania, and four from Dahomey. All the responses from Guinea were completed in 1910; the originals can be found in ANS, 1G 338.

stay with the family of the mother, which does not prevent her from marrying legitimately in the area later on.[54]

The response from Kita and Bafoulabé (Upper Senegal and Niger) supports the impression that this was a new development. So does the response from the *cercle* (administrative district) of Lagunes et Grand Bassam (Ivory Coast), where the temporary nature of such unions was reflected in the establishment of a monthly payment of ten to twenty-five francs to the woman's parents, rather than the more usual single payment of the bride-price.[55] Even so, the French sometimes attempted to justify and legitimize this new 'custom' on the basis that indigenous marriage itself was temporary, formalized only by the handing over of the bride-price. When defending interracial unions in 1910, for example, Lieutenant-Governor Clozel of Upper Senegal and Niger wrote that: 'One might object that such marriages are essentially temporary unions, but that is precisely one of the distinctive features of indigenous marriage, which does not have the immutable character that marriage has in our societies in Europe.'[56]

In many areas, however, the introduction of temporary marriages was resisted. When this survey was carried out in about 1910, the practice did not hold among the Islamic Dioulas of the Ivory Coast, with European or indeed African 'outsiders'. Where relations did occur between Dioula women and outsiders, it was said that they usually involved widows or divorcees who had slipped in society and 'gone to market'.[57] (In the areas of the Ivory Coast inhabited by the Agni people, women found guilty of adultery were said to form another category more likely to be 'available'.[58]) The N'Gans of the Kong region of the Ivory Coast forbade temporary marriages on the basis that they could not lead to the constitution of a family; if such unions did occur, the woman was not allowed to marry legitimately later on. Similar ostracism would follow in the coastal areas of Lahou, Fresco, and Dabou. Here, apparently, Europeans were obliged to look in Jacqueville, Grand Bassam, Moossou, and Assinie, where the French presence was better established, but also—indeed, 'especially'—in the neighbouring British colony, the Gold Coast (Ghana).[59] It is interesting to speculate on whether this could have been linked in any way to the recent attack on interracial unions in the British colonies.

---

[54] *Enquête coloniale*, 368.
[55] Ibid. 368, 395–6, 206. In West Africa, the husband traditionally hands over the bride-price to the wife's parents, which is then held as a guarantee of the daughter's well-being; in some instances this is returnable if the marriage breaks up.
[56] ANS, M 45, Clozel to GG, Bamako, 11 Nov. 1910.        [57] *Enquête coloniale*, 233.
[58] Ibid. 267.        [59] Ibid. 242, 238, 213.

Any resistance to the introduction of temporary marriages may have been determined by the relative strength or weakness of the French position in any given area. Many of the Gouros of Haut-Sassandra (Ivory Coast) disapproved of such arrangements, but, the survey claimed, gave in through fear of the European. In the areas around Ouagadougou and Léo (Upper Senegal and Niger) the marriage of a woman to an employee of the administration or the army was said 'always' to be against the family's wishes, but they would not protest for similar reasons.[60] In Lobi country (Upper Senegal and Niger), an area of prolonged resistance to French rule, interracial unions reflected the violence of colonization in the region, as the local colonial administration continued forcibly to requisition teenage girls as sexual partners for French men until as late as the mid-1940s.[61]

Any woman who became involved with a European man evidently ran a number of risks. In many areas, for example, she was unable later to marry one of her own people. This was true of the strongly Islamic region of Futa Jallon in Guinea, assuming the man was not a Muslim. The survey found that any woman who made such a 'misalliance' in this region was renounced by her own people, 'religion alone establishing a real demarcation between people'.[62] In parts of the Ivory Coast, too, she could be effectively 'mise à l'index'—blacklisted—and would find another man only with difficulty.[63] In certain areas, this would be the result only if children were born of the union. Respondents to the survey in Bas-Sassandra and the *cercles* of Korhogo and Dabakala (Ivory Coast) claimed that abortion was a frequent concomitant of temporary unions,[64] but for presumably similar reasons large numbers of mixed-race children were born and then abandoned, as we shall see in later chapters. The response from the *cercle* of Baoulé-Sud, where Delafosse had been an administrator, considered that the alleged benefits of temporary marriages—bringing foreigners and indigenous peoples into closer contact, 'assimilating' other races, broadening the woman's intelligence and horizons, and opening her mind to the 'civilizing' progress on offer—had to be balanced against the extent

---

[60] Ibid. 220, 387.

[61] The Lobi people inhabit the south-west of what is now Burkina Faso. See the remarkable oral testimony of a Lobi peasant woman set down in Jeanne-Marie Kambou-Ferrand, 'Souffre, gémis, mais marche! Regard d'une paysanne lobi sur sa vie au temps colonial', in Gabriel Massa and Y. Georges Madiéga (eds.), *La Haute-Volta coloniale. Témoignages, recherches, regards* (Paris, 1995), 147–56. The use of force is also alluded to in the Fulani author Amadou Hampâté Bâ's biographical novel, *L'étrange destin de Wangrin* (Paris, 1973), 64, 340, 439; and in the first volume of his memoirs, *Amkoullel, l'enfant peul* (Arles, 1991), 521.

[62] *Enquête coloniale*, 309.　　　[63] Ibid. 213; also 238, 267.　　　[64] Ibid. 217, 285.

to which this 'so-called progress' prepared her for being uprooted and rejected by her own society.[65]

The experience of Amoïn Kré was, according to the findings of the survey, generally replicated across French West Africa, in the sense that a woman who had been involved in one temporary marriage was, when the husband left, very likely to be caught up in a cycle of further marriages to Europeans. There are numerous suggestions in the survey that women saw this as a possible way of avoiding work and acquiring various gifts. It was sometimes claimed that women who had been involved in a union with a European made more material demands than most African husbands could satisfy.[66]

A woman's parents could also profit from the payment of a bride-price of cash, cattle, or whatever could be agreed. One account from French Equatorial Africa shows a young Gabonese girl being 'sold' to a French man for 500 francs, a dog, some sacks of rice and packets of sugar, a demijohn of wine, and a coloured umbrella.[67] The survey assessed the cost of such a union to a French man, in Guinea at least, to have been between 800 and 1,000 francs per year. Yet it is still difficult to say who was exploiting whom, for in the same section it was noted that if the woman was a captive, her owner would take all the profit, effectively turning the arrangement into a form of prostitution.[68] It is all too easy to imagine that the lure of bride-price for a short-term marriage, which did not always have to be returned in these kinds of arrangements,[69] was in some cases enough to ensure that barely pubescent girls were presented for gain.

Temporary wives were often practically inherited by newly arrived colonists when the previous husband had gone, with procurers offering women to French men as they got off the boat which had brought them to Africa.[70] For the woman, however, this pattern could not always be sustained, especially perhaps as she grew past the age of the new colonial recruits. It has already been suggested that she could not always return to the society from which she came, even if that was her desire. Many responses to the survey attested that prostitution was almost the most common outcome in this situation.[71]

---

[65] *Enquête coloniale*, 255.

[66] Ibid. 227, 333, 408–9; see also L. P. Mair, 'African Marriage and Social Change', in Arthur Phillips (ed.), *Survey of African Marriage and Family Life* (London, 1953), 150.

[67] France Renucci, *Souvenirs de femmes au temps des colonies* (Paris, 1988), 175.

[68] *Enquête coloniale*, 294–5; also see 217.        [69] Ibid. 395–6.

[70] See the article by L. Frappier, 'Contre l'article 4 de la Loi sur la Recherche de la Paternité', *La Française*, 18 Feb. 1912.

[71] *Enquête coloniale*, 227, 267, 285, 325, 333, 504, 552.

This section has attempted to give some idea of the kinds of social effects brought about by the spread of temporary marriages in French West Africa. It seems true to say that French men, if that was their desire, generally had little trouble in finding African women for sex, companionship, or both. More specific conclusions are, however, difficult to draw at present. The survey conducted by the Société Antiesclavagiste is a vast document of great complexity, which suggests certain similarities in such relationships but does not, for example, reveal enough about who exactly engaged in them, how Africans viewed them, or how far external factors, such as the strength or weakness of the French position in any given area, determined the way in which they were conducted.

In completing the survey, several respondents registered their disapproval of these relationships, and spoke of their harmful social effects. Though interracial unions, as noted earlier, were never officially condemned by the French in the way they were in the British colonies in 1909 by Lord Crewe, French attitudes towards them do seem to have been changing from the 1910s in particular, and their practice was already in gradual decline. This decline was at least partly due to the fact that an increasing number of French men were arriving in West Africa with their wives; by 1926 there were almost 1,500 European women in Senegal alone.[72] This development can be explained to a degree by a gradual improvement in living conditions, but, as will be seen in the following section, there were ideological considerations at work as well.

### 'THE COLONY IN CURLERS'

Several leading colonial figures expressed serious doubts about the wisdom of encouraging the presence of white women in the colonies. Generals Gallieni and Lyautey, for example, were not in favour of the married colonial officer.[73] Nor was William Ponty, the Governor-General of French West Africa from 1908 to 1915. He believed that half an administrator's efficiency was lost if he brought his family with him to Africa: 'The comfort of the hearth [is] detrimental to good colonial administration.' A biographical novel based on Ponty's career hints that he had African lovers, but in 1910, after twenty

---

[72] Rita Cruise O'Brien, *White Society in Black Africa: The French of Senegal* (London, 1972), 57.

[73] Knibiehler and Goutalier, *La Femme au temps des colonies*, 70.

years in Africa, Ponty himself finally married a French woman and had her live with him in the governor's palace.[74]

In 1916 Louis Le Barbier also decried the development in a book on the Ivory Coast.[75] According to Le Barbier, at the turn of the century it was always said that European women could not live in West Africa, that they would be constantly ill and could not raise a family in such a debilitating and unhealthy environment. But by 1916 many French men had not only their wives but also in some cases their children living with them. In the larger towns there were also 'Aryan girls' living from 'the commerce of their charms'. Le Barbier blamed this 'invasion' of European women on an unnamed Governor-General—could it have been Ponty himself, who died in 1915?—who had the double aim of making life more agreeable for the European man who had come to stay in the colony, and making whites more respectful of 'good morals', cutting down on or even eliminating unions with African women.[76]

In Le Barbier's view, however, white women were a source of trouble: they demanded more than a colonial salary could provide, they instigated hatred and rivalry among young men with 'nerves and senses excited by the climate', they introduced adultery and scandal. African women were far less complicated to deal with, for 'the needs, like the charms of these poor creatures were modest, and their lovers did not have much difficulty in satisfying their taste for luxury'. Nor did they prompt breaches of confidence or 'indelicate acts' committed for love.[77]

Le Barbier concluded, therefore, that virtue had if anything suffered with the arrival of white women. He then effectively inverted the logic offered by the Crewe Circular regarding the harmful effect of 'arrangements of concubinage' on colonial rule. Lord Crewe had argued that an administrator could not take a local woman as his lover without 'lowering himself in the eyes of the natives, and diminishing his authority to an extent which will seriously impair his capacity for useful work in the Service in which it is his duty to set an honourable example to all with whom he comes into contact'.[78] Le Barbier, contrarily, wrote that 'Since the arrival of these women, we have lost much of our prestige among blacks', who, having seen the 'loose conduct' of white women—stretching even to 'depraved European women taking black men in their entourage as lovers'—could not accept

---

[74] See G. Wesley Johnson, 'William Ponty and Republican Paternalism in French West Africa (1866–1945)', in Gann and Duignan (eds.), *African Proconsuls*, 139, 152, 155. Also Conklin, *A Mission to Civilize*, 169.

[75] Louis Le Barbier, *La Côte d'Ivoire* (Paris, 1916), 203–9.　　　[76] Ibid. 204.

[77] Ibid. 205.　　　[78] Hyam, *Empire and Sexuality*, 157.

them as their superiors.[79] By extension, Le Barbier appears to suggest that a union with an African woman was a manifestation of superiority which could actually enhance the European's position.

Le Barbier argued further that even the most chaste and virtuous of European women were unconducive to good colonial administration. He saw them as a divisive influence, blaming them for the creation of two categories of administrator: those who, through the fact of being married, demanded stability and relative comfort; and the bachelors, or those whose families remained in France, who were consequently obliged to perform all the more onerous tasks in the least hospitable parts of French West Africa.[80]

Le Barbier had a very traditional view of the empire as an exclusively masculine preserve, peopled, as it were, by 'real men' who spurned home comforts, slept under the stars, and made do with African lovers. The reporter Albert Londres lamented the decline of this conception of empire in his book *Terre d'ébène*, published in book form in 1929 but based on a series of articles which had appeared in the mass-circulation newspaper *Le Petit Parisien* the previous year as he travelled around West Africa:

He who speaks of a colonial administrator no longer speaks of an adventurous spirit. The career has become dangerously middle class. Gone are the early enthusiasms, the romance of colonization, the risk-seeking, the hut in the bush, the conquest of the negro soul, the little native woman! Nowadays one departs with one's wife, one's children, and one's mother-in-law.[81]

Londres summarized this approach as 'la colonie en bigoudis'—'the colony in curlers'. For Le Barbier and Londres, the empire had represented a place where men could escape metropolitan social restraints and act out various fantasies of power. It was a world where European notions of class seemed less important, where men from humble backgrounds like Louis Gustave Binger, an orphan and a former ironmonger's apprentice, could rise to positions of institutional authority. In Binger's case, this meant the governorship of the Ivory Coast, followed by the naming of its capital after him, Bingerville.

However, Binger the adventurer became Binger the self-made man, who 'dreamt of becoming one of the great capitalists of all time'.[82] He was

---

[79] Le Barbier, *La Côte d'Ivoire*, 206–7.          [80] Ibid. 209.

[81] Albert Londres, *Terre d'ébène* (Paris, 1929), 13. For more on Londres, see Pierre Assouline, *Albert Londres. Vie et Mort d'un Grand Reporter 1884–1932* (Paris, 1989). Maurice Delafosse similarly complained that the 'pioneers' had effectively been transformed into bureaucrats. See Louise Delafosse, *Maurice Delafosse*, 160.

[82] Henri Brunschwig, 'Louis Gustave Binger (1856–1936)', in Gann and Duignan (eds.), *African Proconsuls*, 124.

the governor of the Ivory Coast for fifty months, but spent just nineteen months in the colony; it has been said that 'he started regarding his post in the Ivory Coast as a kind of exile from glamorous Parisian society, where, probably, he was eager to flaunt his success'.[83] Though Londres linked the arrival of French women with a kind of creeping *embourgeoisement*, the process might be said to have begun the moment a career in the colonies could raise a man in society. It was the husbands who made the rules, and the husbands whose class made a difference.

On a similar theme, feminist scholars have recently suggested that European women have been made scapegoats for a perceived deterioration in race relations in the colonies.[84] The stereotype of the destructive colonial wife, Stoler has convincingly argued, has served to obscure the extent to which European women were 'strategic' to 'a realignment in racial and class politics' in the colonies.[85] For Stoler, European women 'became the excuse for—and custodians of—racial distinctions that took the form of class-specific prescriptions for bourgeois respectability and sexual "normalcy"'.[86] This she links to 'an increasing rationalization of colonial management', a tendency which 'seems strongest in the interwar years', connected to the desire to make the empire more productive and economically profitable—what the Colonial Minister, Albert Sarraut, described in 1923 as the 'mise en valeur' of the colonies.[87]

Several works from the inter-war period confirm the extent to which 'bourgeois respectability' was promoted in the colonies, while interracial unions were increasingly stigmatized. A guide to colonial life published in 1929, for example, assumed from the outset that the administrator was married. In his preface, Camille Guy, a former governor of both Senegal and Guinea, stated that 'long experience' taught him that there could not be full understanding between the indigenous population and Europeans unless the authority of the husband was supplemented by the charm and kindness of the French wife. In the colonies, comfort, the 'most agreeable remedy' for illness and boredom, would more and more become the rule. In marked contrast to Dr Barot's 1902 guide, 'comfort' was conceived here in a wide

[83] A. E. Afigbo, 'Men of Two Continents: An African Interpretation', in ibid. 534.

[84] See e.g. the important article by Ann Laura Stoler, 'Carnal Knowledge and Imperial Power: Gender, Race, and Morality in Colonial Asia', in Micaela di Leonardo (ed.), *Gender at the Crossroads of Knowledge: Feminist Anthropology in the Postmodern Era* (Berkeley, 1991), 64–6.

[85] Ibid. 67.

[86] Frederick Cooper and Ann L. Stoler, 'Tensions of Empire: Colonial Control and Visions of Rule', *American Ethnologist*, 16 (1989), 613–14.

[87] Stoler, 'Carnal Knowledge', 86.

variety of recipes—how to make cheese 'dans le genre camembert', for example—and in tips on how to get the most from your kitchen garden.[88] Other books were aimed directly at the women themselves. In *La Femme française aux colonies*, Clotilde Chivas-Baron praised the good works performed by women right from colonial beginnings: they were 'first-class auxiliaries for colonization' and, with their 'feminine solidarity', were precious allies for women living under French rule.[89] The idea that interracial liaisons were an aid to racial understanding was given short shrift: 'As if the native woman would give up her little secrets along with her body!' Support was found in the words of Georges Hardy, who wrote that 'A man remains a man as long as he is under the eye of a woman of his race'. The implication was that the man would otherwise lapse into degeneracy, failing in his colonial duty in the process.[90] In a practical guide to all aspects of colonial life for women, Chivas-Baron presented the French woman as a steadying influence and a way of preventing promiscuity: 'Your presence will keep your husband in his own milieu without him being tempted to cling to a human being, whomever it may be, for the sole reason that it is a human being and because he is alone.'[91]

In this way, French women were charged with the task of providing the home comforts which would help to keep the colonizer separate from the colonized, reminding the colonizer of his racial duty and his purpose as a representative of French authority.[92] As such notions of social distance between the French and West Africans became more deeply entrenched, interracial unions became progressively less socially acceptable in French colonial society, particularly in towns with a discernible European community. Moreover, Alain Tirefort has noted for the Ivory Coast that from the 1920s in particular, métis children seem to have been far more likely to be fathered by French planters, traders, and so on than by colonial administrators.[93] Though interracial relationships were in decline, however, it would be wrong to over-schematize this development. As the following section will demonstrate, in certain areas the temporary marriage was very much alive into the 1920s and beyond.

[88] A. Levaré, *Le Confort aux colonies* (Paris, 1929), p. x, 3.
[89] C. Chivas-Baron, *La Femme française aux colonies* (Paris, 1929), 103, quoting Daniel Marquis-Sébie.
[90] Ibid. 109–10.
[91] J.-L. Faure (ed.), *La Vie aux colonies. Préparation de la femme à la vie coloniale* (Paris, 1938), 29.
[92] See Stoler, 'Carnal Knowledge', 83; also Conklin, *A Mission to Civilize*, 169–71.
[93] Alain Tirefort, 'Européens et assimilés en Basse Côte d'Ivoire 1893–1960. Mythes et réalités d'une société coloniale', Ph.D. thesis (Univ. of Bordeaux III, 1989), 641.

## THE PERSISTENCE OF MÉTISSAGE

In 1922 the liberal administrator and writer Robert Delavignette received his first posting, to Zinder, at that time the capital of Niger. The town was, he wrote, divided in two, with a distinct European or colonial town and an African town:

The natives in our city, the colonial city, were guards and orderlies, cooks and their scullions, boys with their 'small boys' who worked the punkahs [fans]; and women for our need, prostitutes for a night, or concubines for a tour, sometimes servant-mistresses for a lifetime. For the threescore of us Europeans, there were about three hundred servants; a mysterious company, who did what they had to do without bringing us any real contact with the neighbouring world from which they came. And, though they lived with their families in restricted quarters in our buildings, they would slip out at times to recapture in the native city the life which they lacked among us.[94]

Delavignette's description of a socially rarefied 'colonial city' suggests ways in which the nature of the relationship between French men and African women may have developed since the early days of French expansion. His comments on interracial sexual relations place them in the context of a kind of colonial service sector, set up to meet the needs of the French now that their presence had firmly been established. The cooks, the guards, and so on had all adapted to the realities of the new system, trying to find ways of sustaining themselves economically while simultaneously preserving their own culture. Indeed, in this instance it is the Africans themselves who seem most anxious to maintain social distance, while Delavignette is disappointed to find that he cannot get closer to indigenous society.

The suggestion here is that the 'concubines' Delavignette mentioned may have approached French men in much the same way as did the cooks and the orderlies: attempting to extract as many advantages as possible from the system put in place by the French, while maintaining sufficient distance for them always to be able to return to 'the native city' of which Delavignette spoke. To assess the extent to which this may have been true, there is one source, also from Niger, which provides a rare glimpse through the bedroom door, so to speak—or, in this case, past the tent-flap—which sheds more light on the attitudes of African women to temporary unions with French men.

---

[94] Robert Delavignette, *Freedom and Authority in French West Africa* (London, 1950), 3–4. The term 'tour' here could mean either the European's term of office in Africa, or a journey through the district under his control.

André Thiellement was a colonial administrator in the nomadic sub-division of Tahoua in Niger in the mid-1930s. In 1943 he wrote his memoirs, published in 1949 under the title *Azawar*, the name given to a desert region of north-west Niger inhabited by the nomadic Tuareg people. In them, he talks frankly about the process of acquiring a Tuareg wife.[95] Of course, memoir material presents some problems for the historian; one should not perhaps expect unswerving truthfulness from a man's account of his sexual experiences, particularly in cases such as this where they took place in lands where his words were unlikely to be read, with people lacking the ability to reply. Nevertheless, the wealth of detail in this account makes it an extremely valuable source; it does much more than confirm that temporary unions between French men and West African women continued to take place in the inter-war period.

Thiellement's predecessor as commandant, Michier, before leaving recommends that he find a temporary Tuareg wife—'Sleeping dictionnary [*sic*], you understand?'—as the only way to learn Tamachek (the Tuareg language) fairly quickly and to begin to understand 'what goes on beneath those blue veils'.[96] (Indigo veils, worn by both sexes, are the symbol of the Tuareg's identity, varying slightly from tribe to tribe.) She would also help to while away the idle hours of an up-country administrator. The women, according to Michier, are sometimes attractive on French terms; without 'the suntan and the dirt', some would have 'the dull complexion of an Arlésienne'. Michier finally informs his successor that the relatively high status of the woman in Tuareg society is manifested in her refusal of the husband on the first three nights. 'It is necessary to conquer her . . . by force, too.'[97]

There follows a sequence where women are in effect auditioned for the role of Thiellement's wife. The first, named Tawarat, the niece of Thiellement's interpreter, is discovered to have been 'married' previously to three or four whites. Thiellement rejects her because she speaks some French and seems to be a 'femme de luxe', eager for expensive gifts. He is also told that she is from a low artisanal caste; he worries that this may reduce his prestige, but he learns later that as a member of a different race he is outside the caste system and cannot therefore be compromised in this way.[98]

A guardsman presents Thiellement with a second prospective wife, called Tarhedeyt. The intermediary says she is a virgin and the daughter of a chief.

---

[95] André Thiellement, *Azawar* (Saint-Vaast-la-Hougue, 1949), 37–61.
[96] Ibid. 38.    [97] Ibid. 39.    [98] Ibid. 40–1.

She is offered for a bride-price of two four-year-old camels. Thiellement decides to take her, as she cannot speak French. He negotiates the bride-price down to two pregnant cows and some shooting cartridges.[99]

On the first night he tries to engage her in conversation in Tamachek, to no avail. He loses his patience with her, thinking to himself: 'I am the master here. Perhaps violence is needed.' He attempts to untie her intricately knotted veils, but she silently resists, curled up in a ball. Finally, she says 'Eddâza'—'I'm tired'—and he relents. The next night follows a similar pattern. On the third night he has his way; however, he reveals that the guardsman who found her had threatened that her family would all be imprisoned if she continued to struggle. After a month, however, Thiellement sends her back, despairing of ever learning a word of Tamachek.[100]

Later, Thiellement is presented with a woman called Mariama, who meets his specifications. He approves of her fine features, her clear skin, her grace and timidity. Her husband has recently died of pneumonia, her livestock of plague. She is therefore willing to marry a French man who can clothe her, feed her, and provide her with a new herd. Thiellement observes that she is intelligent, and she teaches him Tamachek.[101]

A few months later Mariama becomes pregnant. Thiellement says he had not thought much about this possibility. One day, she falls from her camel. On reflection he realizes that she has done this deliberately to kill the unborn child. His interpreter informs him later that if a woman from Azawar has a child by a French man, she cannot remarry a man from her own country. When their relationship ends, Thiellement signs a declaration drawn up by a marabout (a local Islamic leader) renouncing his proprietorial rights over Mariama, leaving her free to remarry a Tuareg.[102]

This account raises several interesting points. First, the help Thiellement received in searching for a wife, even among the Muslim Tuareg, suggests that it was expected of him that he should take a Tuareg woman as his companion. Michier's comments show that he was following a tradition in doing so.

If Thiellement found it easy to command what he wanted, it would nonetheless be wrong to portray the three women he encountered as entirely powerless. On the other hand, they ran a number of risks in entering into a relationship with him. Tawarat, Thiellement's first prospective wife, is portrayed as exploiting the French in a certain way for material gain. Simultaneously, however, having been with several French men, she seems to have isolated herself from Tuareg society and earned moral disapproval

[99] Thiellement, *Azawar*, 42–3.      [100] Ibid. 43–5.      [101] Ibid. 45–7.
[102] Ibid. 55–7, 60.

from some quarters. The guardsman who later presented Tarhedeyt described Tawarat as a 'putain'—a whore—and 'not a real Tuareg'.[103]

Tarhedeyt, in contrast, represents one unwilling to become detached from the society into which she was born. Faced with her passive resistance, Thiellement was in no doubt that he had mastery over her. Such resistance evidently carried the risk of rape. Yet apparently it was the threats of the guardsman that forced her ultimately to yield. The guardsman himself may well have been motivated by fears of unfavourable repercussions for his (and her) people if the commandant was not served properly, in addition to fears for his own job. Even then, however, Tarhedeyt's continued silence was enough to bring the arrangement to an end relatively quickly.

Mariama can to some extent be located between the two types represented by Tawarat and Tarhedeyt. Temporarily separated by circumstance from her traditional livelihood, she sees some benefit in a short-term union with a French man, though never ceasing to wish to return to her former life, and eventually doing so. Nevertheless, the union carried dangers, as the passage describing her abortion shows. This passage highlights a further point, as it demonstrates Thiellement's ignorance of the traditions of the society he is governing, as well as a relative lack of regard for the consequences of his actions. His main concern in relation to the women he encounters is whether they can teach him Tamachek, but his actions with these women do not suggest that any understanding of the Tuareg language could overcome a lack of ability to understand the society of which they were a part.

CONCLUSION

This chapter has attempted to give some idea of the nature of the relationships established between French men and African women over a considerable period of time. This is clearly a subject which would benefit from much more detailed research. However, certain themes of relevance to the rest of this book have emerged.

First, it has been suggested that colonial actions did not always flow obviously from metropolitan attitudes. Dr Barot's advocacy of 'temporary unions' between French men and West African women was at odds with prevailing French thought on the wisdom of sexual contact between different races, yet it was his work which most accurately reflected what

[103] Thiellement, *Azawar*, 41.

was taking place in West Africa, as highlighted by the survey conducted by the Société Antiesclavagiste de France in 1910.

Secondly, it has been observed that although cohabiting relationships between French and West Africans appear to have declined from about the time of the First World War, as growing numbers of French women joined their husbands in the colonies, such relationships by no means died out altogether. As late as 1939, a guide for colonial recruits could advise 'hardened bachelors' that all urban prostitutes were infected with venereal disease, and that a temporary native wife was consequently a much better alternative.[104] In the more remote parts of French West Africa, such as the area of Niger to which André Thiellement was posted, colonial administrators could still openly form relationships with local women. In urban areas with developing European communities the picture was rather different. There, notions of social and racial distance became more deeply entrenched. Interracial sexual relations did occur throughout the 1940s and 1950s, but tended to take place on a casual basis, and in the words of Cruise O'Brien, 'never acquired the legitimacy and status awarded them during the period of *métissage* and assimilation in the early days of the colonies'.[105]

All this provides vital background information for what was arguably the most important effect of interracial sexual relations in colonial French West Africa: the birth of several thousand mixed-race children. The experiences of these children will provide the focus for the remainder of this book.

[104] André Beauseigneur, 'Le Guide du candidat colonial', quoted in Eric and Gabrielle Deroo and Marie-Cécile de Taillac, *Aux colonies* (Paris, 1992), 92.
[105] Cruise O'Brien, *White Society in Black Africa*, 93.

# 2
# *Abandonment and Intervention*

The lives of people of mixed race in French West Africa were shaped by a paradox. On the one hand, most métis could tell a story of individual rejection. The majority were left behind by their French father while they were still infants, if indeed they ever knew their father's identity, while a smaller number also found themselves abandoned by their mothers. At the same time, however, the French administration expressed great interest in their collective potential. This interest found its most concrete form in the establishment of special institutions for mixed-race children, known as *orphelinats de métis*. This chapter is concerned with this peculiar mixture of abandonment and intervention. It will describe the circumstances which led to the creation of special homes for métis children. It will also consider the factors which determined the actions and attitudes of French men, both as individuals and in the service of colonialism, showing how these actions and attitudes helped to determine the lives of the mixed-race population of French West Africa. This will lead into Chapter 3, which looks at the education given to those taken into the so-called métis 'orphanages', and the types of employment they subsequently found. First of all, however, we must briefly recapitulate the circumstances under which most métis were born.

## SEX AND REPRODUCTION

French sexual activity in West Africa, as suggested in the previous chapter, was influenced by several beliefs concerning male sexuality and the best way to go about establishing the French presence in the region. Interracial sexual liaisons were rarely condemned openly by the colonial authorities, and although they became progressively less socially acceptable as time went on, this disapprobation was mostly restricted to towns with a discernible European community.

French men in the colonies seem either to have decided that the imperatives of male sexual desire were more important than the possibility of reproduction, or barely made the connection between sexual activity and children. Victor Augagneur, a socialist deputy and former Governor-General of Madagascar, was in the minority in describing miscegenation in 1913 as a 'curse' for the reason that it led to the birth of large numbers of mixed-race children whose position in society gave cause for concern.[1] Three years later, Louis Le Barbier considered the wisdom of allowing interracial unions. He saw the birth of métis children, 'these unhappy little creatures', as 'the unfortunate side' of the question, but ultimately did not regard the problem as sufficiently important to advocate an end to *métissage*.[2] In a similar vein, when Henry Filatriau, the administrator in Sakété in Dahomey, wrote in 1938 of 'the inherent needs of our nature in the flush of youth' when disparaging Italian efforts to prevent interracial sexual relations in Ethiopia, his conclusion was that 'There will always be métis'.[3]

Many French men seem to have approached their sexual relations with West African women in this banal and insouciant fashion, with the 'inevitable' offspring as good as condemned in their description as 'incidents de voyage'.[4] As seen in the previous chapter, André Thiellement confessed that he had not thought much about the possibility of his Tuareg wife becoming pregnant; nor does her subsequent self-inflicted abortion appear to have troubled him unduly.[5] Under these circumstances, the widespread abandonment of those children who did survive does not come as any great surprise. Though some French colonials would have objected to one mixed-race writer's description of the métis as the 'cast-off of a great race and a great civilization',[6] any attempts to act in favour of people of mixed race were, broadly speaking, framed by the idea that they were in some way unwanted, the unfortunate by-products of colonial rule. Some administrators, it will be shown, argued for their 'potential' in the overall scheme of colonialism. Even these, however, tended to approach métis as 'a problem'—and a fairly intransigent problem at that. Before considering how this problem was addressed, the following section will examine the response of the colonial authorities to the issue of abandonment.

[1] Victor Augagneur, 'Notre devoir envers les enfants métis', *Les Annales Coloniales*, 11 Jan. 1913.
[2] Le Barbier, *La Côte d'Ivoire*, 210.
[3] CAOM, Commission Guernut 101.
[4] See Georges Hardy, *Une Conquête morale*, 70.
[5] Thiellement, *Azawar*, 55–7. Evidently the forms of birth control advertised in colonial journals such as *Le Journal des Coloniaux et l'Armée Coloniale Réunis* were still far from being in widespread use in the 1930s when this incident took place.
[6] Barthélémy Chaupin, 'Le Métis dans la Société', *L'Eurafricain*, 9 (1950), 36.

## INDIVIDUAL AND COLLECTIVE RESPONSIBILITY

In May 1912 the Minister for Colonies, Albert Lebrun, issued the following circular to the Governors and Governors-General in each of France's colonies.

### *Circular—Abandonment of Illegitimate Children*

Complaints have been referred to me by the Société d'Anthropologie [de Paris] concerning the situation in certain colonies which befalls children born of temporary unions between administrators or soldiers and local women.

It frequently comes to pass that, upon their return to France or their departure for other colonies, the fathers abandon the children born of these unions, without taking any further interest in them.

Though convinced that the cases which have been drawn to my attention represent exceptions from which it would be unfair to generalize, I am writing to draw your attention to the necessity of reminding the administrators and soldiers under your command of the duties which, in individual cases, the strictest principles of humanity impose upon them. Though no other legal sanction obliges them to recognize their illegitimate children, they must at least guarantee their education and put them in a position to provide for themselves.

I would add that from a political point of view we have the greatest interest in avoiding giving any offence which might alienate the mixed-race population from us. The abandonment of illegitimate children represents one of the possible causes of discord among the various elements of this population, besides the fact that it is likely to throw the greatest moral discredit on the principles by which our civilization declares itself to be inspired. I request you to draw the attention of the civil and military personnel in the colony under your authority to these remarks, which will certainly not fail to strike all those who are cognizant of their duty towards themselves, as towards France itself, of which they are in the colonies the accountable representatives.[7]

The practical effect of this circular, as will be shown, was minimal. However, it serves to highlight a number of different attitudes not only towards interracial sexual relations, but also towards the issue of how best to deal with the burgeoning métis population in France's recent acquisitions in West Africa, something which was beginning to arouse widespread concern.[8]

---

[7] ANS, H 25; CAOM, AP 28. The complaints referred to in the first sentence followed a survey conducted by the Société d'Anthropologie de Paris in French West Africa between 1909 and 1911; this survey will be covered in detail in Ch. 4.

[8] For examples of how this concern was manifested in Indochina, see Ann Stoler, 'Sexual Affronts and Racial Frontiers: European Identities and the Cultural Politics of Exclusion in Colonial Southeast Asia', *Comparative Studies in Society and History*, 34 (1992), 514–51.

First, it is striking to compare this circular with that issued against 'concubinage' in the British colonies by Lord Crewe in 1909.[9] In contrast to his British counterpart, Lebrun appears tacitly to have accepted that temporary unions were an inevitable feature of colonial life. There is no suspicion that he wished to follow Lord Crewe's example in clamping down on such unions, or that he considered introducing legislation obliging French men to recognize their illegitimate children as their own. There are similarities, however, in the sense that both Lebrun and Crewe identified the necessity of representatives of the colonial power 'setting a good example', to avoid (in Crewe's words) 'lowering oneself in the eyes of the natives', and facilitating thereby the exercise of power.

One of the central problems here lies in trying to explain why Lebrun's moral strictures were unaccompanied by any real threat of retribution against those who failed to live up to French colonial ideals. The question is more generally applicable to how the French authorities defined 'morality' in the colonies, and why they were not inclined to adopt measures similar to those laid down by Lord Crewe.

An answer may be found by looking more closely at the ideology which underpinned French colonialism. In theoretical terms at least, French colonial expansion involved the imposition of much more than a political structure and an economic system: it also involved the export of the Republican ideals of liberty, equality, and fraternity. Lebrun's circular therefore made explicit reference to the high principles by which French civilization claimed to be inspired, and warned of the dangers of failing to live up to these principles.

The problem lay in the fact that to vest any faith in these ideals in a colonial context, it was also necessary to put faith in the ability of their representatives to behave in a manner befitting them. Legislation against those who failed to live up to these ideals would have represented an affront to the idea that the French were transmitting a morally 'superior' civilization and were consequently able to 'improve' the peoples they dominated. Paradoxically, then, the centrality of Republican ideals in French colonial ideology limited the ability of the authorities to take action against 'immoral' behaviour—particularly, perhaps, in a case such as this which involved large numbers of French men.

As a result, Lebrun's circular was ineffectual. French men could continue to abandon their mixed-race offspring with impunity. Lebrun was wrong, in any case, to contend that cases of abandonment were the exception.

---

[9] See Ch. 1.

To some extent he was displaying an incredulity typical of metropolitan observers when it came to considering certain aspects of colonial life. The realities often raised awkward questions.

ABSENT FATHERS

—But what does one do when children are born?

—There too you behave as you please. You can recognize the child, as some of us do, or you can just leave a little nest egg to the bank to provide for the child when you leave Gabon. The cashier is used to this, by the way: at the beginning of each month, all the women bring their child along with them when they come to pick up their allowance.

(France Renucci, *Souvenirs de femmes au temps des colonies*, 172)

One source estimated in 1916 that French men abandoned their mixed-race progeny in West Africa in nine cases out of ten, usually when the children were still very young.[10] Some would formally recognize these children as their own, having their names inscribed on the lists of the *état civil* (the register of births, marriages, and deaths). This gave the child the rights of any French citizen along with the right to use the father's surname, although this did not of course mean that the father would necessarily stay any longer than one who did not recognize his children. More commonly, the father would provide for his métis children for the duration of his stay, then leave a sum of money to the mother upon departure without having undertaken the process of recognition of paternity. Others would not make any provision at all; members of the military were especially liable to disappear without much likelihood of any further contact with either mother or child.[11] This could be done without fear of legal reprisal, as African women and their métis children were effectively powerless to extract any form of recompense from an absconding French father. Metropolitan modifications to the Civil Code in 1912 giving greater scope for paternity suits were not extended to French West Africa in any meaningful form until 1949, and even then the opportunities for their application were minimal.[12] Most métis children became the black woman's burden, so to speak, or were placed in special homes, as will be discussed later.

[10] Le Barbier, *La Côte d'Ivoire*, 210.   [11] See e.g. ANS, FM: O 175.

[12] This will be treated in depth in Ch. 5.

It is true that some French men, even those in military service, took care to assure the future of their métis children. A series of letters in the Senegalese archives, for example, reveals the concern of a French warrant officer in a battalion of the Senegalese *tirailleurs* in arranging with the colonial authorities in 1918 to make special provision for his two métis children when it came time for him to return to France, as their Mauritanian mother (herself described as an orphan) could not afford to look after them and his own pay was insufficient.[13] But the somewhat surprised reaction to this request on the part of Lieutenant-Colonel Gaden of Mauritania and Governor-General Angoulvant, and the absence of any clear procedure in such cases, suggests that it may be taken as the exception that proves the rule. There were a few rare cases of fathers taking their mixed-race children back to France with them, but the behaviour of the colonial officer who, according to Georges Hardy, sent his five métis sons to a school in the north of France at the rate of one per year, creating 'a curious Franco-Khassonké colony' in the process, was highly unconventional.[14]

Examples of the much more common tendency to abandonment are legion for all the territories of French West Africa, but at this point one instance from Dahomey seems particularly representative. The example is drawn from a survey on 'the métis problem', one of the issues addressed by a colonial commission set up and funded by central government in 1937.[15] The survey reveals that in the subdivision of Natitingou in northern Dahomey in 1938 there were four métis, two male and two female, born of four different French men. The eldest child was a 14-year-old, who lived 'à l'indigène' with his mother having been 'totally abandoned' at birth by his father. The other three children were aged between 3 and 5. Each father had provided for his métis child while he remained in the colony, but all had since departed. None of them had given any further word of their whereabouts, or formally recognized their children. The respondent to the survey observed that this was either because they did not want to establish a legal link with their métis children, or because they were returning to families in France.[16]

[13] ANS, 9G 35.
[14] Hardy, *Une Conquête morale*, 70. The Khassonké people are concentrated particularly in the area around Kayes and Bafoulabé in Mali. See also ANS, FM: 17G 381, report on women and the family in French West Africa by Mme Denise Savineau, 1937–8, report 13: La Guinée Orientale, 24.
[15] See CAOM, Commission Guernut 101, which contains the responses from Dahomey, the French Soudan, and the mandate of Togo. The response from Senegal is in ANS, FM: O 715.
[16] CAOM, Commission Guernut 101.

This pattern seems to have been replicated across the colony of Dahomey. Mixed-race sons and daughters of French administrators, traders, and military men lived with their African mothers or were placed in special homes, misleadingly called 'orphanages'.[17] The survey noted the existence in Dahomey in 1938 of 241 people born of French fathers and African mothers; the rate of recognition on the *état civil* was certainly no higher than 15 per cent, and very probably less than that.[18] The figure was even lower in the French Soudan, where just twenty-two out of 274 métis listed for the purposes of the survey had been recognized by their fathers.[19]

It is not the intention here to suggest that all French men were completely devoid of feelings for their mixed-race offspring. Quite apart from the issue of financial support, some men apparently remained in correspondence with their métis children.[20] Similarly, Albert Londres began his exposé of the plight of French West African métis in *Le Petit Parisien* in 1928 with extracts from letters written by two generals, making enquiries about children they had long since left behind:

You will remember that in 1904 I buried a child at the cemetery in M . . . , close to the fort. On his grave I simply put: Henri. If the sand has not covered everything over, could you . . .

I have never stopped thinking about that time. Oh! my Soudan! What has become of my little hut near Fort Bonnier? Where is my native woman? my son? . . . His name was Robert. He is a man now. Where is he? I must tell you that I have always questioned friends returning from there! They know nothing of him. His mother's name was Aïssa, from the village of Kabara. . . . I would be infinitely grateful if . . .[21]

In this second letter, however, the nostalgic general's métis son seems to stand primarily as a symbol of his experience of Africa. The child enables

[17] The patently inaccurate designation 'orphanage' should hereafter be read as if in quotation marks.

[18] CAOM, Commission Guernut 101; also ANS, FM: 17G 381, Savineau report 6: Dahomey, 27–9. It is not possible to give a more precise rate of recognition for Dahomey because the figures include a number of non-French fathers (mainly other Europeans, Lebanese, or métis). The response from Togo notes the recognition of just one métis from 238. The rate in Senegal was much higher, but the figures are again skewed by the inclusion of non-French fathers, particularly those of mixed race themselves, whose children were almost invariably legitimate: see ANS, FM: O 715.

[19] CAOM, Commission Guernut 101. The figure 274 refers only to Soudanese métis who had been raised in the *orphelinats de métis*, which again prevents the calculation of an absolute rate of recognition.

[20] Ibid.; see the response from Togo, 5.

[21] Londres, *Terre d'ébène*, 66–7; *Le Petit Parisien*, 19 Oct. 1928. Fort Bonnier and Kabara are both in the region of Tombouctou; the second letter was sent to the commandant there.

him to believe that he became a part of the land he ruled, that he had a
right to possess it ('my Soudan!') not simply as a conqueror but also as a
father of one of its inhabitants.

Sometimes years would pass before fathers chose to recognize their métis
children. It has been calculated for the lower Ivory Coast that this gap
was seven years on average.[22] Some fathers would wait until their children
were fully grown before making a decision, allowing time to see how their
personalities were developing. One métisse was reclaimed by her father from
the special home for mixed-race children in Bingerville when she was 19.[23]
A father of two métisses in Guinea in the 1930s chose to recognize just
one of his daughters. She was withdrawn from the orphanage in Kankan,
while her unfortunate sister remained in the institution.[24]

Most métis children, however, had no further contact with their
fathers once they had left. In fact, they were more likely to try to find out
about their missing parent than vice versa. In the late 1930s the colonial
novelist Clotilde Chivas-Baron visited the missionary-run girls' orphanage
in Moussou (just outside Grand-Bassam) during a tour of the Ivory Coast.
Here she encountered a métisse in her late teens, who asked whether she
knew the address of her father. Chivas-Baron was taken aback because she
knew who the father was, but felt unable, despite her deep sympathy for
the girl, to promise to find out his address. She expected him to have since
started a family in France, far from this 'indiscretion'.[25] It was precisely
with the aim of preventing this kind of personal tragedy that Chivas-Baron,
as seen in the previous chapter, was such a prominent supporter of the
presence of French women in the colonies. Similar dramas were being
played out all over French West Africa.

In the absence of any social or legal obligation for French men to ensure
the well-being of the children they fathered in the colonies, it is not
perhaps surprising that the majority failed to make the necessary material
provision for such children. The absence of effective paternity laws was
one determining factor, but behaviour was also increasingly influenced by
the development of special homes for métis. From about the turn of the
century, all French men knew that undesired métis children could be placed
in these so-called orphanages,[26] where they would be looked after by French

[22] Tirefort, 'Européens et assimilés en Basse Côte d'Ivoire', 451.

[23] ANS, FM: O 501, Procès Verbal, Conseil de Perfectionnement, Foyer des Métis de
Bingerville, 4 Mar. 1944.

[24] ANS, FM: 17G 381, Savineau report 13: La Guinée Orientale, 24.

[25] Clotilde Chivas-Baron, *Côte d'Ivoire* (Paris, 1939), 113.

[26] See Joseph-Roger de Benoist, *Église et pouvoir colonial au Soudan français* (Paris, 1987), 160.

people who would also ensure that they received at least some basic education. The motivations behind this development were as much ideological
as they were altruistic, as will be shown. First, however, we must consider
the precedents for administrative action in favour of métis children.

The origins of special care for métis in French West Africa are to be
found in nineteenth-century Senegal. Between 1807 and 1812 Anne-Marie
Javouhey set up the Soeurs de Saint-Joseph de Cluny, dedicated to the
task of educating poor French children. In 1817, however, at the request
of the Restoration government, a few members of the order went to the
Île de Bourbon (now known as Réunion) to help educate the children of
colonial settlers there. In 1818 the order began similar work in Senegal;
Javouhey went to Africa herself in 1821. By 1822 there was a school for
European and mixed-race girls both in Saint-Louis and on the island of
Gorée.[27] The Frères de Ploërmel performed a comparable role for boys
from 1841. These two religious orders maintained a virtual monopoly on the
education of the children of the European elite and the métis bourgeoisie
in Saint-Louis and Gorée (and, a few years later, Dakar and Rufisque) until
the first decade of the twentieth century.[28]

In 1855 the Soeurs de Saint-Joseph de Cluny extended their activities
by opening a crèche for abandoned girls under the age of 7 at N'Dar Toute,
on a peninsula joined by a bridge to the island of Saint-Louis. Some of
these girls were freed slaves or children of captives, while others were
orphaned by epidemics. The largest category, however, was of mixed race.
As the children grew older the institution evolved into an *orphelinat-ouvroir*
(orphanage-workshop). There they were taught how to make their own
clothes, as well as sewing, washing, and ironing, and some rudimentary
schooling in reading, writing, and arithmetic. There were already thirty-five
children at N'Dar Toute in 1856, rising to an average of approximately
fifty, many staying till the age of 21, until the establishment closed in the

[27] Knibiehler and Goutalier, *La Femme au temps des colonies*, 150; Geneviève Lecuir Nemo,
'Mission et colonisation: Saint-Joseph de Cluny, la première congrégation de femmes au Sénégal
de 1819 à 1904', MA thesis (Univ. of Paris I, 1985), 165.
[28] Denise Bouche, *L'Enseignement dans les territoires français de l'Afrique Occidentale de 1817
à 1920. Mission civilisatrice ou formation d'une élite?* (Paris, 1975), 148; David E. Gardinier,
'The French Impact on Education in Africa, 1817–1960', in G. Wesley Johnson (ed.), *Double
Impact. France and Africa in the Age of Imperialism* (Westport, Conn., 1985), 335.

late 1950s.[29] The Pères du Saint-Esprit also cared for mixed-race children—mostly male—in their orphanage at N'Gazobil, where they had founded a mission in 1849, although their intake included roughly equal numbers of black African children.[30]

Why did métis children begin to receive particular attention in the mid-nineteenth century? The reasons are not entirely clear. Geneviève Lecuir Nemo has shown from her work on the lists of children admitted to the orphanage at N'Dar Toute that most carried surnames that were either French, or of well-established Saint-Louisian métis families such as Angrand, Valentin, and Pellegrin. She concludes that the main role of the orphanage was to take in young mixed-race girls who were not necessarily orphans, but who were in all probability illegitimate and increasingly less well accepted by Saint-Louisian society.[31] This would seem to fit in with the picture suggested in Chapter 1 of a socially less confident and economically less secure métis bourgeoisie, and a colonial society whose male members were becoming less willing to accept responsibility for the offspring of their interracial unions.[32] The objectives of the missionaries themselves must also be considered, however; to do this we must look not just at Senegal, but also at other parts of West Africa falling under French influence in the late nineteenth century.

## MISSIONARY OBJECTIVES

If the objectives of colonialism, Joseph-Roger de Benoist has argued, are likely to depend on a range of variables—contemporary ideas and interests, specific factors relating to the colonizers and the colonized, and

[29] Lecuir Nemo, 'Mission et colonisation', 209–13; id., 'Les Effectifs des écoles et des orphelinats des Soeurs de Saint-Joseph de Cluny au Sénégal', MA thesis (Univ. of Paris I, 1986), 3–5, 9–10, 15. A similar institution was opened by the same order on Gorée, closing in 1927 following a yellow fever epidemic.

[30] See Dr d'Anfreville de la Salle, *Notre vieux Sénégal. Son histoire, son état actuel, ce qu'il peut devenir* (Paris, 1909), 207–10; Philippe Gossard, *Études sur le métissage, principalement en A.O.F.* (Paris, 1934), 40; ANS, FM: 13G 93. N'Gazobil is close to Mbour on the coast south of Dakar; Léopold Sédar Senghor was educated at the mission school there between 1914 and 1923. See Janet G. Vaillant, *Black, French, and African: A Life of Léopold Sédar Senghor* (Cambridge, Mass., 1990), 20, 29. At various times there were also missionary-run orphanages in (for example) Dakar, Ziguinchor, and Thiès; see Bouche, *L'Enseignement*, 773.

[31] Lecuir Nemo, 'Les Effectifs', 9–10.

[32] It is unclear whether mixed-race girls were more likely to be abandoned than boys at this time in the old colonial towns of Senegal, although General Faidherbe did authorize a boys' orphanage in Saint-Louis in 1864. See Lecuir Nemo, 'Mission et colonisation', 209.

so on—then, at least theoretically, evangelization has just one objective: to make converts.[33] Missionaries should therefore, in theory, represent a distinctive and non-relativistic strand of colonialism. But de Benoist, a member of the Pères Blancs, himself acknowledges that the nature of missionary work is fundamentally influenced by the personalities and backgrounds of those carrying it out, and by the constraints set by secular objectives. It will be argued in this section that missionaries in French West Africa, particularly outside Senegal, were increasingly obliged to prove their loyalty to the colonial cause in the face of Third Republic anticlericalism by demonstrating that their goals were the same as those of the secular authorities. Their attitude to métis children highlights this very well. It will then be considered why they were nonetheless badly hit by anticlerical legislation between 1903 and 1905. The French Soudan will provide the focus for this section, being at present the area best documented in terms of the standing of missionaries in the decade before the laicization of education.

After a good deal of lobbying of the colonial authorities, unsure about the presence of missionaries in an area still very far from being brought under French control, the first permanent mission in the French Soudan was established by the Congrégation du Saint-Esprit, otherwise known as the Spiritains, at Kita in November 1888. The following year the administration gave them the money to found a school there. The same order further established its presence in August 1893 by setting up in Kayes, the centre of the nascent French administration in the region. They were joined later that year by the Soeurs de Saint-Joseph de Cluny. The Spiritains then set up an orphanage in Dinguira, about twenty-five miles along the railway line east of Kayes, having decided that the climate of Kayes itself—one of the hottest towns on earth—was unsuitable for such an institution. A group of Soeurs de Saint-Joseph de Cluny followed in 1896.[34]

In 1895 responsibility for missionary activity in the French Soudan was handed over to the Société des Missionnaires d'Afrique, more commonly known as the Pères Blancs, an order founded in 1868 by Cardinal Lavigerie, Archbishop of Algiers. By 1901 the Pères Blancs had completely replaced the Spiritains, taking over the schools at Kita and Dinguira, and setting up others in Ségou and Tombouctou.[35]

[33] De Benoist, *Église et pouvoir colonial*, 32.
[34] Ibid. 52–6. I use 'Dinguira' here in preference to 'Dinguiray' as the former was the more common French spelling, and serves to distinguish it from Dinguiray(e) in Guinea, where al-Hajj Umar Tall had his headquarters in the mid-nineteenth century.
[35] See ibid. 152–6.

To serve the evangelical aims of missionary work, the principal objective of mission schools was to form an indigenous clergy, catechists, and
schoolteachers.[36] In order to find the people most likely to fulfil this objective, Christian missions all over Africa tended to give particular attention
to people whose ties to society had been loosened or destroyed. These
included those uprooted by war, disease, or famine, as well as slaves either
liberated by military conquest or bought from captivity by missionaries
themselves.[37]

It is often forgotten, however, that people of mixed race constituted another
category which aroused especial interest among missionaries. Although the
conquest of what became the French Soudan can only truly be said to have
got under way in the early 1880s, interracial sexual relations were such
a part of the process of colonization that by the turn of the century métis
children were a familiar sight in the towns of the Soudan. Monseigneur
Hacquard, vicar apostolic of the Sahara and the Soudan, noted as much
when writing to Governor-General Chaudié in December 1899, adding that
'I cannot, without a pang of anguish, see them wander the streets abandoned,
without anyone to offer sustained care'.[38]

In the same letter, Hacquard gave a neat exposition of why he thought
métis, 'the sons of Frenchmen and Christians', were worthy of special
interest. 'It would be superfluous', he wrote, 'to explain to you what services
these children, perfectly acclimatized and more intelligent than the majority
of blacks, can render to the colony in later life.' Hacquard continued that
although the Pères Blancs had already taken in a few métis, the number was
far too small. He wished those in positions of responsibility to know that the
Pères Blancs were able to look after 'these poor little creatures' from the
moment they no longer required maternal care (which, in his estimation,
was about the age of 2), and that they would set about forming 'future
auxiliaries of French action, intelligent and devoted'.[39]

Hacquard was at pains to frame his request within the terms of secular
objectives, a tendency visible elsewhere in his dealings with the colonial
authorities.[40] He therefore emphasized the services that métis might be able
to render the colony and the 'civilizing mission', rather than their potential
as agents of Christian evangelism. French missionary societies were already
aware that their position was threatened by the anticlerical tendencies of

[36] Gardinier, 'The French Impact on Education', 335.
[37] Philip Curtin, Steven Feierman, Leonard Thompson, and Jan Vansina, *African History* (London, 1988), 525; de Benoist, *Église et pouvoir colonial*, 97–8.
[38] ANS, 17G 33, Mgr Hacquard to GG Chaudié, Ségou, 18 Dec. 1899.      [39] Ibid.
[40] For further examples see de Benoist, *Église et pouvoir colonial*, 145.

the Third Republic. From the early 1880s official aid was only being given to specific missionary projects, such as hospitals and schools, rather than general grants to the various societies and congregations.[41] But there were other reasons, too, for the Pères Blancs to stress that they were working towards essentially the same goals as the lay authorities in the French Soudan. As Christopher Harrison has phrased it in relation to the work of the society's founder, Cardinal Lavigerie, 'however well his charitable activities fitted with the rhetoric of the civilising and liberating mission of colonialism . . . the colonial authorities were nonetheless, with good reason, fearful of the political consequences of allowing the missionaries a free hand in strongly Muslim areas'.[42] After all, Hacquard's residence as vicar apostolic of the Soudan was at Ségou, which the French had captured as recently as 1890 from Ahmadu, sultan of the Islamic Tukolor empire.[43]

Hacquard was not concerned to create any sense of moral obligation for fathers to recognize or take responsibility for their mixed-race offspring. He welcomed any financial contribution that the fathers might make towards the upkeep of their métis children, but stressed that this would only ever be left up to individual discretion.[44] Nor at any stage did he mention the circumstances which led to the birth of these children. Of course, Hacquard may privately have expressed disapproval of the dealings of French men with African women. In this early phase in the colonization of the French Soudan, however, Catholic missionaries were often cut from similar cloth to their secular counterparts. Most famously, Père Auguste Dupuis, who co-founded the mission in Tombouctou with Hacquard in 1895, found Catholic vows of celibacy difficult to maintain among the women of the Soudan. So much so, in fact, that in 1904, after over four years as superior of the mission in Tombouctou, he decided to leave the Pères Blancs and marry a local woman, with whom he went on to have a large family.[45] His friend Hacquard was not best placed in 1899 to preach to secular administrators about their sexual conduct, even if that were his desire.

By July 1902 mixed-race boys in the French Soudan were cared for in the Pères Blancs' orphanages at Dinguira, Kita, Ségou, and at a smaller orphanage in Tombouctou. The girls were looked after by the Soeurs de

---

[41] Gardinier, 'The French Impact on Education', 336.

[42] Harrison, *France and Islam in West Africa*, 18.

[43] On the capture of Ségou, see Thomas Pakenham, *The Scramble for Africa* (London, 1991), 169–72, 361–5.

[44] ANS, 17G 33.

[45] The story of Père Dupuis is best told in William Seabrook, *The White Monk of Timbuctoo* (London, 1934).

Saint-Joseph de Cluny in Dinguira, and by the Soeurs Blanches[46] in Ségou. All these institutions were subsidized from the colony's budget, and the secular authorities were content for the time being to entrust to missionaries those métis children deemed to be in need of care.[47]

Hacquard's successor, Hippolyte Bazin,[48] expressed his desire to offer all the orphans living in the Pères Blancs' school at Ségou a more advanced education than the day-pupils, 'with the aim of providing ourselves with auxiliaries later on in the various regions of the Soudan where we are able to establish ourselves and found schools'. However, he had particular hopes for his métis pupils. Accordingly, they received a higher level of care and attention. Early in 1902 the mixed-race girls in the Soeurs Blanches' home in Ségou were separated from the black African so-called *abandonnées*, with the aim of giving them 'an education apart'. They were taught French, and in dress, diet, and general behaviour were raised as Europeans. Like Hacquard, Bazin was anxious to take in more métis, regarding it as 'unfortunate' that some could not be prized away from their mothers, and that others were not rescued because they lived too far from any missionary establishment.[49] Enthusiasm for what could be done was shortly to be curtailed, however, as the effects of Third Republican anticlericalism began to be felt in West Africa.

## MÉTIS AND THE LAICIZATION OF EDUCATION

The first steps in the process of secularization in France took place during the premiership of the moderate Republican René Waldeck-Rousseau between 1899 and 1902. Motivated partly by the role played by certain religious orders in the Dreyfus Affair, Waldeck-Rousseau drafted legislation obliging all religious orders to obtain recognition by law. This was passed in a rather more extreme form than he had envisaged in July 1901, and

[46] The more common name for the Congrégation des Soeurs Missionnaires de Notre-Dame d'Afrique.

[47] Bouche, *L'Enseignement*, 768; CAOM, SG, Soudan X dossier 4, 15 July 1902, rapport Bazin, 6. The numbers of métis taken in are hard to pin down; Bazin claimed that missionaries looked after over a hundred children in Dinguira and forty in Kita, but gave a figure of a dozen métis living in Kita itself.

[48] Hacquard having drowned in the Niger River in April 1901; see de Benoist, *Église et pouvoir colonial*, 77.

[49] CAOM, SG, Soudan X dossier 4, rapport Bazin, 6. A schools inspector later contested the 'Frenchness' of the girls' education at Ségou; see the case study of the Orphelinat de Ségou in Ch. 3 below.

was put into effect the following year with the closure of over a hundred religious communities, and in turn of thousands of educational establishments. Anticlerical measures proceeded apace when Waldeck-Rousseau's administration was replaced by the more radical Bloc Républicain, first under Émile Combes (1902–5), and then under the more moderate Maurice Rouvier (1905–6). In January 1903 a resolution was passed in the Chambre des Députés calling for the secularization of church schools in West Africa. A law of July 1904 forbade all teaching by religious orders, even those which had received official authorization; and in December 1905 the separation of church and state was finally implemented.[50]

The effects of this wave of anticlericalism were unevenly felt across French West Africa. This was primarily due to the fact that none of the anticlerical legislation passed in the *métropole* was ever actually promulgated in the federation, despite being advocated by such prominent figures as Governor-General Ernest Roume. One key concern was how any legislation might affect relations in Islamic areas, but the colonial authorities also had to consider whether secular alternatives were available if missionary education were to cease.

The attack on congregational education nevertheless came at a time when, with the process of 'pacification' well advanced and the federal structure of French West Africa now in place, ideologies of colonial domination were under particular scrutiny as the French assessed how to make the most of their newly won possessions. In France itself, people weighed up the various merits of the theories of 'assimilation' and 'association'.[51] In West Africa, administrators worked out how to follow military with moral conquest. In terms of education, the latter was a necessity which went beyond the rhetoric of bringing so-called civilization to so-called savages: it was, as Christopher Harrison points out, inextricably linked to political and economic goals.[52] The French needed to educate Africans to cement their standing in the area and to form auxiliaries for colonial rule. Most

---

[50] This paragraph is largely based on Jean-Marie Mayeur and Madeleine Rebérioux, *The Third Republic from its Origins to the Great War, 1871–1914* (Cambridge, 1984), 227–32, and James F. McMillan, *Dreyfus to De Gaulle: Politics and Society in France 1898–1969* (London, 1985), 15–18. More detailed studies are Malcolm O. Partin, *Waldeck-Rousseau, Combes, and the Church: The Politics of Anticlericalism, 1899–1905* (Durham, NC, 1969); Maurice Larkin, *Church and State after the Dreyfus Affair: The Separation Issue in France* (London, 1974); and James P. Tudesco, 'Missionaries and French Imperialism: The Role of Catholic Missionaries in French Colonial Expansion, 1880–1905', Ph.D. thesis (Univ. of Connecticut, 1980), 149–86.

[51] See Betts, *Assimilation and Association*.

[52] Harrison, *France and Islam in West Africa*, 57.

of all, there were economic imperatives; as one writer was to phrase it in 1911: 'To instruct the natives is to augment their economic value.'[53]

This task was too important to be left to missionary groups whose loyalty was doubted by many. Roume was in favour of the secularization of education on the basis that the congregations, though not particularly strong at the time, might grow in influence and pursue objectives which did not harmonize with official policy.[54] Significantly, the pyramidical structure for education in French West Africa authorized by Roume in November 1903 envisaged no role for missionary-run private education.

Laicization therefore got under way at the start of 1903, hastened, it should be added, by pressure put on the Colonial Minister, Gaston Doumergue, by the anticlerical majority in the Chambre des Députés and by the radical press.[55] In Senegal, the process was all but complete by the beginning of the school year in 1904.[56] Though their subsidies were cut, however, the Soeurs de Saint-Joseph de Cluny and the other orders operating in Senegal remained in the country, using other funds to maintain what became clandestine private institutions.[57] In this way the orphanages at N'Dar Toute and N'Gazobil both survived; moreover, in 1909 the Lieutenant-Governor of Senegal observed that in Saint-Louis, Dakar, and Gorée, the Soeurs de Saint-Joseph de Cluny and the Soeurs de l'Immaculée Conception continued to receive the children of officers, administrators, and local notables in unauthorized schools. Those in charge of the newly founded lay schools, not surprisingly, complained bitterly about this unwanted competition.[58]

Indeed, the only order which abandoned its work in West Africa as a result of laicization was the Frères de Ploërmel. In Dahomey, Catholic education not only survived laicization more or less intact, but even managed to develop after 1904, helping to explain the number of Dahomeans (second only to the Senegalese) who went on to the secondary schools of Senegal, set up to serve the whole federation.[59] Léopold Mairot, the Inspector of Education in French West Africa, was by no means pro-clerical, but even

[53] F. Dubois, *Notre beau Niger* (Paris, 1911), 208.

[54] ANS, 17G 33, GG Roume to Ministre des Colonies, no date (probably April or May 1905).

[55] Bouche, *L'Enseignement*, 487.

[56] See ANS, J 84 for further details; also Bouche, *L'Enseignement*, 487.

[57] 'Clandestine' was the word generally used by administrators, although the degree to which they truly were so is debatable.

[58] ANS, J 84, Lt.-G. du Sénégal to GG, Saint-Louis, 11 June 1909. See also ANS, J 28.

[59] Bouche, *L'Enseignement*, 496, 684; J. B. Webster and A. A. Boahen, *West Africa Since 1800* (2nd edn., Harlow, 1980), 221. The position of these schools in the structure of education in French West Africa will be described more fully in Ch. 3.

he was forced in 1905 to concede the merits of the fact that, primarily due to the work of the Société des Missions Africaines de Lyon, '1,600 children in Dahomey and 350 in the Ivory Coast are learning the French language without the colonies concerned having to spend a single centime!'[60]

The picture was different in the French Soudan. The most important figure here was William Ponty, a freemason in the prestigious Grand Orient lodge. He was the Governor-General's delegate in charge of administrating the French Soudan from 1899 until 1904, when he became the first Governor of the colony reconstituted as Upper Senegal and Niger.[61] Ponty had criticized the 'uselessness' of the education offered by the Pères Blancs as early as 1900, and despite acknowledging an improvement in 1903, he nevertheless approved the cessation of subsidies—a total of 14,200 francs—to all six of their schools from 1 January 1904.[62] With this decision the educational activity of the Pères Blancs was brought almost completely to a halt, to the extent that the following year acting Lieutenant-Governor Fawtier of Upper Senegal and Niger wrote that there was simply no need to promulgate the law of July 1904 preventing all religious orders from teaching.[63] The institutions run by the Soeurs de Saint-Joseph de Cluny and the Soeurs Blanches at Dinguira and Kita respectively received money for a further year while alternatives for the children were sought.[64]

It was against this background that, in January 1904, nine girls aged between 12 and 15, mostly of mixed race, fled the orphanage at Dinguira. Following the railway line they ended up in Kayes, where they complained to the local administrator of brutal treatment at the hands of the nuns. Ponty intervened and arranged for them to be housed temporarily in empty huts close to the École Professionnelle de Kayes, for whose pupils they were obliged to cook and mend clothes, under the supervision of a woman named Makaïta Fall. Other girls were admitted—two of them bringing similar claims of maltreatment from Dinguira—and the École Ménagère des Filles de Kayes was born. A teacher, Madame Teissonnière, arrived from France to take charge, and the institution was officially recognized in October 1904.[65]

---

[60] ANS, J 11, 'Rapport sur l'enseignement au Haut-Sénégal-Niger, en Guinée, les écoles coraniques et les congrégations', 56. No date.

[61] For biographical details see Johnson, 'William Ponty', 127–56; also de Benoist, *Église et pouvoir colonial*, 136–7.

[62] The schools involved were at Tombouctou, Ségou, Kita, Dinguira, Ouagadougou, and Koupéla. See Leonhard Harding, 'Les Écoles des Pères Blancs au Soudan français, 1895–1920', *Cahiers d'Études Africaines*, 11 (1971), 106–7; also ANS, J 83, 'Note au sujet de la laïcisation des écoles de l'AOF', June 1904.

[63] ANS, J 83, Fawtier to GG, 3 Apr. 1905.     [64] ANS, J 35.

[65] Ibid.; CAOM, SG, Sénégal X dossier 26; de Benoist, *Église et pouvoir colonial*, 155.

Even at the time the girls' allegations of brutality were treated with a degree of scepticism, most notably by Governor-General Roume himself; and the Inspector of Education, Mairot, was later to describe some of the girls as having 'singular moral principles'.[66] But Roume accepted the findings of an inquiry set up by Ponty which produced medical evidence of beatings, and suggested that the children had been overworked, poorly nourished, and kept in unhygienic conditions.[67] Roume wrote to Colonial Minister Gaston Doumergue in June 1904 that the grant to the Soeurs de Saint-Joseph de Cluny at Dinguira was given in large measure because most of the children they looked after there were born of 'unions accidentelles'—an exquisite euphemism—between European men and African women. He recognized the need for special care, based on the belief that there was genuine hostility towards métis on the part of black Africans, arguing that if they were not taken in by some charitable institution straight away they risked being abandoned or even 'suppressed'. In any case, he felt that African families were incapable of offering the requisite level of care. Despite these fears, Roume was unsure whether the colony of Upper Senegal and Niger had the resources necessary to take on the role played by the sisters at Dinguira; but the Minister, unconcerned by such practicalities, brusquely informed him that the administration had a duty to perform which was too important to be left to nuns who mistreated children and struck the sick.[68]

The establishment of the École Ménagère de Kayes and the mixed orphanage founded at Ségou in October 1904—an institution we shall be looking at in depth in the following chapter—signalled the beginning of a direct involvement in the upbringing of métis children by the French colonial administration in West Africa that was to continue until independence. Other special homes exclusively intended for métis children offering schooling as well as a bed, food, and so on were to follow in other colonies, for example at Bingerville in the Ivory Coast in 1910, and at Porto-Novo in Dahomey in 1913.[69] These institutions became the focus for the French

---

[66] ANS, J 35, report on the École Ménagère de Kayes, 13 Jan. 1905. Apparently more than one girl had become pregnant. See ANS, FM: O 685, 'Note sur les orphelinats de métis du Soudan français'.

[67] Some of these allegations had been made previously in a report by the *commandant de cercle* of Kayes, who described the results achieved by the mission at Dinguira as 'absolutely inadequate'; see ANS, J 35.

[68] CAOM, SG, Sénégal X dossier 26. GG Roume to Ministre des Colonies, Gorée, 14 June 1904; Ministre des Colonies to Roume, Paris, 9 July 1904.

[69] CAOM, Direction du Contrôle 962 dossier 81; ANS, FM: O 53. A table providing some basic detail on all such institutions can be found in Owen White, 'Miscegenation and Colonial Society in French West Africa, *c.*1900–1960', D.Phil. thesis (Univ. of Oxford, 1996), 332.

administration's 'policy' towards métis, such as it was. They were also the places where any theories regarding the potential of people of mixed race to serve as auxiliaries for colonial rule could be put into practice. Much more lay behind the intervention of the secular administration than anti-clerical distaste or a guilty kind of altruism; to assess the motives of the administration, we must now examine more closely how French colonials perceived people of mixed race.

## WHY INTERVENE?

In his *Guide pratique de l'européen dans l'Afrique occidentale* of 1902, as described in the previous chapter, Dr Barot encouraged French men to form temporary unions with African women. He went beyond this, how-ever, to express optimism, even excitement, about the children which would result from such arrangements. Not only could they be 'beautiful, strong, and intelligent'; they would also play an integral role in a radical method of colonization which might be described as biological assimilationism. In Barot's mind: 'The whole problem of adapting our races to these climates lies there; it is by creating mulatto races that we most easily Gallicize West Africa.' Tempering his tone slightly, he suggested that the initial contact between Europeans and Africans should be followed by unions between whites and métis, leading to perfect acclimatization.[70]

Barot's enthusiasm was typical of his time, when French rule in West Africa was still only in its formative stages. French aims had to take account of insecurities resulting from expansion into an unfamiliar environment with its attendant medical hazards. Yet Barot's vision of métis potential can be seen at least as late as 1938, when the administrator for the subdivision of Grand-Popo in Dahomey wrote that '*Métissage* is not to be encouraged unless it leads to a French race born in the colony and perfectly adapted to life in the tropics'.[71]

Barot was aware that his vision would require vigorous intervention if it were not to do more harm than good. Observing that French relations with people of mixed race had often been strained, he ascribed this partly to their social isolation between blacks and whites: 'they have had to become inflexible to defend themselves; we are responsible for their state of mind, and must do all we can to correct it.' Thus he was in favour of

---

[70] Barot, *Guide pratique*, 331. For more on the acclimatization issue, see Ch. 4 below.
[71] CAOM, Commission Guernut 101.

the subsidies for the missionary institutions at Kita and Dinguira, though convinced that the level of assistance remained inadequate.[72] Barot's views on métis typify the heady rhetoric of the 'civilizing mission', where the grand schemes and quasi-evangelical language used to promise improvement by contact with a 'superior' civilization sat somewhat at odds with the racially deterministic attitudes which structured them.

This self-justifying and self-aggrandizing language was less in evidence by 1916 when another advocate of interracial unions, Louis Le Barbier, considered how the 'unfortunate' by-products of such unions should be treated. The pressing concern now was to follow the *mise en place* of the colonial structure with an effective system of administration and, increasingly, to think of ways of enhancing the economic worth of French West Africa—a process referred to as the *mise en valeur*.[73]

Le Barbier prefaced his remarks with familiar observations on the social isolation of métis; he then expressed his desire for 'the white community' to make up for the faults of certain of its individual members. There, however, his humanitarian assessment of the situation ended, because in truth he regarded métis primarily as an exploitable resource. He envisaged separating them from black African children from a young age (their mothers' wishes did not merit a mention in his plan), and placing them in specially created schools in each colony. The less intelligent would be guided towards manual professions, while the more gifted would be encouraged to take up commerce and industry. (Presumably this was intended only for the boys; he foresaw only a school of domestic science for the girls.) In doing this, Le Barbier argued, the French would be able to create a pool of skilled workers, shopkeepers, and so on, who would be 'good servants'—unlike, for example, the 'lazy and thieving' Wolofs, who, he claimed, virtually monopolized these functions in Senegal and the French Soudan. Then, by encouraging mixed-race men and women to intermarry, it would be possible to create an 'intermediate race' which would understand European civilization while remaining in contact with the local population.[74] What he was advocating, as will be seen in the next chapter, was for métis to form a kind of petty bourgeoisie in a racially conceived class structure—a prospect which continued to motivate policy-makers until at least the 1940s.

[72] Barot, *Guide pratique*, 330–1.
[73] Most famously in Albert Sarraut, *La Mise en valeur des colonies françaises* (Paris, 1923).
[74] Le Barbier, *La Côte d'Ivoire*, 210–15. Le Barbier thought this scheme could be financed at least in part by the money then being spent on bringing white women to Africa, expenditure he considered useless. Other colonial theorists were very much opposed to the idea of an 'intermediate' race, as will be shown in Ch. 3.

An importance difference in emphasis is seen in Georges Hardy's *Une Conquête morale: L'Enseignement en A.O.F.*, published in 1917. Hardy's views are of considerable significance. He was Inspector-General of Education for French West Africa from 1914 to 1919, and his writings were not just presented as official texts—in the estimation of Governor-General Gabriel Angoulvant in 1919, they served as the 'credo' for the colonial administration's education policies.[75]

Hardy, a prominent supporter of the presence of white women in the colonies, was not in favour of interracial unions. He painted a bleak picture of métis children, abandoned by their fathers, growing up virtually as vagrants and 'being corrupted rapidly'.[76] Ostracism by blacks and whites was again seen as a major problem, but Hardy's fears outweighed any optimism he may have felt for a solution via social engineering. In his view, there was a risk that métis would become 'a race of true rebels, hostile to both whites and blacks, intelligent and perverse, armed for evil, because we have not oriented them towards good. And it is to ward off this danger that, in French West Africa, we have undertaken to gather in these abandoned métis children. It is also out of pity . . .'[77]

No one could be in any doubt, however, that Hardy's support for the *orphelinats de métis*—somewhat reluctantly given, it should be added—was based on an essentially negative appraisal of métis potential. He had no grand schemes for what could be done with them, only the wish that they be guided towards 'good, modest occupations'.[78]

The attitude of the administration towards abandoned métis children, therefore, was characterized by an ambivalence concerning their potential to become either indispensable auxiliaries or dangerous *déclassés*. As will be shown in the following chapter, this ambivalence shaped the treatment of the children gathered together in the orphanages.

The French were not slow, however, to congratulate themselves on what they saw as the munificence of their policy towards abandoned métis children. Not only does it seem likely that the orphanages lessened the guilt

[75] Tirefort, 'Européens et assimilés en Basse Côte d'Ivoire', 456. For more on Hardy's incumbency as Inspector-General of Education, see Prosser Gifford and Timothy C. Weiskel, 'African Education in a Colonial Context: French and British Styles', in Prosser Gifford and Wm. Roger Louis (eds.), *France and Britain in Africa* (New Haven, 1971), 690–4.

[76] Stoler again has noted in Indochina (and, indeed, the Dutch Indies) this fear of 'a new underclass of European paupers, of rootless children who could not be counted among the proper European citizenry'; 'Sexual Affronts', 525.

[77] Hardy, *Une Conquête morale*, 71. Similar views had been expressed by the administrator François de Coutouly in 'La question des métis en Afrique occidentale française', *La Revue Indigène*, July 1912, 545–9.

[78] Hardy, *Une Conquête morale*, 72.

felt by an absconding father, but they were also presented as an example of the caring nature of the French administration.[79] Once again, some peculiar relative value judgements were employed. Louis Le Barbier, for example, hailing the generosity of his plan discussed above, felt that if it were put into practice then métis children would be so grateful to whites in general that they would be able to forget their individual grudges against their French fathers.[80] Almost thirty years later, Governor Toby of Niger seems to have been thinking the same way when he wrote that:

The French administration considers the métis question from a sentimental point of view. It is in the nature of the French, who are not steeped in racial prejudice, to take pity on these little children, often deserted by their father through cowardice or necessity, and abandoned by their mother, and whose lot is indeed pitiful. That is why orphanages for métis are generously open to children in every colony, and they are cared for there with complete devotion by those in charge of them.[81]

Both these examples seem to suggest that the actions of individual Frenchmen could be excused by the collective ideals of French colonialism, as if these ideals gave the individual some kind of immunity against doing wrong. In fact, this represents another possible explanation for the absence of official sanctions against the individuals who treated their métis children with such apparent insouciance. Having considered some of the reasons why the colonial authorities decided that métis children were worthy of special attention, the following section will focus on the principles developed by the administration to regulate their involvement.

## PRINCIPLES OF ADMINISTRATIVE INTERVENTION

From its beginnings in the French Soudan, secular care for métis children soon spread to the other colonies of French West Africa. The only exceptions to this were Senegal and Mauritania. In Senegal, missionaries continued to operate unofficially until 1922, when a decree reorganizing private education in the federation enabled them legally to recommence their activities. Several years before this date, however, the Mauritanian government was sending its métis children to the institution run by the Soeurs de Saint-Joseph de Cluny at N'Dar Toute, suggesting that the

[79] To cite a few examples among many possibles, see the article 'A l'Institut colonial', *La Presse Coloniale*, 17 Nov. 1926; CAOM, Direction du Contrôle 941 dossier 17; Robert Cornevin, 'Les Métis dans la colonisation française: l'hésitation métisse', college thesis (École Nationale de la France d'Outre-Mer, 1941–2), 57.

[80] Le Barbier, *La Côte d'Ivoire*, 212–13.

[81] ANS, FM: 17G 187, Dec. 1943 or Jan. 1944.

authorities had fairly rapidly realized that missionaries played an indispens-able role.[82] Similarly, the administration in the Ivory Coast began placing mixed-race girls in the orphanage run by the Soeurs de Notre-Dame des Apôtres at Moussou just after its foundation in 1911, but did not formally authorize the institution until 1923.[83]

When the secular authorities began their own programmes of assistance, intervention in favour of métis children who were either completely abandoned or considered to be in need of extra-familial attention began to take on a kind of missionary zeal. Some of the children admitted to the orphanage at Bingerville in the Ivory Coast, for example, were brought in by one or even occasionally both parents. Most, however, were handed over by district administrators, who had been charged with the task of finding them in the areas under their control.[84]

Until now, the term 'abandonment' has been used only in so far as it applied to the departure of the fathers of mixed-race children. Administrators frequently used the word while disregarding the fact that the children's mothers had in many cases by no means 'abandoned' them in the way most of their fathers had. This is not necessarily to suggest that the position of métis in West African society was always secure; as will be suggested in Chapter 6, métis tended to be associated in some way with the colonial power, which may at times have left them vulnerable within indigenous society.

The general formula for administrators to take action was set out in a text from May 1924 reorganizing education in French West Africa. In this text, each colony was instructed to take in as many métis children of both sexes as possible who were 'morally and materially abandoned'.[85] This phrase was to reappear in the founding texts of every *orphelinat des métis* which followed, although administrators had been applying the principle for some time for the institutions which pre-dated it, such as those at Bingerville and Porto-Novo.[86]

---

[82] *Journal Officiel de l'Afrique Occidentale Française*, 1 Apr. 1922, 208; Lecuir Nemo, 'Les Effectifs', 19.

[83] CAOM, Direction du Contrôle 962 dossier 81.

[84] Ibid., report by M Sorin, 8 Mar. 1938. Parents who brought their children in were obliged to pay for their upkeep; those presented as 'abandonnés' were admitted free.

[85] See Paul Moreau, *Les Indigènes d'A.O.F. Leur condition politique et économique* (Paris, 1938), 86.

[86] The first use I have been able to find of this phrase in French West Africa comes in a series of proposed alterations to the education system in 1912 and 1913; see ANS, J 13. In France itself, under the 1889 law on the 'moral abandonment' of children, public author-ities could take in children adjudged by civil courts to be neglected or abused by their par-ents. There too, however, these criteria were open to interpretation. See Sylvia Schafer, *Children in Moral Danger and the Problem of Government in Third Republic France* (Princeton, NJ, 1997).

What this meant, in effect, was that métis children could be removed from the care of mothers deemed by an administrator to be unworthy or lacking sufficient financial resources. These criteria were so vague that even apparently loving homes could be broken up. In 1950, for example, one métis reflected on his experience of separation in an article entitled 'Mon entrée à l'Orphelinat':

I was very young in 1927. Still so young that I could hardly keep upright on my little legs, and yet that first journey I made to Adjatché [Dahomey] made such an impression on me that it is still present in my memory.

Mother was away from home during the day, and, my father not having had the goodness to leave us his address, I passed the greater part of the first years of my life with my grandparents.

I remember my grandmother best of all; tender and understanding as only grand-mothers know how to be with little children with whom they discover affinities.

For some time, I had been the object of special attention. I was hardly reasoning, but I had felt a gnawing unease.

I could not, of course, have guessed that the commandant had taken the decision to send me far, far away from my family.[87]

In this particular instance, we do not know the mother's reaction to the separation, and we cannot rule out the possibility that she had given her permission for it. For some women, struggling to provide for their métis children, placing them in an orphanage was the best available option.[88] Sometimes, however, pressure was put on mothers to hand over their children. This was the case when two *orphelinats de métis* were created in the colony of Niger in 1923. In an effort to recruit children for these institutions, a circular was issued to district administrators, asking them to

persuade [the parents] to send the children, from the beginning of the next school year, either to Zinder or Niamey, where they will receive education and care free of charge. You will be particularly insistent when it concerns young girls, for whom the future is more uncertain and from whom the mothers sometimes do not want to be separated.[89]

This 'persuasion' had mixed results. A 1938 report on the orphanage at Zinder gave the background to the admission of some of its boarders, suggesting ways in which the phrase 'morally and materially abandoned' may have been interpreted:

[87] From *L'Eurafricain*, 7 (1950), 8.
[88] See the cases cited by Savineau in ANS, FM: 17G 381, report 6: Dahomey, 27–8.
[89] ANS, FM: O 175. Circular by Adminstrateur en Chef Jore, 5 Apr. 1923.

The parents [*sic*] of these two little métis are in agreement and their children would only gain from being admitted into this establishment instead of wandering the streets of Tahoua.

(Commandant, Tahoua district, to Governor of Niger, March 1931)

He was almost unclothed, very dirty and with unkempt hair. Very timid, he seemed to me almost completely abandoned. His transfer to the Orphanage is imperative.

(Perruchot, Schools Inspector, note from June 1932)

These two children live in Madaoua; they have been abandoned, and their destitute mothers have many difficulties in feeding and looking after them.

(Commandant, Konni district, to Governor of Niger, June 1935)

It would be sad to see this young child soon follow the example of her mother, who engages in the basest prostitution in the village of Tanout.

(Commandant, Tanout district, to Governor of Niger, August 1935)[90]

The commandant of the *cercle* of Agadez, on the other hand, an area with a strong military presence and a correspondingly high proportion of mixed-race liaisons, took a different perspective. When the mothers of five métis children strongly opposed the sending of their children in 1932 to the orphanage at Zinder, 250 miles distant, the commandant supported them, on the basis that although it was a duty of the administration to take an interest in the future of métis children, it was nevertheless only humane to respect the fact that mothers had more rights over their children than anyone else. In this respect, it may be relevant to mention that most of the women involved in interracial unions in this particular area were Tuaregs, whose descent is matrilineal; as such, the French colonial state's assumption of paternal authority ran counter to local custom. In other West African societies, the mothers of métis children may not, in indigenous law, have had custodial rights over them. Among the patrilineal Abbeys (or Abbés) of the Ivory Coast, for example, regular marriages between local women and outsiders were resisted precisely because the break-up of the marriage left the children to the father by right.[91]

Many French administrators evidently disapproved of métis children being raised by African women. The term 'abandonment', as Stoler has pointed out, seems often to have referred to 'cultural rather than physical neglect', where the métis child was left to inhabit a native milieu considered an unfit environment in which to raise children in a seemly

---

[90] All examples from ibid. For an instance of separation against the mother's will, see Kambou-Ferrand, 'Souffre, gémis, mais marche!', 156.

[91] *Enquête coloniale*, 206.

fashion.[92] Contemporary commentators often employed highly emotive language to describe the plight of métis children, and blamed the mothers for a host of real or imagined wrongs. They used the mothers' shortcomings as justification for the intervention of the colonial authorities, whose generosity was freely praised, while the fathers' actions were exempted from scrutiny. Then, almost buried in sentimental rhetoric, they would discuss the plans devised to make the most of these unhappy circumstances: the formation of auxiliaries, a bourgeoisie, an elite, and so on. The following passage well represents this racist, high-handed, and ultimately self-serving brand of humanitarianism.

Solitude, isolation, and nostalgia are the mistresses of desire: children are born in the village home, in huts in the bush, and there find food and shelter, even tenderness, for as long as the man is present. But the eagerly awaited day arrives [for the man] to go on leave, to a different post, to other places of work, and the child remains in the care of the mother, who, unable to provide him with what he needs, abandons him. He is an orphan thrown on his own devices, a plaything of chance, of inexorable fate, he is an unfortunate with no means of support and no hope, who would go under in the unequal struggle [for life] if the local administration did not show the concern to take him in and guarantee his upkeep and his education.

All this preceded the author's assessment of a proposed reorganization of education for métis which would contribute to the formation of 'a limited elite', for 'the greater good of the community'.[93]

Those involved in providing care for métis children would seem often to have preferred their complete separation from their African backgrounds. Where was the point, complained Governor Legendre of Dahomey in 1947, in spending money on métis children if they went back to their families the moment they were old enough to be useful?[94] It is true that some children's mothers would try to reclaim them, and many made efforts to remain in contact whatever the circumstances. This was so to the extent that in 1915 the head of the orphanage at Porto-Novo in Dahomey felt the need to restrict their visiting rights.[95] There were even instances of

[92] See Stoler, 'Sexual Affronts', 526; also 532, where the author wonders whether concerns about a lack of paternal discipline and 'the threat of single-mother families' expressed at the same time in Europe and America may also have been at work here.

[93] Daniel Legrand, 'Pour les métis en AOF', *Revue des Questions Coloniales et Maritimes*, Apr.–May–June 1939, 31–3. He was actually writing in support of the Charton/de Coppet plan discussed below.

[94] ANS, FM: 2H 22. Conseil Général du Dahomey, Procès Verbal de la séance du 4 sept. 1947.

[95] ANS, J 47. See also de Benoist, *Église et pouvoir colonial*, 227.

mothers moving to the towns where their children had been placed in special homes.[96] After all, as the Head of Primary Education in Guinea noted during an inspection of the orphanage at Kankan in 1937: 'These are not for the most part abandoned children, but children who have been entrusted to us. The mothers come to see them at the orphanage and by no means forget about them.' The children went back to their mothers during the holidays too, at least to those deemed suitable by the local *commandant de cercle*. The Inspector complained that they often needed special attention on their return to Kankan, but accepted that they could hardly be prevented from going home to mothers who wanted to see them.[97] Some métis children would travel long distances to see their mothers during school holidays; two from the orphanage at Ségou, for example, made a round trip of over 800 miles to Tombouctou in July 1912.[98]

Even so, the basic information that most of these children were not orphans often seems to have been ignored or simply forgotten. An example of the latter instance came in a plan devised in 1936 by the Inspector-General of Education in French West Africa, Albert Charton, to rationalize the assistance given to métis children across the federation. The plan was approved by the Popular Front's appointee to the position of Governor-General, Jules Marcel de Coppet. It proposed to create three federally funded 'Maisons de Métis', one in Senegal, one in the French Soudan, the other in the Ivory Coast. This would have involved sending children from Niger hundreds, sometimes thousands of miles to Bamako, and children from Guinea all the way to Bingerville.[99] Both Governor Blacher of Guinea —himself a métis from the French West Indies—and Governor Court of Niger immediately pointed out the opposition that the administration would encounter from mothers unwilling to allow their children to be sent so far away, ending the possibility of their visiting them, and perhaps even of journeys home during the school holidays.[100] The proposals were never put into practice due to a combination of lack of money, prevarication, and the Second World War, but the example serves to highlight the extent to which the rationalizing, 'modernizing' tendencies of some of the Popular Front's appointees sat somewhat at odds with their avowed intention to rule the colonies more humanely.

[96] ANS, FM: 2H 1, 'Note au sujet des métis', Nov. 1937.     [97] ANS, FM: O 685.
[98] Institut de France (IF), Fonds Terrier, 5940 vol. 2.
[99] ANS, FM: 2H 17; ANS, FM: O 128.
[100] ANS, FM: 2H 1, 'Note au sujet des métis', Nov. 1937. Before the creation of the orphanages at Zinder and Niamey, Nigerien métis were sent all the way to the institution at Porto-Novo, with unhappy results. See ANS, FM: O 175.

The most obvious denial of the fact that most métis were not orphans, of course, was in the application of the word 'orphelinat' to institutions housing mixed-race children. The patent absurdity of this was widely acknowledged; as Albert Londres put it: 'They constitute the strangest category of orphans: orphans with a mother and father.'[101] However, the designation reinforced the self-justifying logic of intervention: these children had no one in the world to care for them, therefore grouping them together and giving them a direction was a supremely generous act. Only in the late 1930s and 1940s did some of these institutions cease to call themselves 'orphanages'; the one at Bingerville set the trend for them to be called 'foyers de métis' in 1939.[102] Though clearly more appropriate, it could be argued that the word 'foyer' equally implied the necessity for an alternative 'home', particularly when, as will be seen in the following chapter, demands were made of the French women running such institutions to offer themselves up virtually as surrogate mothers.

This chapter has shown how métis were identified by the colonial authorities as worthy of special attention, and has traced the development of institutions for them. In examining the principles drawn up to regulate the intervention of the French administration, it has also shown that many métis moved at a young age from the milieu of their mothers into the cultural milieu of their (absent) fathers. The effect this separation had on the children was hinted at by Barthélémy Chaupin, the secretary of a society set up by West African métis in the late 1940s, in an article written in 1950.

Here then is our young presumed Durand or Dupont in an establishment baptized 'Orphanage'. . . . It would have been even better to leave him to the loving affection of his mother, where, if he would not have acquired a perfect education, something which is no less lacking in these government homes, he would all the same have benefited from the maternal tenderness which, whatever anyone says, has a great influence on children. Numerous examples demonstrate it: at times a bitter melancholy, a deep spiritual sadness spontaneously overcomes them.[103]

The *orphelinats de métis* will now be looked at in detail: the living conditions and education offered therein, and what became of the children who were placed in them.

[101] Londres, *Terre d'ébène*, 68.
[102] *Journal Officiel de la Côte d'Ivoire*, 15 Apr. 1939, 365.
[103] From 'Le Métis dans la Société', *L'Eurafricain*, 9 (1950), 35.

# 3
## Education and Employment

French commentators offered a dual justification for the existence of special homes for métis children. Above all, they argued, such institutions were natural expressions of the humanity of the colonizing power. This was always followed, however, by a utilitarian justification, which emphasized the potential of métis to serve as auxiliaries for French rule. These justifications are well captured in an inspector's report on the orphanage at Porto-Novo in Dahomey in 1928:

> The generous tendencies of our race incline us to want the best for the populations we have taken it upon ourselves to guide. This moral obligation becomes all the more pressing where it concerns the métis whose care we have undertaken as a collective responsibility.
>
> These idealistic sentiments are joined by preoccupations no less legitimate and worthy for being more pragmatic: instead of making malcontents of those who have something of the two races in contact, would it not be better, if possible, to make use of them to reach the great indigenous mass?[1]

This chapter will concentrate particularly on issues raised in this second paragraph. By looking at the education given to the children housed in state-funded orphanages and the careers they were encouraged to pursue, it will attempt to discern what the 'legitimate preoccupations' of the colonial authorities were in relation to métis. French aspirations for the children in their care will be compared with the conditions in which they lived, with the aim of establishing whether French policy was motivated primarily by the desire to create a pool of willing auxiliaries for colonial rule or through the fear of creating a group of 'malcontents' or 'déclassés'. The chapter also features case studies of two different orphanages. First of all, however, some background details on the colonial system of education in French West Africa are needed.

---

[1] CAOM, Direction du Contrôle dossier 71, 'Rapport fait par M Le Gregam concernant l'Orphelinat des Métis du Dahomey à Porto-Novo', 27 Dec. 1928.

EDUCATION IN FRENCH WEST AFRICA

The French government first involved itself in education in West Africa as
early as 1816.[2] Throughout the nineteenth century, however, this involvement was inconsistent and unregulated by any particular 'system'.[3] This
changed in 1903, when a secular school system was finally established,
offering free education to African children. The system was organized in a
pyramidical structure. At its base were the *écoles de village*. The intention
was to open these in places possessing thirty potential pupils under the age
of 11.[4] The primary objective of these schools, clearly stated when the system was reorganized in 1924, was to 'diffuse spoken French among the
mass of the population'.[5] Even with the youngest children at the preparatory level, therefore, the French language was the medium used to impart
notions of hygiene and morality—obedience, courtesy, and so on—along
with some basic schooling in the three Rs.[6]

At the elementary level, children were introduced to the metric system, simple geometry, and general science, along with some history and
geography. They also received theoretical and practical instruction in
agriculture. These subjects were developed for the more able pupils at the
*écoles régionales*, which were created—in theory at least—in the capital
of each administrative district or *cercle*. A small number of students were
then able to progress to the *écoles primaires supérieures*, which gradually
appeared in the capitals of each colony from the 1910s. These schools sought
to train primary school teachers and clerks for the administration or for
commerce. Beyond these centres lay the federal schools based in Senegal,
accessible only to a chosen few, which trained teachers for advanced
primary education as well as medical personnel.[7]

---

[2] The most comprehensive treatment of French education in West Africa remains Denise
Bouche, *L'Enseignement dans les territoires français de l'Afrique Occidentale de 1817 à 1920*
(Paris, 1975); also see Conklin, *A Mission to Civilize*, 73–141. The post-1920 period has not
yet been covered in as much detail, though Paul Désalmand gives a thorough survey of the
archival material for one colony in the two volumes of his *Histoire de l'éducation en Côte d'Ivoire*
(Abidjan, 1983).

[3] On nineteenth-century education policy see Bouche, *L'Enseignement*; Joseph Gaucher, *Les
Débuts de l'enseignement en Afrique francophone* (Paris, 1968); Georges Hardy, *L'Enseignement
au Sénégal de 1817 à 1854* (Paris, 1920).

[4] Raymond L. Buell, *The Native Problem in Africa*, ii (New York, 1928), 52.

[5] Cited in Georges Hardy, 'L'Enseignement aux indigènes: possessions françaises d'Afrique',
in Bibliothèque Coloniale Internationale, *Rapports Préliminaires* (Brussels, 1931), 332.

[6] On the arguments for and against using French as the language of instruction, see Buell,
*The Native Problem*, ii, 57–61.

[7] These paragraphs are based primarily on Buell, *The Native Problem*, ii, 49–64, and
Gardinier, 'The French Impact on Education in Africa', 333–44.

The avowed objective of the system, as expressed by Governor-General Jules Carde, was to 'instruct the masses and extract the elite'.[8] The masses, however, remained largely untouched. Raymond Buell calculated that only 1.2 per cent of children of school age attended schools run by the colonial authorities in 1925.[9] Nor did this situation change greatly until after the Second World War. In fact, as several studies have suggested, the system was intended primarily to provide the functionaries required by the colonial administration. Moreover, even smaller in number were those sufficiently educated to be justifiably described as forming part of a 'French-educated elite'.[10] Despite the wishes of many French observers, generally speaking this held true for métis just as much as it did for black Africans. Nevertheless, there were differences in approach towards the métis children gathered together in the orphanages.

### EDUCATION AND CLASS FORMATION

If the French fashioned the education system for the purpose of producing the auxiliaries they required, then they had particular expectations of métis children. This was expressed consistently throughout the period in question, and was influenced by two key lines of thought. One of these was the implicit belief that an 'abandoned' child was more easily moulded to fulfil a specific requirement than one whose position in society was more secure. Of greater importance, however, were ideas stemming from beliefs in the racial characteristics of métis.

First, for reasons which will be detailed more fully in the next chapter, racially deterministic arguments were regularly applied in attempting to distinguish the aptitudes of people of mixed race. One common suggestion was that métis were somehow more intelligent than black Africans by virtue of their 'French blood'. A mutant offshoot of the same root argument, however, maintained that they were physically weak and unsuited to perform manual labour. As Jacques Mazet put it in 1932,

---

[8] Quoted in L. P. Mair, *Native Policies in Africa* (London, 1936), 215.

[9] Buell, *The Native Problem*, ii, 53–4. The figures were 30,000 (2,500 of whom were girls) out of a possible 2,500,000. Buell omitted from this percentage the 6,000-odd pupils educated in mission schools.

[10] Bouche, *L'Enseignement*, 895; Gifford and Weiskel, 'African Education in a Colonial Context', 675; Gardinier, 'The French Impact on Education', 334.

The European imprint which they bear leads them towards occupations where physical strength is less important than skill, patience, or reason. Must we allow these individuals, the partial issue of our race, to undergo an undeserved penalty due to our lesser resistance to fatigue? On the contrary, should we not teach them a trade, make accessible to them a profession better in tune with their aptitudes?[11]

Secondly, although there was much disagreement over the idea of treating métis as an intermediate class, it was recognized that a racially 'intermediate' group in society might have its uses. One respondent to a survey on 'the métis problem' in 1938 stated, for example, that métis were naturally bilingual. This, he argued, gave them 'a complete understanding of two mentalities', which could be used to facilitate the reconciliation and mutual comprehension of Europeans and Africans.[12]

This belief in their ability to understand two *mentalités* was practically an article of faith throughout the colonial period, and sometimes took on an almost mystical hue. As late as 1946, for example, Robert Delavignette weighed up the role played by métis in the history of French West Africa and concluded that: 'Their function is not yet at an end. They are still the only people, among blacks and whites, who can tap the hidden sources of an existence where Africa and Europe blend so intimately.'[13]

This assessment of the potential of métis to be useful to the French in many cases manifested itself in their orientation towards a variety of occupations which might be described as 'petty bourgeois'. There were precedents for this. 'Why . . . should we not encourage the formation in our new colonies of a race of métis?', wondered the Institut Colonial Français, a body which existed to promote development in the colonies, in a statement issued in 1926. 'Do they not constitute the very honourable and very intelligent basis of the local bourgeoisie in the French West Indies?'[14]

The extent to which there was ever a concerted effort to create a similar 'bourgeoisie' in French West Africa is debatable, but in certain areas the Institut Colonial's wishes seem partially to have been fulfilled. Attempting to reach this outcome, however, involved significant differences in treatment for mixed-race boys and mixed-race girls.

---

[11] Jacques Mazet, *La Condition juridique des métis dans les possessions françaises* (Paris, 1932), 9–10.

[12] ANS, FM: O 715. Senegalese response to Commission d'Enquête dans les Territoires d'Outre-Mer, Aug. 1938.

[13] Delavignette, *Freedom and Authority in French West Africa*, 30.

[14] See the article 'A l'Institut colonial', *La Presse Coloniale*, 17 Nov. 1926.

## EDUCATING MÉTISSES

Most of the *orphelinats de métis*, funded as they were from the budgets of colonies permanently short of money, lacked sufficient resources to offer a proper 'in-house' education. Mixed-race boys, therefore, were generally taught at local schools, following the curriculum described earlier. The girls, on the other hand, in most cases received at least part of their education within the orphanages themselves.

The education of métisses is of particular interest, because for many years they were disproportionately represented among females receiving an education in French West Africa. Education for girls was very slow to develop in the aftermath of the French conquest. This was true to such an extent that by 1917 the Governor of Senegal could still put in a plea for the administration to set up any kind of system of education for African girls.[15]

Any attempts to increase the number of girls receiving an education in West Africa faced the major obstacle of trying to convince parents of the worth of allowing their daughters to be educated outside the family home. For this reason, orphans or the abandoned formed a large proportion of those in a position to receive schooling.[16] At least until laicization, however, the administration seemed content to leave this task in the hands of missionaries.

Education for girls was of central importance to missionary orders, who hoped to increase the number of Christian marriages with the aim of establishing the gospel more securely in West Africa. The education they offered, however, was as limited in scope as this objective implies, treating female pupils primarily as future wives and mothers. Moreover, in the service of 'preparing children for the future', they might be put to work from a young age, which helped to subsidize their upkeep. The following passage from the 1870s, though referring specifically here to female orphans, sets out many of the aims of nineteenth-century missionary education for girls.

The Soeurs de Saint-Joseph de Cluny still maintain a crèche [on Gorée]. Its goal is to rescue from poverty and vice any poor little orphan girls that can be taken in, and to give them, along with an education in keeping with their station in life, habits of orderliness, piety, and work, and to make of them good workers or good servants.[17]

---

[15] See Bouche, *L'Enseignement*, 775.    [16] Ibid. 768.
[17] *Annales religieuses de Gorée*, report on Goréen schools by Père Meyer, 1 Nov. 1873. Quoted in Lecuir Nemo, 'Mission et colonisation', 212.

Such institutions were often accused of exploiting children for their labour. Some such complaints were made by anticlericalists with a grudge, but even these accusations frequently carry the ring of truth.[18] Official reports also suggested that since mission-run educational establishments for girls offered more tuition in washing and ironing than reading and writing, it was stretching a point to use the term 'school' to describe them.[19]

The administration took pains to avoid any accusation of exploitation when it began its own orphanages for métis in the wake of the secularization of education. In 1917 Georges Hardy wrote that 'we are seeing to it that the general instruction of métis children is in no way neglected', but stressed that 'above all we are taking the greatest care to avoid any organization of labour which might arouse the suspicion of child exploitation'.[20]

In spite of these assertions, the education offered to mixed-race girls in these new institutions often bore more than a passing resemblance to what had gone before. The very name École Ménagère de Kayes, for example, hardly promised a revolution in thinking about the role of women in French West Africa, even though Léopold Mairot, the Inspector of Education, enthused in 1905 that this school and its counterpart in Ségou served as the 'avant-garde' for girls' education in the federation.[21]

In fact, the rest of Mairot's comments on the École Ménagère de Kayes, wherein about half the pupils were of mixed race, highlights how limited was the administration's view of its potential. The emphasis was on teaching infant hygiene, cookery, sewing, ironing, and manual work appropriate to women, with one session given over to teaching everyday spoken French, along with some basic reading and arithmetic. The main aim was to fashion workers and domestics capable of supporting themselves; essential, in Mairot's estimation, 'if these young girls are not to turn to debauchery'.[22]

In practice, one of the few differences at Kayes was that all the education was given in French, whereas the girls who had come from the mission school at Dinguira, for example, had previously received instruction in the local language, Bambara. This was practically a heresy in the eyes of the laicizers, for whom the French language was the principal instrument of secular evangelism. Meanwhile, as Mairot was to note somewhat gloatingly, the mission school in Dinguira, along with similar establishments in the French Soudan, was heading into 'an inevitable decay'.[23]

---

[18] See e.g. ANS, J 28, report on the École des Filles de Dakar, Première Classe, 1907–8.
[19] See Bouche, *L'Enseignement*, 423.
[20] Hardy, *Une Conquête morale*, 72.      [21] ANS, J 11.
[22] ANS, J 35, 'Rapport d'inspection sur l'École Ménagère de Kayes', 13 Jan. 1905.
[23] Léopold Mairot, 'Les Écoles du Haut-Sénégal et Niger', *Revue de l'Enseignement Colonial* (1905), 135. On the importance attached by Republicans to teaching in the French language see Conklin, *A Mission to Civilize*, 84.

The advent of secular education for girls did not, therefore, represent much of a break from the established traditions of missionary education. The administrators wanted their new charges to become dutiful housewives, though precisely who for is not always clear. Part of the aim, as Stoler has argued for South-East Asia, was to avoid the creation of 'a future generation of . . . paupers and prostitutes, an affront to European prestige and a contribution to national decay'[24]—hence the additional emphasis on the skills which might enable the métisses to find some form of gainful employment. However, in spite of the disquiet which colonial administrators, in common with their missionary predecessors, expressed about the sexuality of métisses, when one reads such lines as 'it would be useful to teach them European cuisine',[25] it is difficult not to speculate whether some had any greater aspiration for these so-called *orphelines* than that they become companions for French men.

In 1917 Georges Hardy admitted that education for girls had been neglected in French West Africa. 'We attended to the most urgent things first', he wrote. To produce the auxiliaries needed in the early stages of colonization, almost exclusive attention had been paid to educating boys. Hardy now lobbied for the balance to be redressed, noting the ways in which French rule could thus be strengthened in the long term:

When we bring a boy to the French school, we gain an individual; when we bring a girl there, we gain an individual multiplied by the number of children she will have.

To ensure the cohesion of our empire, to make relations easier and bring the natives closer to us, we need to spread the use of the French language. When the mothers speak French, the children will learn it without difficulty and will come to us already roughly formed; for them, French will become, in the true sense of the word, a mother tongue.[26]

Here, as before, the measure of a woman's utility lay in her capacity to bear children and raise them in a suitable fashion, with secular objectives replacing the religious aims of the missionaries. Ironically, it was about the same time that heightened colonial involvement in the early stages of motherhood had a significant impact on many métisses, as they were encouraged to become midwives in an expanded medical service. This will be covered in detail in the next section. At this point, however, mixed-race boys must also be brought back into the picture.

[24] Stoler, 'Sexual Affronts', 525.
[25] ANS, J 35, report on the École Ménagère de Kayes, 3 Aug. 1907.
[26] Hardy, *Une Conquête morale*, 74–5.

THE INTER-WAR YEARS: 'LA MISE EN VALEUR DES MÉTIS'?

By the end of the First World War, special homes for métis children had been in existence long enough—and the children themselves were old enough —to be turning out significant numbers of métis seeking employment. Employment statistics represent perhaps one of the best available methods to discern whether métis were being treated as a special case. Official statistics on this subject appear only irregularly, and can be misleading, as will be argued later. Even so, trends do appear which suggest that métis children were being oriented towards particular careers. After all, in creating state-funded orphanages the colonial authorities were, so to speak, controlling the means of production, and their influence on the lives of their charges was constantly evident.

Between 1918 and 1934, according to official statistics, ninety-one girls and ninety-three boys left the official orphanages in the French Soudan. Mixed-race girls were grouped together in the mixed orphanage in Kayes from 1918 to 1923, the date at which they were transferred to a new, single-sex *orphelinat* in Bamako, an institution which will be the subject of a case study later in this chapter. The employment subsequently found by the boarders of these two establishments was as follows:[27]

| | |
|---|---|
| Midwives and nurses (serving any colony in A.O.F.) | 51 |
| Local nurses (serving colony of origin only) | 15 |
| Schoolteachers | 8 |
| Seamstresses | 2 |
| No profession (married) [*sic*] | 15 |

The range of occupations followed by the boys was more diverse. From 1918 to 1932 métis boys from the French Soudan were based in Kayes. In 1932 this official orphanage, which had become dangerously dilapidated, was closed, and, like their female counterparts a few years earlier, the boys were moved to Bamako. The boarders of the latter institution attended school during the day at the École Régionale de Bamako. Then, if they passed their *certificat d'études primaires indigène*, they were able to progress to the nearby *école primaire supérieure*.[28] The following jobs were found by

---

[27] Figures from ANS, 2H 13, GG Brévié to Ministre des Colonies, 30 Mar. 1934. Also in Gossard, *Études sur le métissage*, 38.

[28] ANS, FM: O 128, 'Arrêté du Lt.-G. réorganisant les orphelinats de métis du Soudan français', 11 Aug. 1932.

these ninety-three métis when they completed their schooling and came to leave the orphanages at Kayes and Bamako:[29]

| | |
|---|---|
| Schoolteachers | 19 |
| Auxiliary doctors | 10 |
| Auxiliary pharmacists | 7 |
| Auxiliary veterinary surgeons | 4 |
| Nurses | 3 |
| Employed in commerce or industry | 13 |
| Clerks | 8 |
| Railway employees | 14 |
| Naval engineers | 4 |
| Agricultural service employees | 4 |
| Topographers | 2 |
| Legal secretary | 1 |
| Postal worker | 1 |
| No profession | 3 |

These statistics do not always reveal very much about the nature of the occupations followed. It is likely that the occupation dignified here with the rubric 'agricultural service employee' was that of sheep-farmer, into which form of employment entered four of the five boys who left the orphanage at Kayes in 1930.[30] Moreover, the word 'clerk' (*commis*) was ill defined in a colonial context, although it may be significant that having studied the use of the word, Ada Martinkus-Zemp summarizes the role of the *commis* simply as an 'intermediary between whites and blacks'.[31] Likewise, it would be interesting to know exactly what functions métis performed on the railways, to shed some light on Robert Cornevin's comment that they were particularly suited to this form of employment.[32]

What is clear is that métis in the French Soudan were being particularly encouraged to enter the education and medical services as auxiliary workers. Both services had difficulties in attracting trained French personnel to the colonies, and just as much trouble in keeping them there. There was considerable discontinuity in the education system—as métis children were

[29] The total number cited in the documentation is ninety-four, but the figures in fact only add up to ninety-three.
[30] CAOM, Direction du Contrôle 941 dossier 17, mission Sol: report on the Orphelinat des Métis de Kayes by M. J. Chastenet de Gery, 20 Apr. 1930.
[31] Ada Martinkus-Zemp, *Le Blanc et le Noir. Essai d'une déscription de la vision du Noir par le Blanc dans la littérature française de l'entre-deux-guerres* (Paris, 1975), 124.
[32] Cornevin, 'Les Métis dans la colonisation française', 54.

often only too aware—due to the high turnover of French staff who found their tasks too arduous, fell ill, or even, in some cases, died while in service.[33] Moreover, in order to create schools in areas isolated from centres with a European population, teachers living 'à la mode indigène' were rapidly identified as essential for the system to function at all.[34] The need to train auxiliaries at least to fill subordinate posts therefore became a matter of some urgency. The fact that it was far cheaper to employ Africans in these posts was another compelling argument in its favour— besides, in passing, being a good reason for the French to continue to define métis as 'African', rather than 'white' or 'European'.

Concerning métisses in particular, the figures cited above suggest strikingly that they were urged to enter medical service as midwives or nurses. Indeed, at first glance one might even think the numbers falsely inflated; but they are corroborated by other sources,[35] and in any case were the result of a particular set of circumstances.

In 1905 the French administration began a program of medical aid known as the *assistance médicale indigène* (AMI). Its early impact, however, was limited. During the First World War military doctors were shocked to discover the poor general state of health of West Africans recruited to fight in the French cause. When the war ended, these same troops brought back new disorders (smallpox, venereal diseases) to add to pre-existing maladies like yellow fever, bilharzia, and plague, which continued to exact a heavy toll. Most significantly of all, tuberculosis began to spread at an alarming rate, its incidence rising from less than 12.5 per cent to over 40 per cent of the population of French West Africa between 1914 and 1930.[36]

Such a state of affairs was not just damaging to France's image: it also threatened the French West African federation's tax base and productivity levels. Improving standards of health care consequently became one of the most pressing concerns of the post-war administration—a fundamental problem, in fact, for the 'mise en valeur' of French West Africa.

[33] See e.g. IF, 5940 vol. 2, doc. 747; ANS, FM: 2H 1, Lt.-G. du Dahomey to GG, 28 Jan. 1937.

[34] e.g. ANS, J 11, 'Rapport de l'inspecteur de l'enseignement en A.O.F., 1905–6', 31; see also Conklin, *A Mission to Civilize*, 81. By 1946 the education department employed 200 European and 650 African teachers in French West Africa; see Delavignette, *Freedom and Authority in French West Africa*, 30.

[35] ANS, FM: 23G 22, report by Frédéric Assomption, Inspecteur des Écoles en Soudan français, 22 Mar. 1927; ANS, FM: 2H 17, Lt.-G. du Soudan français (Rougier) to GG, 9 Apr. 1937.

[36] See Jacques Thobie, Gilbert Meynier, Catherine Coquery-Vidrovitch, and Charles-Robert Ageron, *Histoire de la France coloniale*, ii (Paris, 1990), 156. For more on the AMI, see Conklin, *A Mission to Civilize*, 49–50, 69–70, 221–2.

To succeed in this aim required personnel. In 1918, therefore, a medical school was created in Dakar to train Africans as auxiliary workers for the AMI. The school proved to be quite a success, impressing foreign visitors with its high standards. One British observer described it in the 1930s as 'the crowning achievement of the French West African educational service'.[37]

Maternity and child care having been singled out as areas in need of special attention, a midwifery section was annexed to the École de Médecine de Dakar at its inception. The ideal was to be able to place in every sizeable village a midwife belonging to the local ethnic group and speaking the same language. The authorities envisaged the expansion of schools for girls in order to recruit suitable candidates for this venture.[38] In fact, due primarily to financial constraints, these developments took place only slowly, and never quite to the degree imagined.

Since métisses constituted a significant percentage of the small number of women who, by 1918, had received any kind of education from the colonial power, they were correspondingly well represented in the midwifery section, the results of which were described as 'brilliant' by one British doctor in the mid-1920s.[39] The section selected 18- to 25-year-olds by means of an examination testing spelling, French composition, and arithmetic. In the 1930s an average of seventy candidates competed annually for twenty vacancies. The official orphanages in the French Soudan and the mission-run institution at Moussou in the Ivory Coast were particularly successful in supplying students.[40] Indeed, getting pupils admitted seems to have developed into something of an obsession. Moussou was as much a workshop as a school, but written by the names of several of its pupils on a list from 1929 one finds such hopeful phrases as 'a prospect for Dakar' . . . 'very dedicated for Dakar' . . . 'for Dakar when she is old enough'.[41]

[37] W. B. Mumford and G. S. Orde-Brown, *Africans Learn To Be French* (London, 1937), 47.

[38] Bouche, *L'Enseignement*, 775–6. The *école primaire supérieure* at Bingerville had actually started its own midwifery section a few years before the foundation of the medical school at Dakar. See Tirefort, 'Européens et assimilés en Basse Côte d'Ivoire', 222. These developments might also be placed in the context of pro-natalist currents in the *métropole*; see Conklin, *A Mission to Civilize*, 164–5.

[39] See Buell, *The Native Problem*, ii. 38.

[40] See Dr Blanchard, 'L'École de Médecine de l'A.O.F. de sa fondation à l'année 1934', *Annales de Médecine et de Pharmacie Coloniales* (1935), 93; also Mumford, *Africans Learn to be French*, 139–40. Between 1918 and 1927, forty-two girls from the orphanages of the French Soudan went on to train as midwives; see ANS, FM: 23 G 22, report cited in n. 35.

[41] ANS, FM: O 501, 'État nominatif des métisses, pupilles de la Colonie, à l'orphelinat de Moussou, du 31 août 1928 au 31 août 1929'. Also see Tirefort, 'Européen et assimilés en Basse Côte d'Ivoire', 455, 744.

In 1923 the French woman in charge of the midwifery section at the Dakar School of Medicine, Madame Nogue, wrote in cheerfully racist fashion about the ethnic composition of the class she taught. Some colonials, she breezed, might doubt the results she had obtained with her pupils, having been more familiar with blacks who were either 'primitive' or 'led astray' by a civilization 'too complex for their rudimentary mentality'. But in her class, she continued, there were daughters of chiefs or native civil servants from Guinea, Dahomey, or Senegal, whose 'fairly evolved' families had allowed them to acquire a basic education.

These black African students, however, were still in the minority in Nogue's class. They were outnumbered by two to one by métisses from across French West Africa. Nogue offered her own opinion of the worth of these métisses as 'intermediaries':

These young girls have retained, albeit to varying degrees, a fairly deep maternal imprint which explains their sympathy for the milieu of the mother's side of their family and their determination to dedicate themselves to the regeneration of the black race. In this way, they are destined to become the happy link between ourselves and the peoples under our protection. For they feel very French and proud to belong to us. Entrusted for the most part at a tender age to lay or religious French teachers, who become their adoptive mothers, they are, through their paternal heredity, neces- sarily very close to us. From the first months of their stay in our school they feel the pull of our attraction so strongly that, in each class, they help to give birth to that collective spirit into which comes to be incorporated the more fragile personality of our black students. In this way the latter gradually submit to the disciplines to which their half-sisters so easily apply themselves. And each class soon forms a whole so like-minded, so similarly receptive to our suggestions, that in my mind I cannot distinguish the true daughters of Africa from those we might claim as our own.[42]

Nogue saw herself as helping to create 'what one might call an indigenous feminine elite', describing her students as 'our future little missionaries'.[43] The example of the midwifery section, coupled with the employment statistics given earlier, might appear to support the idea that, in the post-war period in particular, métis of both sexes were being moulded into an 'indigenous elite'—even if, within the broader structure of colonial society, this equated at best to forming a kind of petty bourgeoisie. In reality, however, their status was more ambiguous and complex.

[42] Mme Maurice Nogue, 'Les Sages-Femmes auxiliaires en Afrique Occidentale Française', *Bulletin du Comité d'Études Historiques et Scientifiques de l'Afrique Occidentale Française*, 2 (Apr.–June 1923), 321–2. For more on the idea of 'race regeneration', see Conklin, *A Mission to Civilize*, 221–2.

[43] Nogue, 'Les Sages-Femmes auxiliaires', 318, 348.

UNEQUAL OPPORTUNITIES

Much of the previous section focused on the employment found by people of mixed race in the French Soudan. Though significant in itself, this nevertheless risks distorting the picture for French West Africa as a whole. Indeed, much that was written about official policy towards métis chose the same focus, precisely because the French Soudan was in many ways the colony most advanced in terms of the local administration's provision for 'abandoned' mixed-race children.[44] This had something to do with the fact that it had been more thoroughly 'laicized' than other colonies, partly as a result of fears stemming from the strength of Islam in the area. This can only be a partial explanation, however, particularly in view of the fact that the French Soudan was one of the poorer colonies of the federation.

In the treatment of métis children, as in other matters, it seems likely that the French acted according to the relative strength or weakness of their position in any given area. In Senegal, for example, the care of 'abandoned' métis children was left to missionaries. But there the French presence was well established and comparatively secure, and 'auxiliaries' were consequently perhaps easier to come by than in the French Soudan. Each of the eight colonies which comprised French West Africa had different needs at different times, so it is not surprising that there were divergences in the treatment of métis children.

In any case, even in the French Soudan the image of a production line turning out midwives and teachers by the dozen is misleading. For a start, the orphanages only released métis who had already found a situation.[45] Moreover, an inspector visiting the boys' orphanage at Kayes in 1930 not only described it as 'the most run-down of the Education Service's establishments that I have seen in the Soudan', but also commented on the fact that all five of the boys who had left that year had gone to work in agriculture, four of them in sheep-farming. This, he continued, was because many of the children were physically and intellectually underdeveloped—not altogether surprising in view of the 'sordid' and demoralizing conditions in which they lived.[46]

---

[44] See e.g. 'La Condition des métis au Soudan français', *Bulletin d'Information et de Renseignements Coloniaux de l'A.O.F.*, 8 Mar. 1937.

[45] ANS, FM: 23G 22, report by Frédéric Assomption, Inspecteur des Écoles du Soudan Français, Bamako, 22 Mar. 1927.

[46] CAOM, Direction du Contrôle 941 dossier 17, mission Sol: report on the Orphelinat des Métis de Kayes by M. J. Chastenet de Gery, 20 Apr. 1930.

Admission to the school of medicine in Dakar became increasingly competitive throughout the 1920s and especially the 1930s. Soudanese métisses who failed to get into medical school or to become schoolteachers were initially found employment as auxiliary nurses, but when the recruitment of these was suspended in the mid-1930s the administration went back to the stand-by of the old École Ménagère de Kayes by putting them to work as seamstresses, embroiderers, and so on. Others were not considered capable of these tasks. In the utilitarian language of one report from 1938, 'those incapable of use in any branch of human activity are returned to their families and can be maintained on public funds until the day they free themselves from administrative protection, often by marriage'.[47] According to the logic of administrative intervention, which looked to take the 'morally or materially abandoned' into orphanages, to return métis to their families represented a kind of reabandonment.

Institutions for mixed-race girls often looked to secure the futures of the children in their care by marrying them off, rather than training them for particular kinds of employment. The staff of the girls' orphanage at Kankan in Guinea took charge of introducing their métisses to young men, especially graduates of the teacher-training college. In the course of the school year 1935–6, ten young women from the Kankan orphanage left to get married, no fewer than seven of these to teachers. Of the four other leavers, two were returned to their families having reached the age of 21. Just two continued with their education, one at the midwifery section in Dakar.[48] At the missionary orphanage for métisses at Moussou in the Ivory Coast in the 1930s, the Mother Superior dealt with marriages. A prospective suitor would offer her a gift of money. In return, she would present the young women in her care to him, one after the other. He would then make his choice; the views of his intended did not come into play. The Mother Superior also dealt with the bride-price and other costs arising from the wedding.[49]

In fact, the principal objectives of education for métisses remained essentially the same for all colonies throughout the colonial period— namely, to prepare them for their eventual role as 'prudent housewives' and 'enlightened mothers',[50] and to fulfil Hardy's objective stated earlier

[47] CAOM, Commission Guernut 101, response from the French Soudan to survey on 'le problème des métis', 2 Sept. 1938.

[48] ANS, FM: O 685; ANS, FM: 17G 381, Savineau report 13: Guinée Orientale, 24.

[49] ANS, FM: 17G 381, Savineau report 11: Abidjan, Bingerville, Grand-Bassam, 28–9; report 18: Rapport d'ensemble, 164–5.

[50] ANS, FM: 17G 219, 'La Question des enfants métis au Soudan', no date (probably 1932).

in this chapter to increase the number of West Africans with French as their mother tongue. More generally as it related to education for girls in French West Africa, the administration's ambitions never extended much beyond simply giving a greater number of children the same kind of missionary-style education.[51] Even when the École Normale de Jeunes Filles de Rufisque was set up in Senegal in 1938, a teacher-training college open to candidates from each colony, the central aim was to form 'good housewives, [and] auxiliaries for girls' education'.[52]

The case of Dahomey provides another instance of how the end-results of education for métis did not always match the stated aims. The administration's policies were often short-lived and exhibited great inconsistency of purpose. Dahomean métis housed in the orphanage in Porto-Novo, for example, according to an inspection in 1928, attended local schools until they could sit examinations allowing them to become midwives or typists or, in the case of mixed-race boys, until they could join the local *école primaire supérieure* which trained a variety of administrative employees, from printers to local schoolteachers.[53] In 1935, however, the institution at Porto-Novo was closed down. The boys were either summarily sent back to their families, or—a cause of great unhappiness for the children, who missed Porto-Novo and the friends they had made there—to one of the *écoles régionales* at either Savalou or Bembéréké. The girls were entrusted to missionaries in seven different locations.[54]

Lieutenant-Governor Bourgine hinted in 1935 that finding employment for the children kept in the orphanage had been becoming increasingly difficult, particularly where métisses were concerned. 'The jobs of mid-wife and typist are tending to become scarce and are only accessible to a minority', he wrote, suggesting that black Africans were increasingly pre-dominating in these roles. He added wryly that 'soon there will be too many dressmakers'.[55]

Just two years later, in 1937, the colony created a new boys' orphanage in Abomey. The worth of this institution was itself soon questioned by the director of education, who complained in 1942 that the local *école*

---

[51] A point made by David Gardinier in *Brazzaville. Janvier–février 1944. Aux sources de la décolonisation* (Paris, 1988), 196.

[52] Désalmand, *Histoire de l'éducation en Côte d'Ivoire*, i. 209.

[53] CAOM, Direction du Contrôle 940 dossier 71; Gardinier, 'The French Impact on Education', 337.

[54] CAOM, Commission Guernut 52, B17, report from 1930–1; also ANS, FM: 2H 1, Lt.-G. du Dahomey to GG, Porto-Novo, 28 Jan 1937, which noted that the métis children in the school at Bembéréké were harassed by their black African peers.

[55] ANS, FM: O 685, Lt.-G. Bourgine to GG, Porto-Novo, 19 Mar. 1935.

*régionale* only taught basic manual labour and agriculture, and, as a result: 'This orphanage no longer responds to Dahomey's needs.'[56]

As for the fate of the métisses, Lieutenant-Governor Bourgine offered a plausible if self-serving defence of missionary education in 1937:

> these establishments offer guarantees which the Administration can only with difficulty assure: close supervision and continuity of direction by Europeans who have, to all intents and purposes, set up home for good in the colony; an advanced domestic education; ongoing contact with the young woman and moral guidance after she leaves the establishment.[57]

Five years later, however, in 1942, the director of education, accepting that mixed-race girls were receiving a worthy and 'unpretentious' education from the missions, nevertheless felt that the results were not all that might be expected. 'We have no control over their orientation', he wrote: 'many of them vegetate in trivial jobs, after a very long period of schooling, because we have not encouraged them to do any better.'[58]

Finally, just after the Second World War, in technocratic language typical of the time, Governor Legendre reasserted the desire to make métis useful to the colony of Dahomey. The colonial state should, he wrote, rationally decide on the orientation of each child's studies, with a view to them becoming the technicians or native workers required by the territory.[59]

What emerges most clearly from the above is that métis were generally regarded as a potentially valuable resource, but that there was great disagreement as to how this resource should be managed. Métis were trained to meet the needs of the colonial administration for particular types of labour at particular times, but often when the administration's labour needs changed, so too did its policy towards the *orphelinats de métis*. As a result, the childhoods of métis could be extremely unsettled, subject to the needs and whims of a colonial administration whose own plans were constantly limited by the finances at their disposal. To understand better the lives of métis under colonial rule, we now need to penetrate deeper into the heart of the administrative ambivalence which characterized French 'policy' towards them.

[56] ANS, FM: O 53.     [57] ANS, FM: 2H 1, Lt.-G. to GG, Porto-Novo, 5 Jan. 1937.
[58] ANS, FM: O 53, Directeur-Général de l'Instruction Publique to Haut Commissaire de l'Afrique Française, 7 Nov. 1942.
[59] ANS, FM: 2H 22, Conseil Général du Dahomey, Procès-Verbal de la séance du 4 sept. 1947.

## THE FEAR OF *DÉCLASSEMENT*

Up until now, this chapter has concentrated on positive visions of métis as 'auxiliaries' or 'intermediaries' in the service of the colonial power. But there was a dark side to this debate which was just as influential in the lives of métis: the idea that they could turn out to be a socially and politically dangerous group of *déclassés*. One encounters this idea more or less constantly throughout the period in question, and about twice as often as its more optimistic counterpart. This reflects a general sense of nervousness felt by the French in West Africa about the security of their rule there, even though the region was never to cause them the same trouble as some of their other overseas possessions, most notably Indochina, Madagascar, and Algeria.

Of course, the fear of *déclassement* was not applied solely to métis. It was also a common theme in the debate concerning the sort of education that should be given to Africans. In the 1890s and 1900s in particular, many cautioned against over-educating 'the masses' to avoid removing them from their traditional way of life, and creating 'scholars, that is to say *déclassés*'.[60] Even so, the education system set up in 1903, in which provincial students attended schools progressively further from their villages the more successful they were, seemed almost to encourage these fears. Yet it was in relation to métis that the idea of *déclassement* most obviously influenced people's lives.

*Déclassement* was a central concept in the ideology of administrative intervention in favour of mixed-race children. Numerous administrators felt that to leave such children with their African families was to invite trouble. This stemmed partly from the view that 'the native family . . . considers [the métis child] as a *déclassé* in relation to local society',[61] and partly following a more racially deterministic line of reasoning. In 1908, for example, an education inspector, Jules Mariani, wrote that, 'despite the care which he generally receives from his mother's family', the abandoned métis was 'deprived of his share of paternal inheritance and will find himself with a generally higher level of intelligence in a situation inferior to that of a native. We are therefore duty-bound to take care of him.'[62]

---

[60] CAOM, SG, Soudan X dossier 4, rapport Bazin, July 1902. See also Georges Hardy, *Ergaste, ou la vocation coloniale* (Paris, 1929), 34; Michael Adas, 'Scientific Standards and Colonial Education in British India and French Senegal', in Teresa Meade and Mark Walker (eds.), *Science, Medicine and Cultural Imperialism* (Basingstoke, 1991), 25; Nogue, 'Les Sages-Femmes auxiliaires', 342.

[61] ANS, M 45, Lt.-G. du Sénégal to GG, Saint-Louis, 24 Mar. 1919.

[62] CAOM, SG, Soudan X dossier 7, Inspecteur de l'Enseignement Musulman Mariani to GG, Dakar, 15 Jan. 1908.

Rather than creating separate homes for métis, Mariani instead favoured the idea of offering them special assistance in their education, which would, he hoped, avoid the creation of a group of *déclassés* or privileged people. Others, of course, did not agree, and the creation of French-run 'orphanages' became a standard method of attempting to restitute something of the abandoned métis child's 'paternal inheritance'.

This development did little to allay the fears of some influential observers. The respected colonial legislator Arthur Girault was particularly concerned that métis should not be allowed to form a separate class. He invoked a historical precedent as a dire warning in the following passage, which was often quoted by subsequent writers on the subject:

Treat métis as a class apart and ask yourselves what feelings will germinate in the minds of these men. Rejected by all sides, they will become *déclassés*, and, I would add, the most dangerous *déclassés* from the point of view of maintaining European domination . . . We in France must not forget that failure to understand this has in the past had disastrous consequences for us. The basic reason for France's loss in the eighteenth century of Saint-Domingue, which was her finest colony, was the division of whites and mulattoes. The former did not know how to accept the assistance which the latter loyally offered them. If they had accepted it, the island of Saint-Domingue would without doubt have remained a French colony.[63]

There was another way of looking at the same problem which carried just as much credence. The socialist deputy Victor Augagneur, an opponent of *métissage* and a former Governor-General of Madagascar, agreed that métis should not form a separate class in colonial society, but did not share Girault's view that they should be assimilated by the French. He predicted that special treatment for métis would create a caste of half-educated *déclassés*, who would think themselves superior to 'the natives'. The latter, suffering from the former's 'pretentions', would hate them and hold the French responsible. In short, a class of métis interposed between Europeans and Africans would be 'a disruptive element, serving to isolate the one from the other'. If métis were to be treated like any other group of 'indigènes', however, they would be 'lost in the mass'.[64]

These opinions had in common a general sense of unease which fed directly into the treatment of mixed-race children in the *orphelinats de métis*. Were they to be treated as Europeans, or as 'indigènes'? In 1916 the head

---

[63] From Institut Colonial International, *Compte Rendu de la session tenue à Brunswick les 20, 21 et 22 avril 1911* (Brussels, 1911), 315.

[64] Victor Augagneur, 'Notre devoir envers les enfants métis', *Les Annales Coloniales*, 11 Jan. 1913.

of the orphanage at Porto-Novo complained about the uncomfortable bedding that her 'delicate' boarders had to endure, and suggested that they should not be housed 'à la mode indigène'. Her superiors responded by warning that her charges should not be allowed to grow accustomed to luxury that they might not have later on in life; rather, 'they should be raised in the conditions of the milieu in which they must evolve'.[65]

A report on the same orphanage at Porto-Novo in the late 1920s offers a further insight into the confusion which held back the development of a consistent approach to the treatment of métis. Here, the inspector, Monsieur Le Gregam, noted that the question of what was to be done with Dahomean métis seemed to be deferred, with 'policy' effectively reduced to the phrase: 'We will see when these children are older.'[66] Le Gregam continued that

it is not without reason, in these conditions, that the children in the care of the orphanage are raised in the native style: if their beds are hard and their meals manioc-based, if the most glorious disorder reigns in their dubious and parasite-infested lodgings . . . it is so that they do not lose contact with their milieu of origin, that they find themselves 'at home'.[67]

What becomes clear is that this bizarre defence of insect-infested dormitories resulted primarily from a case of unknown identity. Neither Le Gregam nor, apparently, anyone else with any influence over the lives of métis children seemed able to decide precisely who or what they were. Were they black, or were they white? Would they return to 'native traditions', or were they, 'by atavism',[68] more receptive to French ideas? Who could say on which side of the line between public servants and public enemies they were likely to fall? Part of this confusion resulted from the mischievous influence of a lingering form of racial determinism, which will be the main subject of the next chapter. But the undefined class of métis caused as much concern as any racial doubts. This is evident in a supplement to Le Gregam's report by the Chief Inspector of Schools in Dahomey:

The boarding regime for the métis of Porto-Novo, a halfway-house between native customs and the European way of life, is adapted to the needs and aspirations of the children. No one will oppose more frequent cleaning, the eradication of bugs, or if we try to vary and spice up their daily diet. It is a financial question—but let

[65] ANS, J 47, annual report on the Orphelinat Mixte de Porto-Novo, 27 July 1916.
[66] The phrase was originally that of Arthur Girault; see *Principes de colonisation et de législation coloniale*, ii (Paris, 1929), 522.
[67] CAOM, Direction du Contrôle 940 dossier 71, report by M Le Gregam, 27 Dec. 1928.
[68] Ibid.

us be careful not to allow ourselves to get carried away by our egalitarian passions. It is a fact that we are heading towards the integration of métis into our legal system.[69] We must treat them as Europeans, something I wish to happen. However, we must not forget that even in Europe, there is a world of difference between the children of a labourer, those of a skilled worker, and those of a banker. To treat them in the manner of a white child from a very well-to-do family would be to develop aspirations in them which they would not all be able to satisfy. They are not all of the same intelligence, and if some of them are destined for higher levels, others will become no more than labourers or petty employees with meagre salaries. After a happy childhood, these people will be embittered potential communists.[70]

In taking métis children into special homes, the French made themselves responsible for their 'class' just as much as they had, in a sense, helped to create their 'race'. But in the end, the ambivalence of the French administration towards métis effectively brought about the creation of the separate class which many had hoped to avoid. Pulled confusingly in several different directions, métis frequently felt socially isolated. Their attempts to find an identity in colonial society will be the subject of Chapter 6. At this point, however, the lives of métis children can be brought into sharper focus by looking more closely at two different orphanages.

CASE STUDY ONE: L'ORPHELINAT DE SÉGOU

Ségou, lying about 150 miles east of Bamako on the south bank of the River Niger, was captured by the French in 1890, and incorporated into the colony created and named Soudan Français that same year. The first educational establishment founded in Ségou was an orphanage for métis and black African children run by the Pères Blancs. But in October 1904 this institution was laicized, with the colonial administration taking over responsibility for its running.[71] Mixed-race boys in the institution, of whom there were twenty-nine in 1907, received an education at the local *école régionale*, while the girls (thirteen métisses and twenty 'indigènes' in 1907) were taught 'in house'.[72]

By 1908, however, the institution could barely claim to represent much of an improvement on the care offered previously by missionaries. Though

---

[69] He was referring to proposed legislation to allow unrecognized métis to become French citizens; details in Ch. 5 below.
[70] CAOM, Direction du Contrôle 940 dossier 71, comments by Potebon, Inspecteur des Écoles, 13 Jan. 1929.
[71] See ANS, J 36.          [72] Ibid.

the education inspector, Jules Mariani, accepted that the rationale of the establishment was 'a question of assistance rather than instruction', he was far from impressed by the results of the administration's investment. He found that while many of the girls knew how to sew, only two were beginning to speak French.

Likewise, standards of care were not always of the highest order. The African women employed as monitors were accused of neglecting their duties unless an official inspection was imminent. Conjunctivitis and ear infections were endemic, and the children were constantly dirty. Part of the problem lay in the fact that the orphanage took in children of all ages; as a result, the two French women employed to run the home were 'reduced practically to the role of wet-nurses'. Mariani, however, expected more from the 13,000 francs spent annually on personnel.[73]

This serves to put into perspective the comments of one of Mariani's predecessors, who, filled with triumphal pride at the extent of laicization in the French Soudan, had written in 1905 of what little was left of the missions' work with 'orphans': 'As for the orphan girls of Ségou, if they hardly understand anything except Bambara [the language of the main local ethnic group], at least they know how to sew and pound couscous.' And later:

What decay, what apathy I found in the schools run by missionaries in the Soudan! Classrooms, dormitories, everything breathes neglect. . . . I could . . . prove that in the Soudan the Pères Blancs are completely losing interest in their pupils . . . what purpose was served by the large grants received by the Pères Blancs before 1 January 1905?[74]

The main reason for singling out the secular Orphelinat de Ségou for special attention, however, is because of the existence of a very unusual source. In January 1911 Auguste Terrier, a leading metropolitan supporter of the French presence in Africa, visited Ségou during a tour of the federation. Here, Terrier, who two years later became secretary-general of the colonial pressure group, the Comité de l'Afrique Française, met Madame Pion-Roux, who had just been appointed to run the orphanage. Terrier took a special interest in the 'troubling question' of métis, and the two remained in contact. Thus it was that in 1912 he received a selection of letters written by children at the orphanage either to Madame Pion-Roux's daughter, or to Madame Pion-Roux herself when she had

---

[73] CAOM, SG, Soudan X dossier 7, report by Mariani, Inspecteur de l'Enseignement Musulman, 15 Jan. 1908; ANS, J 36, 'Notice sur les écoles de Ségou', 1907.

[74] ANS, J 11, pp. 9, 49.

returned to France on leave. These letters, which offer a fascinating insight into the lives of the children, survive as part of the Fonds Terrier at the library of the Institut de France in Paris.

Madame Pion-Roux was sent to Ségou in the aftermath of an unspecified 'compromising incident' involving her predecessors. By that time there were fifty-three children at the school, thirty-five male and eighteen female, of whom all but three were of mixed race.[75] While she ran the orphanage, her husband was appointed head of the nearby *école régionale*.[76] With the aim of creating some continuity and stability in the education service, married teachers from France were often given posts in the same town. The husbands of two previous heads of the Ségou orphanage had also been in charge of the local boys' school.[77]

The priority for Madame Pion-Roux was to make sure that the children in her care were healthy. This preceded her desire to teach them in a practical fashion.[78] In fact, she saw herself as a surrogate parent; as she was to write to Terrier, 'at Ségou I endeavoured with these poor children to replace the father who forgot them and the mother who could not and did not want to take care of them'.[79] This idea was evidently encouraged among the children in her care, for many of them addressed her in their letters as 'My dear second mother', and signed off 'Your beloved son'.[80] The notion that a French woman could act as a mixed-race child's mother became an established ideal in homes for métis across French West Africa.[81] This is not to decry the efforts of these women in the task that was set them. However, the concept undoubtedly created a confusion of identities for métis children from an early age.

This confusion was exacerbated by the fact that most children returned home to their African mothers during the school holidays. In the summer of 1912 children from the Ségou orphanage travelled great distances to stay with their mothers in Koutiala, Koulikoro, Sikasso, Bougoumi, and even as far as Tombouctou. A smaller number were genuinely abandoned.

---

[75] ANS, J 12, 'Inspection des écoles de Ségou', no date (probably early 1911).

[76] IF, 5928 vol. 2, 'Note sur les instituteurs de l'A.O.F.', no date.

[77] Namely M and Mme Niénat and Imbert. ANS, J 36, Bulletin d'inspection: École Régionale de Ségou, 21 July 1913. This report was written by the regional inspector of education, J.-L. Monod, whose own wife ran a school for girls in Bamako.

[78] IF, 5928 vol. 2.

[79] IF, 5906, Mme Pion-Roux to Terrier, Amélie-les-Bains, 5 Sept. 1912.

[80] IF, 5940 vol. 2.

[81] To cite just a few examples, see CAOM, SG, Sénégal X dossier 26, GG to Ministre des Colonies, 14 June 1904; ANS, J 35, report on the Orphelinat Mixte de Kayes, 9 June 1918; ANS, FM: O 685, report on the orphanage at Kankan, 21 June 1937; ANS, FM: 17G 381, Savineau report 18: Rapport d'ensemble, 154.

These had the misfortune to remain in the institution throughout the summer.

One such child provides an additional example of the contrary world which métis inhabited. This 14-year-old chose to style himself in letters to his 'second mother' as Paul Gouraud, using the surname of his father, a captain in the colonial infantry. Since his father had not recognized him, however, Madame Pion-Roux referred to him as Paul Coulibaly—the surname of his true mother, who had also abandoned him. Meanwhile, he and his peers in the orphanage continued to refer to black Africans as 'the natives'.[82]

Identities were simultaneously being created and denied, therefore, at the point when métis children's awareness of their social situation was awakening. In such circumstances, the comment made by an inspector at Ségou in 1910 that métis should be formed into 'a class of superior natives, rather than inferior whites, that is to say *déclassés*',[83] comes across as virtually meaningless. Such fine distinctions were simply no longer available to be made: métis were already, in a sense, everything and nothing. It was entirely natural that a committed colonialist like Auguste Terrier should write during his visit to Ségou: 'One feels uneasy watching them.'[84]

This collection of letters throws additional miscellaneous sidelights on the lives of the children. One of their main topics of conversation, for example, was the success of the crops they had planted in the grounds of the orphanage. Discipline in the institution could seem harsh; one child wrote in error-strewn French: 'I tore four sheets out of my exercise book and Sir stopped my holidays when I was a bit better behaved Sir let me go.'

The letters also reveal that the Pères Blancs were still in evidence in Ségou. In the words of 14-year-old Réné Ahmoudou: 'Now there are many métis who are baptized and they gave us our baptism certificate. They gave us our first communion. Every Sunday we go to mass. Paul Diarra, Paul Kourouma and Étienne want to be baptized they have already passed the exam.'[85] Paul Kourouma states elsewhere that Étienne was baptized

[82] IF, 5940 vol. 2. This child was also one of the subjects of an anthropological survey in 1910, providing details on his family background. See 'Enquête sur les croisements ethniques', *Revue Anthropologique*, Sept.–Oct. 1912, 392.

[83] Quoted in Bouche, *L'Enseignement*, 771.

[84] IF, 5922, *carnet de voyage*, entry from 28 Jan. 1911.

[85] IF, 5940 vol. 2, 3 June 1912. In other orphanages, too, for example at Ouagadougou in the 1930s, the children would attend mass every Sunday. In the girls' orphanage at Bamako at the same time, the girls would recite their litanies together in the evening; at Kankan in Guinea, on the other hand, while the girls described themselves as Catholics, none expressed much interest in attending mass. See ANS, FM: 17G 381, Savineau report 1: Bamako, 17; report 8: Ouagadougou, 24; report 13: La Guinée Orientale, 25.

Joseph by Père Courteille, while he himself was baptized Pierre, the name
also given to Paul Diarra. In fact, the latter does not appear to have used
his new name; in 1934 he was recognized as a French citizen under the
name Paul Diarra.[86]

At the age of 12 Paul Kourouma was already being oriented towards
a particular career. In his case, he had been earmarked for the medical
profession:

Now they are teaching me to do many things at the dispensary. Sir gave me an
exercise book. Every morning if I go to the dispensary I take this exercise book
with me to make a note of all that they teach me. It is Dr Moreau who is now
giving me lessons in medicine because before I only knew how to do dressings.[87]

The same Dr Moreau was responsible for circumcizing the younger
children, and quite possibly he was also involved when, as Jacques Traoré
explained to Madame Pion-Roux, 'they purged us twice'.[88]

Most of these letters were written when the orphanage at Ségou was
about to close. During the course of 1912, girls aged 12 or over were
sent to Bamako, while the boys and younger girls went to the new mixed
orphanage at Kayes. The buildings at Ségou were beginning to collapse
around the few boys left in the summer of 1912. A combination of termites
and a tornado meant that, in Jacques Traoré's words: 'Our dining room
is the classroom now because the classrooms have almost fallen down . . .
the wall which is next to our toilet has fallen down.'[89]

Later that summer these remaining children joined the others in
Kayes, and the institution at Ségou finally closed. Madame Pion-Roux,
while concerned that her former charges would find the climate in Kayes
extremely unpleasant, was pleased that they were now in a town promising a broader range of employment when they were old enough to leave.[90]
Fourteen-year-old Pierre Kamara did not seem so happy. Although he
was working hard towards his ambition of becoming a teacher—an aim in
which he eventually succeeded[91]—he revealed that the older children had
formed a delegation to complain that their plates had holes and that they
were badly fed. 'They even wanted to hit the monitors. Monsieur Cros
became angry, and gave them a severe punishment. . . . We don't have much
fun here.'[92]

[86] See ANS, FM: 23G 23.　　　[87] IF, 5940 vol. 2.
[88] Ibid.　　　[89] Ibid.　　　[90] IF, 5906.
[91] See ANS, H 25. In 1918 he was teaching at the École Professionnelle de Bamako.
[92] IF, 5940 vol. 2.

CASE STUDY TWO: L'ORPHELINAT DES MÉTISSES DE BAMAKO

The first home for mixed-race girls in Bamako was founded in 1912. Three years later, due to a personnel shortage created by the First World War, this institution was forced to close, and its boarders were sent to the mixed orphanage at Kayes.[93] In 1923, however, the Orphelinat des Métisses was re-established in Bamako.

This new institution soon developed a reputation as one of the most successful homes for métis children in French West Africa. Its renown stemmed largely from the number of pupils who went on to become schoolteachers or who were accepted by the midwifery section in Dakar, which, one inspector noted with little consideration for the reasons why, seemed to hold a particular attraction for métisses.

Girls could be admitted to the orphanage from the age of 6. The youngest would follow the preparatory and elementary courses during the day at the École des Fillettes Indigènes de Bamako. They would then pursue their studies either in the orphanage itself, which offered a 'general' education along with the typical domestic education, or in an annexed section which trained teachers for the girls' schools of the French Soudan.[94]

The institution received some very favourable notices in the early 1930s. The buildings were well appointed, spacious, and clean, with a light and properly aired dormitory protected from mosquitoes. The food was well prepared and sometimes complemented by dishes cooked 'à l'européenne', and the staff, under the direction of Madame Assomption, who had been teaching in the French Soudan with her husband for almost twenty years, made sure the children were properly looked after.[95]

This was in marked contrast to the impression created by the boys' orphanage at Kayes, which an inspector described as 'intolerable'. Its buildings were dilapidated and its hygienic precautions insufficient, with many of the children suffering from skin problems and eye infections. Not only was the children's health poor; they were also said to lack the 'gaiety' of the métisses. This, it was suggested, may have been linked to the fact that they were kept more or less in confinement; the orphanage courtyard was described as 'their complete horizon'. It was perhaps this, the inspector continued, which gave them 'the sullen air of children who have nothing

[93] ANS, FM: O 685, 'Note sur les orphelinats de métis du Soudan français', 1923.
[94] ANS, FM: O 128, 'Arrêté du Lt-G réorganisant les orphelinats de métis du Soudan français', 11 Aug. 1932; *Journal Officiel du Soudan Français*, 1 Apr. 1925, 138.
[95] CAOM, Direction du Contrôle 941 dossier 16, inspection of 22 Feb. 1930; also ANS, FM: 17G 219, 'La Question des enfants métis au Soudan', no date (probably 1932).

to do and who do not know how to play'. Even so, he felt that it was 'hardly advisable' to allow them to return to African society, even during school holidays. A major part of the rationale for such establishments was the supposed 'lack of comfort, hygiene, and the poor clothing and dietary regime' in African homes. The institution at Kayes in 1930 seemed to offer much the same, but without the family support the child might have been able to expect if he had not been 'rescued'.[96] The situation was even worse in the orphanage at Zinder in Niger, where an inspection in 1929 noted that its buildings were infested with termites, the dormitories were like prisons, and that one child had recently died during an outbreak of beri-beri, which suggests that the children were malnourished.[97]

Mixed-race girls at the Bamako orphanage were not, however, completely isolated from other Africans. In fact, the institution also accepted as day-pupils local girls who had already completed the *cours élémentaire*, and who, in general, wished to work in education or for the Assistance Médicale Indigène.

One person who fell into the latter category was Aoua Keita, whose autobiography makes her one of a very small number of West African women to have published their experiences of the colonial period.[98] Keita's father, a native civil servant in the health service, defied her mother—for whom sending a girl to school was a 'scandal'—in enrolling her at the École des Filles de Bamako. Having proved her intelligence, Keita continued her education in 1926 by following the courses given at the Orphelinat des Métisses. Here, as she explains, her success was not always welcome.

In these classes, in the midst of big métisses who had been at school for four or five years longer than us, I hovered between fourth and sixth place in the class, never lower. I was in a 'blue funk' about these big girls who, what is more, were always threatening me. Sometimes they would wait in a corner to say to me: 'If you ever come top of the class here, we'll break your ribs.' On one occasion, when I came second in the class, they came close to actually doing this. After taunts followed by slaps in the face, I hurried to the laboratory to inform my father of my anxiety as to the pursuit of my studies.

The matter was resolved when her father and brother went to see Frédéric Assomption, referred to here as the *Inspecteur*, who was also the husband

---

[96] CAOM, Direction du Contrôle 941 dossier 16; also dossier 17, inspection dated 20 Apr. 1930.

[97] CAOM, Direction du Contrôle 938 dossier 20.

[98] Aoua Keita, *Femme d'Afrique: La Vie d'Aoua Keita racontée par elle-même* (Paris, 1975). Also see La Ray Denzer, 'Gender and Decolonization: A Study of Three Women in West African Public Life' in Ajayi and Peel (eds.), *People and Empires in African History*, 217–36.

of the head of the orphanage. Assomption called together all the parties concerned. Disbelieving the improbable tales told by the métisses, he scolded Keita's aggressors, and insisted that everyone shake hands. Keita states that some of them eventually became her friends, while she herself went on to finish first among candidates from the French Soudan for the midwifery section in Dakar.[99]

Aoua Keita's story raises the general question of the extent to which métis children were segregated from black Africans. In 1938 an inspector complained that the orphanage for mixed-race boys in Bamako was an integral part of the local *école primaire supérieure*, meaning that 'in the classroom and the refectory, as in the dormitory, the métis are mixed in with the native students. In terms of their dietary regime and their school clothes, there is hardly any difference between the two.'[100]

This did not mean, of course, that their treatment was entirely the same. A similar situation had obtained in Bingerville in the 1910s, but there the authorities insisted that métis were 'better monitored, surrounded with more care and attentively looked after in case of illness'.[101] Eventually, something approaching full segregation was achieved in Bingerville, with separate classrooms and dormitories for métis and for their black African contemporaries, and instruction given by European teachers.[102] In general, until the 1940s most colonies appear to have maintained distinctions between métis and black African children just as far as their budgets allowed them to make separate provision in terms of buildings, personnel, and so on.

The segregation of the sexes was another contentious issue, illustrated by the scandal created by two métisses in Bamako, one aged 15, one 18, who became pregnant in 1937. Within a fortnight the matter came to the attention of the Governor-General himself, Jules Marcel de Coppet, who was concerned to know whether the administration could be held responsible. There were good reasons for de Coppet to express concern. Still fresh in the memory of staff at the orphanage was the fate of Marie Camara, who in 1931 was expelled from the institution when she fell pregnant. She went

---

[99] Keita, *Femme d'Afrique*, 25–6. While serving as a midwife in the 1930s, Keita became increasingly involved in political activity, rising to prominence in the Soudanese section of the Rassemblement Démocratique Africain; in 1958 she became the first woman to be elected as a deputy to a national assembly in a francophone West African territory. See Denzer, 'Gender and Decolonization', 218.

[100] CAOM, Direction du Contrôle 962 dossier 75, Inspecteur-Général des Colonies Coste to Ministre des Colonies, 20 July 1938.

[101] Tirefort, 'Européens et assimilés en Basse Côte d'Ivoire', 454.

[102] CAOM, Direction du Contrôle 962 dossier 81, report concerning the effects of the closure of the Orphelinat des Métis de Bingerville, 8 Mar. 1938.

to live in town with her mother, who apparently encouraged her to take up a life of prostitution. Less than two years later she died, suffering from tuberculosis and syphilis. Her child also died.[103]

Both the 1937 pregnancies occurred outside the orphanage, during the summer holidays when most métisses were left in the care of parents or guardians whose fitness to look after them had been approved by the head of the institution. Their suitability was rechecked by the local authorities following these incidents, even though Governor Rougier admitted that 'an accident is always possible'. As no one knew of the whereabouts of the mother of the younger of the two métisses, she was entrusted to the care of a 'respectable' mixed-race family to await her mother's consent for her to marry her African lover. The 18-year-old refused to reveal the identity of her paramour, though the prime suspect was a married métis. She was sent to live with her stepfather and was found work as a dressmaker under a European woman.[104]

The woman in charge of the orphanage when these incidents took place, Madame Demurat, complained of the difficulty of keeping the boarders occupied and properly monitored, particularly during the holidays. (Similar problems were blamed for a pregnancy in the orphanage at Porto-Novo in 1935, where some of the métisses were also accused of bribing their monitors to allow them to receive visitors.[105]) In recognizing these problems, the chief inspector of schools, Charles Cros, saw the development of community life as the most effective safeguard against similar occurrences. 'The life of the boarding school', he wrote, 'must in effect become family life for these orphan girls.' To this end, he welcomed the return of a métisse, Madame Richard, to teach at the orphanage where she had been raised. Cros hoped that, like Madame Pion-Roux at Ségou, she could become, as far as possible, 'the "mother" for a whole family of nearly fifty young orphan girls'.[106]

The response of the administration to these incidents serves to highlight some of the fears of the French authorities concerning the sexuality of the mixed-race girls in their care. Administrators, as noted earlier, had expressed such concerns right from the early days of the École Ménagère de Kayes, just as Governor Rougier now spoke of the necessity of creating

[103] ANS, FM: 17G 381, Savineau report 1: La Femme et la Famille à Bamako (25 Nov. 1937), 18.
[104] Details in ibid. 17–20; also report 18: Rapport d'ensemble, 155–6.; ANS, FM: 2H 1; FM: O 685.
[105] ANS, FM: 2H 1, Lt.-G. du Dahomey to GG, 5 Jan. 1937.
[106] ANS, FM: O 685, report of 17 Oct. 1937.

work for unmarried métisses if they were not to turn to prostitution.[107] This, of course, was one profession which did not figure on the colony's employment statistics. While difficult to quantify, however, numerous allusions to the problem testify to its reality.[108]

Even so, many administrators were aware that if some métisses became prostitutes, this was inextricably bound up with the behaviour of the French themselves. As late as the 1940s, one administrator complained that European men too often represented 'an obstacle to the healthy intellectual development of mixed-race girls'.[109] Similarly, in 1950 the president of a society for métis observed that everyone knew that, in colonial society, the word 'ménagère' or 'housewife' effectively meant 'maîtresse-servante' or 'mistress-servant'.[110] By raising métisses separately, moreover, the French may have increased their forbidden allure among black African men.[111]

Although the efforts of the French Soudan in providing for métis children continued to receive praise throughout the 1930s, one nevertheless gains the impression that the Orphelinat des Métisses de Bamako was an institution in decline, with a staff whose commitment to the task in hand was at times questionable. In one report from 1937 we find the headmistress, Madame Assomption, giving her classes in curlers. At the end of the school day she removes them with impatience, readying herself for the social life to which she seems to attach more importance.[112] The same report compared the faces of the heavily disciplined children in Bamako with those of the girls in the materially less well-off institution at Kankan in Guinea. While the métisses in Bamako seemed 'hostile' and 'suspicious', the inspector found the girls in Kankan much more open and confident, concluding that they were 'by far the more Europeanized'.[113]

Plans drawn up in the late 1930s to modernize the orphanages in Bamako were abandoned when war broke out. And it was during the Second World War that special homes for métis entered their final phase of development.

---

[107] ANS, FM: 2H 1, Rougier to GG, 1 Nov. 1937.

[108] See e.g. ANS, FM: 17G 381, Savineau report 6: Dahomey, 27–8.

[109] ANS, FM: 17G 186, 'Étude du Programme de la Conférence de Brazzaville, Colonie du Niger', Dec. 1943 or Jan. 1944. Also ANS, FM: 17G 381, Savineau report 13: La Guinée Orientale, 25.

[110] From *L'Eurafricain*, 9 (1950), 12. For a South-East Asian parallel, see Stoler, 'Carnal Knowledge', 89.

[111] Black African attitudes to métis are covered in more detail in Ch. 6 below.

[112] ANS, FM: 17G 381, Savineau report 1: Bamako, 19.

[113] Ibid., report 18: Rapport d'ensemble, 153–4.

CONCLUSION: BRAZZAVILLE AND BEYOND

The assistance given to métis children by the colonial authorities from just after the turn of the century may have been sporadic, unevenly distributed, and ideologically contradictory. Yet even when, on the surface, the material conditions and education reserved for métis barely differed from that of their black African counterparts, there was a distinctive attitude towards them which set them apart from the mass. Métis children were quickly made aware that they were 'different'. They were told that they were not 'natives'—even though they found out when they were older that, in the eyes of the law, that was precisely what they were.[114] They were constantly the subject of schemes to regulate their treatment, even though the majority of these never got beyond the planning stage. 'The métis problem' was always there, a constant reminder of difference.

Only in the 1940s was there a concerted effort by the colonial authorities to challenge this concept. The key figure in this shift in attitudes was, in fact, the Governor-General of French Equatorial Africa from 1940 to 1944, Félix Éboué. While French West Africa came under the control of the Vichy regime, in August 1940 Éboué took French Equatorial Africa over to de Gaulle's Free French—making it practically the only territory enabling de Gaulle to claim that France was still fighting the war. As a result, Éboué's views took on a greater significance than might otherwise have been the case.

A black Guianan, Éboué had always resented favouritism shown to people of mixed race in the Caribbean.[115] In his important General Circular of 8 November 1941, he envisaged a new approach to métis in French black Africa. He believed that anything which served to differentiate them from indigenous society could only bring about 'a pernicious rivalry' between the two groups, to the benefit of no one. He saw French citizenship (discussed in Chapter 5) as a poor substitute for the family life and security the métis had lost. He therefore questioned the necessity of placing in 'orphanages' those children whose fathers had abandoned them but who continued to live with their mothers. Indeed, he found the whole idea of having special homes reserved for métis to be questionable, suggesting instead that black African children should be admitted on equal terms. He was in favour of encouraging all other measures likely to reincorporate métis into African society, of which he felt they had to form a part.[116]

[114] See Ch. 5 below for more on the legal status of métis.
[115] Brian Weinstein, *Éboué* (New York, 1972), 271.
[116] *Journal Officiel de l'Afrique Française Libre et de l'Afrique Equatoriale Française*, 1 Dec. 1941, 692.

The issues raised by Éboué were presented for discussion among the French West African Governors in the run-up to the Brazzaville Conference of January 1944. The Brazzaville Conference was an attempt to re-examine and establish the priorities of French colonial doctrine and policy in Africa, although in the end, due to lack of time, the 'métis question' was not debated at the conference itself.

Not everyone was in agreement with Éboué. The Governor of Guinea, for example, wanted to maintain orphanages for métis alone, to raise them 'with a view to a possible assimilation with the European colonial element'.[117] In general, however, Éboué's ideas were embraced. Governor Assier de Pompignan of Dahomey agreed that métis would have to owe any success to their intelligence and merit, rather than their bloodline.[118] The Gaullist Governor of the Ivory Coast, André Latrille, brought a typically radical thrust to his response. Latrille acknowledged that métis had suffered in the divided society set up by racist French colonialism, squeezed between the supposedly superior white race and the exploited and 'inferior' black race. But these ideas, he claimed, no longer had any place in French Africa. 'Our policy which tends to place Africans and Europeans on the same footing automatically resolves the métis question', he argued. 'They will no longer find themselves isolated between two racially distinct groupings. They will merge into the society in common which will know no difference other than individual worth.'[119]

The key factor in prompting this shift in attitudes was the growth of a class of Gallicized black Africans known as *évolués*, whose aspirations were seen as potentially far more hazardous to French rule than those of métis, whose numbers were no longer on the increase. To continue to be seen to show favouritism to people of mixed race in these circumstances was clearly becoming dangerous. 'From now on', wrote Robert Attuly, head of the judiciary in French West Africa, 'the métis problem merges with that of the "évolués".'[120]

A prominent member of the latter category, Léopold Sédar Senghor, who went on to be the first president of independent Senegal, expressed a similar view in a 1947 newspaper article entitled 'There is no métis problem'. Senghor argued that the problems faced by people of mixed race were no different from those faced by any black African minority. Like Éboué, he favoured treating abandoned métis children in the same way as any other orphan or abandoned child. Instead of creating a bourgeoisie or

---

[117] ANS, FM: 17G 186.    [118] ANS, FM: 17G 187.
[119] ANS, FM: 17G 186.    [120] ANS, FM: 17G 187.

a privileged class, he felt that the role of the state should be limited simply to enabling every abandoned child to occupy a position in society in line with his or her ability and individual merit, rather than the colour of his or her skin.[121]

The new rhetoric embodied in Éboué's circular was generally presented without pause to reflect on the damage the administration's policies towards métis may have done over the preceding fifty years or so. René Pleven, de Gaulle's Commissioner for the Colonies in his cabinet in Algiers, nevertheless came close to admitting that these policies had failed when, in backing the new approach, he wrote that it was: 'Better to turn the métis child into a fairly well-adapted native than a badly adapted European.'[122]

In practical terms, however, the desire to treat métis in the same way as black Africans does not appear to have effected a particularly profound change. Métis children were still liable to be singled out for special treatment, even though the reasoning behind such measures is not now always clear. In March 1944, for example, the head of the École Professionnelle d'Abidjan agreed to discriminate in favour of métis in admitting students for the section of the school which trained printers.[123]

In fact, despite the apparent orthodoxy of Éboué's ideas, little seems to have changed beyond the names of a few institutions. In 1947 Governor Louveau of the French Soudan grandly announced the intention to create an 'orphanage for abandoned African children' (*orphelinat des enfants africains délaissés*), to replace the old 'foyer des métis' in Bamako. The latter was now in a very poor state, with tuberculosis rampant. Indeed, the President of the Republic himself, Vincent Auriol, had displayed 'the most animated emotion' upon witnessing the 'physical poverty' of the children in the foyer des métis during a visit to Bamako earlier that year.[124] The new institution, continued Louveau more cautiously, would take in 'abandoned African children in possession of sufficient intellectual aptitudes'. However, a search for abandoned black African children was not a success. In fact, they could find only one. Louveau may have blamed Africans for the diseases suffered by métis children, but he accepted that 'There is not a race nor a religion in the Soudan which accepts the abandonment of the child by the father. The only abandoned children are the products of the white race.'[125]

---

[121] Léopold Sédar Senghor, 'Il n'y a pas de problème du métis', *Réveil*, 8 May 1947.

[122] ANS, FM: 23G 22, Pleven to M Seignon (Délégué à l'Assemblée Consultative), Algiers, 9 May 1944.

[123] ANS, FM: O 501.

[124] ANS, FM: 2H 22, Gvr. du Soudan français to GG, 4 May 1947.

[125] ANS, FM: 2H 22, Louveau to GG, 19 Aug. 1947. The 'Foyer des Métis de Bamako' in fact became the 'Foyer des Enfants Abandonnés' in 1948.

# 4
# *Race and Heredity*

In the previous two chapters, the ambivalence of French attitudes towards métis was shown to have been a crucial factor in determining their treatment. This ambivalence, it was argued, was conditioned by both the potential benefits and the potential dangers which their perceived racial and social 'intermediacy' was thought to present the French administration in West Africa, with the essential problem being one of classification.

To explain the disproportionate interest shown in people of mixed race, however, and to understand more fully why they were treated as they were, we need to go beyond the immediate concerns of an insecure colonial administration. For miscegenation and its consequences interested many writers in metropolitan France before the conquest of West Africa. Indeed, in the writings of such thinkers as Arthur de Gobineau and Paul Broca from the 1850s can be found many of the stereotypes which later attached themselves to métis in West Africa, stereotypes which influenced their treatment by the representatives of French rule.

In the first part of this chapter, therefore, we relocate to mid-nineteenth-century France, to trace the development of ideas concerning *métissage* and its effects. We will then look to see how far these ideas became part of the intellectual baggage of French people in West Africa, and how far they affected the lives of métis themselves.

## MISCEGENATION AND DEGENERATION

Though Count Arthur de Gobineau was by no means the first French writer to make use of a racialist conception of society, his work is nevertheless a natural starting point for any assessment of the significance of miscegenation in French racial theories from the mid-nineteenth century. His four-volume *Essai sur l'inégalité des races humaines*, published between 1853 and 1855, occupies this central position due to the originality of its thesis that race is the fundamental determinant of the course of human history.

Gobineau contended that miscegenation inevitably involved racial degeneration, in the sense that the intrinsic value of a people was adversely affected

by 'adulterations' to the blood. For members of the 'white race', contact
with blacks 'disarms their reason, diminishes the intensity of their practical faculties, and deals an irreparable blow to their energy and physical
strength'.[1]

Gobineau's theory, however, was sealed within a fatalistic paradox.
As he saw it, civilization itself was dependent on the vitality that brought
'superior' races into contact with their 'inferiors', despite the harmful consequences of such contact. The avoidance of miscegenation therefore offered
no escape from the crushing inevitability of decadence, for the 'purity' of
those unable to conquer their distaste for racial mixture served in reality
as a measure of their stagnation and lack of vitality. Gobineau's organic
conception of history, as Michael D. Biddiss has shown, saw 'death in life
itself'. Lacking the prospect of divine or supernatural intercession, the body
would continually prevail over the spirit, leading logically to Gobineau's
pessimistic conclusions.[2]

Such fatalism, as Tzvetan Todorov has pointed out, 'ought not to have
spawned any political activists proposing to rid the world of inferior races',
and indeed, judged on his writings alone, there is a significant difference
between the 'romantic pessimism' of Gobineau and the forward-looking
activism of later thinkers such as Vacher de Lapouge, who put their faith
in eugenics and positive selection.[3] Gobineau was apparently uninterested
in the uses to which his theories might be put, and disclaimed moral responsibility for ideas he insisted were 'scientific'. Alexis de Tocqueville, whom
Gobineau had previously served as secretary during his time as Minister
for Foreign Affairs in 1849, criticized this attitude as disingenuous and
ill-advised in the course of their extensive correspondence.[4]

Tocqueville's fears about the work of his former protégé were well founded.
Despite the reservations expressed by many contemporary scientists and
social thinkers about Gobineau's work, particularly his almost nihilistic
determinism, the idea that there was a link between miscegenation and
degeneration became a common assumption in late-nineteenth-century

---

[1] Joseph-Arthur de Gobineau, *Essai sur l'inégalité des races humaines* (Paris, 1853–5), i. 39;
ii. 149.

[2] Michael D. Biddiss, *Father of Racist Ideology: The Social and Political Thought of Count
Gobineau* (London, 1970), 99, 116.

[3] Tzvetan Todorov, *On Human Diversity* (Cambridge, Mass., 1983), 140; Taguieff,
'Doctrines de la race et hantise du métissage', 76–7. For more on eugenics, see William H.
Schneider, *Quality and Quantity: The Quest for Biological Regeneration in Twentieth-Century
France* (Cambridge, 1990).

[4] Biddiss, *Father of Racist Ideology*, 149; Todorov, *On Human Diversity*, 127–9; Larry
Siedentop, *Tocqueville* (Oxford, 1994), 126–8.

French thought. Furthermore, as will be shown later, many of the qualities Gobineau attributed to the various races, both separately and in conjunction, proved to be remarkably durable, even in the face of empirical evidence to the contrary. It comes as no surprise to find the *Essai sur l'inégalité des races humaines* listed as one of a small number of works of non-fiction available to colonial civil servants in their library at Koulouba, the administrative capital of the French Soudan.[5]

Around the same time as Gobineau's historical speculations, the concept of degeneration was being elaborated in a more scientific environment. In 1857 Bénédict-Augustin Morel, head doctor at an asylum near Rouen, associated racial decline with heredity and the environment in his *Traité des dégénérescences physiques, intellectuelles et morales de l'espèce humaine*. Morel added a new social dimension to the theory of evolution which prevailed in nineteenth-century France, based on Jean-Baptiste Lamarck's belief that evolution progressed by the inheritance of acquired characteristics.[6]

Morel held that defects caused by an unhealthy environment, bad diets, or an immoral way of life could be passed on from parents to their children, accumulating over time in a regressive process that would produce sterility in the fourth generation. A wide range of physical defects, from blindness to squints, or personality traits such as apathy and melancholy, were adduced as pathological manifestations of degeneration. In Morel's system, 'the drunkenness of the father became the homicidal mania of the son', while 'the penchant for shoplifting in the mother propelled her daughter into a life of prostitution'.[7] Rather as in Gobineau's work, the spirit was seen to be progressively subordinate to the body, although Morel was concerned to retain a Christian framework for his ideas. As such, as Ruth Harris has phrased it, he 'may be said to have provided a scientific assessment of how "the sins of the father were visited on the sons"'.[8]

Morel's ideas were rapidly transposed from their individual or familial setting to find a much broader application. In fact, in the words of Robert A. Nye, the theory of degeneration became 'so culturally useful that it could explain persuasively all the pathologies from which the nation suffered'. Furthermore, Nye points out that the theory linked biological and social

---

[5] IF, 5922, catalogue of the Bibliothèque des Fonctionnaires de Koulouba, 1910.

[6] See Peter J. Bowler, *Evolution: The History of an Idea* (Berkeley, 1984), in particular 81.

[7] Robert A. Nye, *Masculinity and Male Codes of Honour in Modern France* (Oxford, 1993), 77.

[8] Ruth Harris, *Murders and Madness: Medicine, Law, and Society in the fin de siècle* (Oxford, 1989), 51–6, at 54; see also Daniel Pick, *Faces of Degeneration: A European Disorder, c.1848– c.1918* (Cambridge, 1989), in particular 50–2.

thought so closely together that they became virtually indistinguishable from each other.[9] These tendencies became particularly visible in the aftermath of the debacle of the Franco-Prussian War of 1870, as the response of Gobineau to this national disaster serves to highlight:

Evidently this situation could not have been brought about simply by the collaboration of a few able Prussians. For a country to disintegrate like this, the disease must wreak its work from within; the wounds inflicted by the foreign assailant produce cuts, but never this purulent liquefaction of the marrow and the blood.[10]

The defeat in 1870 ushered in a period of morbid self-examination wherein Germany was held up as a measure of France's own decadence.[11] The applicability of the ideal type of German racial 'purity' seemed to grow exponentially with Germany's galloping birth rate, while the French became increasingly aware of their underpopulation. Although the essential difference, as Nye has shown, was the low rate of fertility within marriage, the issue was conceptualized as a problem of national vitality, typified in the conclusion of the prominent economist (and advocate of colonial expansion) Paul Leroy-Beaulieu:

The children of our families, one or two in number, surrounded with indulgent tenderness and debilitating care, are inclined to a passive and sedentary existence, and only exceptionally manifest the spirit of enterprise and adventure, endurance and perseverance that characterized their ancient ancestors and which the sons of prolific German families possess today.[12]

The problem was posed in more starkly racialist terms by Georges Vacher de Lapouge, who drew a direct link between miscegenation, degeneration, and depopulation. Lapouge argued in 1887 that both the degeneration of the French people and the declining birth rate could be explained by the preponderance in France of people of 'mixed blood', who were less fertile than the racially 'pure'. Though French demographers generally gave little credence to race-based theories,[13] Lapouge reflected widely held assumptions (however poorly demonstrated) about the biological and social effects of *métissage*.

---

[9] Robert A. Nye, *Crime, Madness and Politics in Modern France: The Medical Concept of National Decline* (Princeton, NJ, 1984), 119.
[10] Biddiss, *Father of Racist Ideology*, 214.
[11] See Claude Digeon, *La Crise allemande de la pensée française, 1870–1914* (Paris, 1959).
[12] From Paul Leroy-Beaulieu, *La Question de la population* (Paris, 1911), and cited in Nye, *Masculinity*, 78. The population of Germany increased by 58% between 1872 and 1911, as opposed to 10% in France. See also id., 'Degeneration and the Medical Model of Cultural Crisis'.
[13] See Spengler, *France Faces Depopulation*, 138.

The ideas of Lapouge were not based on the tripartite racial division (i.e. 'white', 'yellow', and 'black') used by Gobineau; instead, he was especially concerned with the mixture of the racial types said to inhabit France: *Homo Europaeus*, *Homo Alpinus*, and the intermediate 'Mediterranean' type.[14] Gobineau was a precursor, however, for Lapouge's belief that the amount of 'Aryan' blood was the principal determinant of the rung on the ladder of civilization occupied by any given people. 'Aryans', close cousins of *Homo Europaeus*, were characterized as a tall, dolichocephalic (long-headed), blue-eyed, blond-haired people who spread civilization, usually through the vehicle of war. 'Aryanness', claimed Lapouge, could be measured scientifically by means of the cephalic index—a figure which could be obtained by multiplying the breadth of the skull by 100, then dividing the result by the skull's length.[15]

Lapouge was concerned to show how the combination of contrasting heredities produced an unstable offspring, the métis, which was both a symbol and a further cause of decadence. In many ways his ideas were no more than the logical outcome of the introduction of the term 'race' into the theories of degeneration propounded by psychiatrists like Morel and Valentin Magnan, where the concern to avoid unsuitable or 'dysgenic' sexual unions saw the development of what Nye has called 'a kind of reproductive eugenics *avant la lettre*'.[16] The idea of 'good' and 'bad' racial mixture was itself not new, however, and although Lapouge and his 'anthroposociology' rapidly became unpopular with French anthropologists,[17] his ideas can nevertheless be shown emerging from an older debate conducted by the French anthropological establishment over the possible links between miscegenation and degeneration.

## POLYGENISTS AND MONOGENISTS

Between 1749 and 1767 Georges Louis Leclerc, comte de Buffon, published the fifteen volumes of his *Histoire naturelle, générale et particulière*,

[14] See Linda L. Clark, *Social Darwinism in France* (Birmingham, Ala., 1984), 148–9; also Benoît Massin, 'Lutte des classes, lutte des races', in Claude Blanckaert (ed.), *Des sciences contre l'homme*, i (Paris, 1993), 139.

[15] Georges Vacher de Lapouge, 'La Dépopulation de la France', *Revue d'Anthropologie*, 10 (1887); also Taguieff, 'Doctrines de la race', 77–81. For more on phrenology, see Theodore Zeldin, *France 1848–1945*, ii (Oxford, 1977), 10–12.

[16] Nye, *Masculinity*, 76.

[17] See Clark, *Social Darwinism in France*, 143–54. Both Lapouge and Gobineau were frequently accused of being too pro-German.

in which he concluded that: 'Every circumstance concurs in proving that mankind is not composed of species essential different from each other; that, on the contrary, there was originally but one species.'[18] A biological species was defined by its members' ability to interbreed; the scientific basis for Buffon's belief in monogenesis lay, therefore, in the knowledge that whites and blacks were capable of procreation.[19]

By the time of the foundation of the Société d'Anthropologie de Paris in 1859, however, there was considerable dispute among human scientists over this point. During the early years of the society's existence the problem of human hybridity was regarded as one of the most pressing issues to be discussed. Indeed, the subject was broached by founder and first president Paul Broca in the very first paper presented to the society, a piece entitled 'Recherches sur l'ethnologie de la France'.[20] Though Broca insisted that the society was 'neither monogenist nor polygenist',[21] his own belief in polygenesis was the view most widely shared among his fellow members.

Broca's ideas on this subject are set out most clearly in his *Mémoire sur les phénomènes d'hybridité dans le genre humain*. This reveals him to have been neither dogmatically polygenist—'[It seems impossible to] re-establish the Ethnology of our planet as it was in the beginning'[22]—nor violently opposed to miscegenation, such as it was understood from what he accepted were the imprecise definitions of 'race' available at the time.

Broca was more concerned to establish gradations in the possibilities for fertile unions between different races. In France itself, for example, the various (white) 'races', in 'pure' or 'mixed' form, were seen as perfectly able to reproduce amongst themselves indefinitely, a process referred to as 'eugenesic hybridity'. Explicitly rejecting Gobineau's vision of relentless decay, Broca asserted that France, 'this hybrid nation', 'far from presenting a decreasing fecundity . . . grows every day in intelligence, prosperity, and numbers'.[23] The contrast between Broca's apparent optimism and the later work of Lapouge is striking.

---

[18] Quoted in Todorov, *On Human Diversity*, 97.

[19] See Nancy Stepan, 'Biological Degeneration: Races and Proper Places', in J. Edward Chamberlin and Sander L. Gilman (eds.), *Degeneration: The Dark Side of Progress* (New York, 1985), 105.

[20] See *Mémoires de la Société d'Anthropologie de Paris* (1860–1), 1–56. For more on Broca see Francis Schiller, *Paul Broca: Founder of French Anthropology, Explorer of the Brain* (Berkeley, 1979).

[21] Paul Broca, 'Proceedings of the Anthropological Society of Paris', *Anthropological Review* (1863), 303.

[22] Paul Broca, *On the Phenomena of Hybridity in the Genus Homo*, 11. This work was first published in the *Journal de Physiologie* between 1859 and 1860.

[23] Ibid. 21–2. Broca reasserted these views in a paper entitled 'Sur la prétendue dégénerescence de la population française' in 1867; see Schneider, *Quality and Quantity*, 16.

Between races deemed to be further apart in a racial hierarchy held as axiomatic, Broca saw a corresponding decline in the potential for successful hybridization. In the first instance, he reiterated the commonplace claim that: 'The union of the Negro with a white woman is frequently sterile, whilst that of a white man with a negress is perfectly fecund.' Despite acknowledging the paucity of evidence for the first assertion, he offered in support the 'anatomically correct' observations of Antoine Serres, to the effect that the length of the penis and the uterine canal in the men and women of the 'Ethiopian race' ensures that the union of white men and black women is easy, whereas during intercourse with a black man 'the neck of the [white woman's] uterus is pressed against the sacrum, so that the act of reproduction is not merely painful, but frequently non-productive'.[24]

Broca further drew on the work of the American polygenist Josiah Clark Nott, who in the mid-1830s had studied medicine and natural history in Paris. Nott, whose theories were turned in his own country to the defence of slavery and vigorous opposition to interracial sexual contact, argued in 1843 that since the races of man actually represented separate species, interracial unions produced a genuine 'hybrid'—'a degenerate, unnatural offspring, doomed by nature to work out its own destruction'.[25] Broca, for his part, quoted from an essay published by Nott in 1854, the conclusions to which are worth reproducing in full.

1. Mulattoes are the shortest lived of any class of the human race.

2. Mulattoes are intermediate in intelligence between the blacks and the whites.

3. They are less capable of undergoing fatigue and hardships than either the blacks or whites.

4. Mulatto women are peculiarly delicate, and subject to a variety of chronic diseases. They are bad breeders, bad nurses, liable to abortions [*sic*], and their children generally die young.

5. When mulattoes intermarry, they are less prolific than when crossed on the parent stock.

6. When a Negro man married a white woman, the offspring partook more largely of the Negro type than when the reverse connection had effect.

7. Mulattoes, like Negroes, although unacclimated, enjoy extraordinary exemption from yellow fever when brought to Charleston, Savannah, Mobile, or New Orleans.[26]

[24] Broca, *On the Phenomena of Hybridity*, 28. See also Georges Pouchet, *The Plurality of the Human Race*, ed. Hugh J. C. Beavan (London, 1864), 53–4.
[25] Stepan, 'Biological Degeneration', 107.
[26] In Broca, *On the Phenomena of Hybridity*, 33.

Although Broca manifested his usual degree of scepticism towards
these claims, he nonetheless seems to have disregarded the social background for Nott's comments. This is particularly interesting in the light
of Broca's remark that, since France and England, 'the two most civilised
nations', had emancipated their slaves, scientists could now speak freely
'without caring for the sophisms of slaveholders'.[27] Though well aware
of the social uses of science, Broca appears to have regarded Nott as
an impartial participant in an international debate. Some of Nott's conclusions will already be familiar to the reader, as examples of the kind of
stereotype applied to French West African métis. This is not necessarily
to suggest that Nott was the originator of these particular stereotypes.
However, a more general point does seem to emerge: that observations made
in quite specific social contexts could, through the conduit of 'science',
find outlets in areas remote from the original source.

Unlike such thinkers as Gobineau and Lapouge, Broca cannot be neatly
categorized as an opponent of miscegenation. In many ways, too, he proves
the wisdom of George W. Stocking's comment that polygenism 'was an
alternative which intelligent—and even humane—scientists could, and
did, reasonably embrace'.[28] Despite this, Broca's conclusions were not far
removed from Nott's catalogue of 'mulatto' degeneracy, as he suggested
that people born of unions between the 'higher' and 'lower' races were liable
to shorter life-spans and, in many cases, sterility.[29]

What Broca serves primarily to highlight, however, is the prevalence by
the late 1850s of a racialist scientific culture which could, on the flimsiest
and most anecdotal evidence, convict people of mixed race of being
'very often inferior to the two parent stocks, both in vitality, intelligence,
or morality'.[30] In short, his work exhibits many of what Todorov has
described as 'the sedimentations . . . of the ordinary anonymous racialist
ideology of the period, a sort of racial common sense that could have
appeared in a "Dictionary of received ideas" of the time'.[31] As the following
section will show, however, this ideology cannot be explained simply as
an attempt to promote or legitimize colonial expansion, even if that was,
in many cases, precisely the purpose it served.

[27] Broca, *On the Phenomena of Hybridity*, 69.
[28] George W. Stocking, Jr., *Race, Culture and Evolution: Essays in the History of
Anthropology* (New York, 1968), 42.
[29] Broca, *On the Phenomena of Hybridity*, 60.
[30] This comment was made by the military physician Jean Boudin. See *Bulletins de la Société
d'Anthropologie* (1860), 206; also cited in Broca, *On the Phenomena of Hybridity*, 39.
[31] Todorov, *On Human Diversity*, 106.

## THE PERILS OF *ÉGALITÉ*

The use of the concept of 'race' by such writers as Gobineau was as much a metaphorical means of addressing contemporary social and political fears as it was a 'scientific' attempt to paint the world in different colours.[32] Pierre-André Taguieff has highlighted the centrality of this theme in what he terms 'mixophobic' discourse, wherein *métissage*, as a cause of the homogenization of the human species, was thought to lead ineluctably to uniformity and mediocrity. For Gobineau, as Taguieff goes on to show, the ideals of egalitarian democracy were no more than the outward manifestation of the 'ethnic confusion' which resulted from the degeneration caused by racial mixture—a confusion which spelt the end of aristocracy.[33] Despite his reluctance to declare Gobineau as a source, and while his ideas on the subject were not based on race, Ernest Renan was arguing along related lines in seeing democracy, with its egalitarian and supposed socially homogenizing tendencies, as 'unnatural'.[34]

These tendencies are embodied in the work of another important late-nineteenth-century French thinker, Gustave Le Bon. Le Bon was something of an anti-establishment figure,[35] but his influence was no less widely felt for that. His *Lois psychologiques de l'évolution des peuples* (1894), for example, was a best-seller in its day, translated eventually into sixteen different languages.[36]

Le Bon shared many of Gobineau's beliefs: his racial determinism, his opposition to the mixture of races and classes, and his virulent dislike of democracy. As Nye has shown, however, he was less concerned to defend the hereditary aristocracy *per se* than the composite military-industrial elites which held sway at the time he was writing.[37]

---

[32] See Biddiss, *Father of Racist Ideology*, 132.

[33] Taguieff, 'Doctrines de la race', 53. I use the terms 'democracy' and 'aristocracy' here as they were understood in nineteenth-century France, i.e. as descriptions of types of society. See e.g. Siedentop, *Tocqueville*, 25–8.

[34] Taguieff, 'Doctrines de la race', 67; also Todorov, *On Human Diversity*, 110. More surprisingly, Lapouge was also loath to cite Gobineau. For his part, Lapouge thought democracy was 'suicide' for humanity, and suggested that 'Determinism, Inequality, Selection' should replace the formula 'Liberty, Equality, Fraternity'. See Massin, 'Lutte des classes', 141; Clark, *Social Darwinism in France*, 141, 153.

[35] See Susanna Barrows, *Distorting Mirrors: Visions of the Crowd in Late Nineteenth-Century France* (New Haven, 1981), 164–5.

[36] Robert A. Nye, *The Origins of Crowd Psychology: Gustave Le Bon and the Crisis of Mass Democracy in the Third Republic* (London, 1975), 52.

[37] Ibid. 43.

Le Bon's fear of mass society, given particular impetus by the Paris Commune of 1871, led him to develop the idea that people regressed morally and psychologically when they gathered together. The crowd was seen as possessing an irrational, unconscious mind of its own which it was vital for the elite to control.[38] Daniel Pick writes that: 'The move from a Morel to a Le Bon marks an important shift of emphasis from the degenerate individual or family to the crowd, or rather to crowd civilisation.'[39] In both cases, however, we might also perceive the existence of an intellectual continuum between these ideas and 'mixophobic' discourse, represented in Morel's threat of sterility, and Le Bon's fear of homogeneity and loss of individuality.

These fears merged more closely with Le Bon's views on race during his involvement in the debate over the merits and demerits of the colonial doctrine of assimilation. Whereas Gobineau had condemned colonialism for hastening the process of degeneration, Le Bon regarded such expansion as inevitable, directing his energies instead to undermining what he saw as the dangerously humanistic notion of assimilation, challenging its application in colonial situations.

Le Bon viewed miscegenation as a prime danger, leading to 'direct racial disorientation in the offspring'.[40] However, the meeting of cultures was likely to be just as harmful as the meeting of bodies. At the International Colonial Congress of 1889, Le Bon insisted that 'every institutional system represents the needs of a particular people and, consequently, ought not to be changed'.[41] Thus he criticized the British for training Indians for use in the civil service, as well as French education policy and missionary activity in Algeria.[42]

These were not heartfelt pleas for a greater appreciation of cultural difference; rather, Le Bon rejected the idea that it was possible to 'improve' people whose 'racial characteristics', as he saw it, differed so profoundly from those of Europeans. Léopold de Saussure, a naval lieutenant who attacked assimilation in an influential volume, similarly contended that the unity of mankind and the Enlightened rationalism upon which the theory depended simply did not square with the laws of evolution.[43]

---

[38] See Pick, *Faces of Degeneration*, 90–3; also Barrows, *Distorting Mirrors*, 162–88; J. S. McClelland, *The Crowd and the Mob: From Plato to Canetti* (London, 1989), 196–236.

[39] Pick, *Faces of Degeneration*, 95–6.    [40] Nye, *The Origins of Crowd Psychology*, 50.

[41] Quoted in Betts, *Assimilation and Association*, 68.

[42] Nye, *The Origins of Crowd Psychology*, 50–1.

[43] Léopold de Saussure, *La Psychologie de la colonisation française*; also Betts, *Assimilation and Association*, 70–1.

For Le Bon, racial characteristics were immutable, and he predicted that they would atavistically be reasserted in future revolts. In support of his arguments, he stated the belief that the final, fatal confirmation of the decadence of the Roman Empire had come when the barbarians were granted citizens' rights.[44]

It is important to stress how, in Le Bon's somewhat paranoid world-view, metropolitan and colonial concerns were inextricably interwoven. Todorov notes Le Bon's 'tendency to identify the hierarchy of race with the hierarchies of sex and class', where workers and women were also regarded as incorrigible possessors of a primitive mentality.[45] His denunciations of assimilation provide just one example of how his theories were intended to defend a beleagured conservative elite fearful of a society whose apparently inexorable tendency towards homogeneity represented a real threat to their power.

In these circumstances, the *idea* of miscegenation—regardless of reality—carried enormous force, and was an obvious subject for debate. Those who opposed miscegenation in the *métropole* could perhaps be characterized, therefore, as being primarily concerned with a loss of identity which would not or could not be stemmed by a system of government which held the ideal of equality as one of its most precious guiding principles.

### LITERATURE AND MISCEGENATION

Before placing these ideas more directly in a colonial context, it is worth briefly considering the role which literature may have played in reflecting and disseminating similar attitudes towards miscegenation and métis. In general, nineteenth-century French fiction asserted the impossibility or at least the undesirability of miscegenation. In William B. Cohen's words: 'Interracial sex was presented as the violation of the distance between two species; the failure of such unions was proof of the unbridgeable biological gap.'[46]

This 'failure', particularly when it involved the relationship between a black man and a white woman, was often symbolized by the violent death of one or both of the parties involved. Cohen presents a range of examples to support this observation, finding only two exceptions wherein miscegenation is depicted as natural, namely *Georges* (1848) by Alexandre

---

[44] Nye, *The Origins of Crowd Psychology*, 51.
[45] Todorov, *On Human Diversity*, 113.
[46] Cohen, *The French Encounter with Africans*, 235.

Dumas—himself an *homme de couleur*—and *Le Chat Maigre* (1879) by
Anatole France.[47]

Pierre Loti—the pseudonym of a naval officer named Julien Viaud—was
probably the most popular exponent of novels which had interracial sexual
contact as a significant theme. The hugely successful and much imitated
*Roman d'un spahi*, first published in 1881, was typical of Loti's work in
revolving around a predominantly sensual relationship between a European
and a native woman of a far-off land, in this case Senegal.[48]

The relationship between the spahi, a soldier in the Senegalese colonial
cavalry, and his young mistress, Fatou-Gaye, is portrayed as unnatural, the
result of a moral weakening on the part of the spahi caused by a combination of the effects of the heat and Fatou's animal allure. The spahi, Jean,
from the Cévennes and described as being of the 'pure white race', attempts
to break away from Fatou to escape the degrading effects of his transgression,
to recover his 'white man's dignity, soiled by contact with this black flesh'.[49]
This attempt is unsuccessful, however. When Jean next encounters Fatou,
on an ill-fated military expedition along the Senegal River, he meets for the
first time the child produced by their union. Jean is immediately struck that

The child had rejected his mother's blood; he was entirely Jean's own... 
He stretched out his hands and watched, furrowing his brow, wearing a solemn
expression—as if seeking to understand why he had been born, and how his blood
of the Cévennes had come to be mixed with this impure black race.[50]

This description, in which Jean and Fatou's child appears as the embodi-
ment of their transgression, shortly precedes the novel's violent climax.
When Jean is killed in an ambush, Fatou strangles their child, filling his
mouth with sand to stifle his cries, then takes her own life with poison.
The three lie dead together, their 'unnatural' relationship worked out to
its conclusion.[51] The violent failure of Jean and Fatou's relationship might
be taken as a literary equivalent to the anthropological belief in the sterility
of interracial unions.

[47] Cohen, *The French Encounter with Africans*, 247. In both these instances the central male
character is a métis. West African novelists have not always proved any more optimistic about
the potential for interracial unions to succeed; see e.g. Ousmane Socé, *Mirages de Paris* (Paris,
1937); Bâ, *L'Etrange destin de Wangrin*, 394–421.
[48] For studies of Loti see Alec G. Hargreaves, *The Colonial Experience in French Fiction:
A Study of Pierre Loti, Ernest Psichari and Pierre Mille* (London, 1981); Todorov, *On Human
Diversity*, 308–23. Louis Charles Royer's *La Maîtresse Noire* (Paris, 1928), for example, serves
to confirm the durability of Loti's archetype.
[49] Pierre Loti, *Le Roman d'un spahi* (Paris, 1974), 210.
[50] Ibid. 243.          [51] Ibid. 277–8.

The idea of the degeneration and inner conflict produced by contrasting heredities, embodied by Jean and Fatou's métis son, is equally manifested in the characteristics of the mixed-race lover taken by Jean earlier in the story. When Jean discovers that she is being unfaithful to him, her civilized veneer fades away and her 'true' nature is atavistically reasserted: 'The *mulâtresse*, granddaughter of a slave, had reappeared in all her atrocious cynicism, beneath the outward form of an elegant woman of refined manners.'[52] In fact, the journal of Julien Viaud reveals that the real-life Loti had had a relationship with a métisse named Félicia Morel during his time in Saint-Louis in the early 1870s. 'The perversity and incoherence in the heart of a *mulâtresse*', Viaud had concluded then, 'would confound Satan.'[53] Such was the *mentalité* of the age that this typical assessment of the psychological make-up of people of mixed race could easily be dressed up in more academic language. To cite, on this occasion, the philosopher and sociologist Alfred Fouillée:

Cross a Bushman with a European woman, and the struggle of antagonistic elements, instead of existing among diverse individuals, will be transported into one and the same individual. You will have a personality divided against itself, incoherent, which will obey first one instinct, then the opposite, without being able to adopt a consistent line of conduct.[54]

Loti, Fouillée, Broca, Le Bon, and all the other writers considered here were therefore entirely representative of their time in finding miscegenation a subject of interest in the latter half of the nineteenth century. This series of debates, however, should not be allowed to become too detached from the real-life colonial context. It is essential to 'humanize' these ideas, by asking how far the lives of people of mixed race were affected by serving as the focus for such intense speculation—whatever 'scientific' justification was being claimed—as to their physiological and psychological qualities. We can begin to answer this question by assessing how far these predominantly metropolitan-based theories influenced observers in the colonies themselves.

[52] Ibid. 50.

[53] See Henry Bordeaux, *Nos Indes Noires. Voyage en Afrique Occidentale* (Paris, 1936), 105–19, in particular 113–15. Similar stereotypes existed in British colonial literature; see Abena P. A. Busia, 'Miscegenation and Metonymy: Sexuality and Power in the Colonial Novel', *Ethnic and Racial Studies*, 9 (1986), in particular 367: 'Where there are children born of such a union who live, they are frequently the most morally degenerate of beings: villainous, treacherous, manipulative degenerates who . . . manage to inherit both the most repulsive physical and spiritual traits of their parents.'

[54] Alfred Fouillée, 'Le Caractère des races humaines et l'avenir de la race blanche', *Revue des Deux Mondes* (July 1894), 96.

## THE COLONIAL DIAGNOSIS

In 1879 Dr L.-J.-B. Bérenger-Féraud, Médecin en Chef de la Marine, published his book *Les Peuplades de la Sénégambie*. An open advocate of French expansion in West Africa, he considered the extent to which métis might assist in this process in a chapter bluntly entitled 'On the utilization by France of the peoples of Senegambia'.

Bérenger-Féraud prefaced his remarks on this subject with the disclaimer that he had been acquainted personally with 'numerous mulattoes who were assuredly better than whites or blacks'. He insisted, however, that he would not allow this to impair his claims to anthropological correctness.[55] As such, he felt it necessary to point out that

Even those mulattoes of blooming health, ample constitution, and athletic build become infertile, sometimes by the second generation, most often by the third generation, and certainly by the fourth generation at the latest. This is not to mention the fact that their offspring, instead of inheriting the combined elements of resistance [to disease, etc.] of whites and blacks, have only their physical and moral imperfections.

The result of an error of nature, or rather of a deception of this nature, mulattoes born of the intercourse of whites and negresses are insufficiently balanced to gain the right to exist and perpetuate their line on the coast of Africa; I could say the same of the Antilles, and it is in vain that one pins any hopes on the creation of a population of this kind; their existence is too ephemeral to constitute anything serious. They are in unstable equilibrium, and one feels that nature, anxious to put an end to their existence as quickly as possible, gave them enough imperfections to condemn the race to a rapid extinction.[56]

The similarities between these claims and the theories considered earlier hardly need to be pointed out: sterility by the fourth generation, degenerates condemned to self-destruction, and so on. To this list one might also add his later contention that mixed-race women were particularly prone to miscarriages.[57]

There is a further continuity between Bérenger-Féraud's ideas and those current in the *métropole* in his equation of race and class. Métis in Senegambia, 'speaking the language of blacks and of whites', represent for Bérenger-Féraud the bourgeoisie, with Europeans (naturally) constituting

---

[55] Dr L.-J.-B. Bérenger-Féraud, *Les Peuplades de la Sénégambie* (Paris, 1879), 396–7. Bérenger-Féraud used the word 'mulâtres' in the original text.

[56] Ibid. 397. See also id., 'Note sur la fécondité des mulâtres du Sénégal', *Revue d'Anthropologie* (1879), 580–5, for a detailed table 'proving' his findings.

[57] Bérenger-Féraud, *Les Peuplades*, 399. As in Nott's work cited earlier, the word used was *avortement*, not *fausse couche*, but the sense is of a miscarriage rather than an abortion.

the nobility, and blacks forming 'the proletariat at the bottom of the ladder'.[58] Here one might point out, for example, that Renan had posited a similar racial division of labour eight years earlier: 'Nature has created a race of workers, the Chinese race . . . a race of field-hands, the Black race . . . a race of masters and soldiers, the European race.'[59] Bérenger-Féraud concluded, however, that the evanescence of the mixed-race population precluded it from any significant long-term role in the exploitation of Senegambia. The French role in Senegambia, as he saw it, should be strictly limited. A scattering of unequivocally dominant whites—'the nobility'—would force the mass of the black indigenous population to produce the raw materials useful to French industry. Sterility, argued Bérenger-Féraud, would rapidly bring about the failure of any system based on closer interracial contact.[60]

How are we to explain the process whereby an experienced colonial doctor, well aware of the existence of a long-established mixed-race community in his area of interest, could claim that this selfsame community was infertile *inter se*? Two possible explanations present themselves.

First, Bérenger-Féraud has to be located at a particular moment in the history of the colonization of West Africa. In the early 1860s the métis community of Senegal appears still to have been regarded as something of a special case. In 1860, for example, one member of the Société d'Anthropologie de Paris, a Monsieur Simonot, stated that

In our colony of Senegal, the mulattoes are almost the equals of the whites. This is because the Yoloff race [*sic*], to which their mothers belong, is at the same time the most beautiful and the most intelligent of all the black races, and also because colour prejudice is less important in Senegal than anywhere else, to the extent that men of colour there are treated by whites on an equal footing.

Simonot explained further that Senegalese *mulâtres* were 'superior' to those found in America because the latter were mainly descended from blacks from Guinea, it being an 'established fact' that blacks declined in quality the closer they lived to the Equator. As for the 'Yoloffs', 'their facial features and body shape differ little from our own'.[61] A similar appraisal was offered by Dr Thevenot, a member of an old Saint-Louisian family: 'The mulatto can do whatever the white man can do. His intelligence is as developed as our own.'[62]

[58] Ibid. 398.
[59] Ernest Renan, *La Réforme intellectuelle et morale de la France* (Paris, 1871), 93–4.
[60] Bérenger-Féraud, *Les Peuplades*, 400–1.
[61] See *Bulletins de la Société d'Anthropologie de Paris* (1860), 211.
[62] Quoted in J.-A.-N. Périer, 'Essai sur les croisements ethniques', *Mémoires de la Société d'Anthropologie de Paris*, 2 (1863–5), 355–6.

By the 1870s, however, this view was not so common. (In fact, even by 1865 Simonot was more guarded in his praise, stating that, in general, métis were physically inferior to blacks, and that moreover they were a confusion of passions, 'a mixture of inertia and violence'. They were essentially 'transitory', their fortunes linked solely, as Bérenger-Féraud himself was to write, to the fortunes of the white population of each colony.[63]) The connection made by Bérenger-Féraud between race and class suggests that, even if it had not existed before, some notion of social distance was now definitively in place in Senegal. This fits quite neatly into the chronological pattern of colonial expansion in Senegal, with the transitional phase represented by Faidherbe's governorship giving way to open colonial exploitation of the type advocated by Bérenger-Féraud, and the development of a more formally stratified society. Moreover, as the similarity noted with Renan's work of 1871 suggests, Bérenger-Féraud's comments might also perhaps be tied into a metropolitan chronology, as part of the conservative backlash which followed the defeat in 1870 and especially the Paris Commune.

It is not wholly satisfactory, however, to see Bérenger-Féraud's work as serving a purely normative purpose. It can also be analysed as a manifestation of a problem of scientific method. This point can better be illustrated by examining the work of Dr Armand Corre, a colleague of Bérenger-Féraud who had helped the latter with his *Les Peuplades de la Sénégambie*.

Corre addressed the issue of *métissage* in the colonies in his book *L'Ethnographie criminelle* (1894), which attempted to draw a link between race and criminality. On the subject of métis born of whites and black Africans, Corre wrote that their brain capacity was greater than that of blacks. On the other hand,

The mulatto has an intelligence which is sometimes brilliant, but in general very superficial; he possesses an egoism which is only equalled by an enormous pride, and if the latter drives him in certain cases towards very laudable goals, through vain emulation, often too, ruled by the former, he is led into selfishness and criminality. He is truly the man for contemporary political situations, scheming, verbose, pretentious, little encumbered by scruples . . .[64]

Here one sees the anti-democratic critique of miscegenation in action: the métis is a chattering degenerate, incapable of decisive action, superficial,

[63] See *Bulletins de la Société d'Anthropologie de Paris* (1865), 114–7; Bérenger-Féraud, *Les Peuplades*, 399.
[64] Corre, *L'Ethnographie criminelle*, 30.

and with criminal tendencies; in short, 'a disruptive social element',[65] and, Corre seems to be saying, rather suited to Third Republican political life. Just a few pages later, however, Corre contradicts himself when writing about the specific case of the *créoles* of Senegal, who are 'all métis to varying degrees':

They have equally easy relations with blacks and whites, are little agitated by political questions, and direct their activity towards commerce, if they do not embrace careers in the army or as civil servants. These are, in general, calm people, among whom outrages are quite rare or limited to minor criminal acts.[66]

It is not enough simply to dismiss Corre and Bérenger-Féraud as bad scientists. Rather, there seems to have been a real struggle here to reconcile theory with empirical observation. Each writer chose a different but equally unsatisfactory solution: Bérenger-Féraud asserting the primacy of theory over observation, Corre apparently opting for inconsistency and making little effort to assimilate what he knew with what he wanted to say (or thought he ought to be saying). Neither was willing or able to challenge the dominant discourse on miscegenation which had, by and large, been formulated in the *métropole* without the benefit of much empirical observation.

Nineteenth-century racial theorists were not famed for the internal logic of their arguments, but there is a more general point to be made. Todorov has described in relation to Renan the tendency in late-nineteenth-century thought towards 'the submission of the good to the true (or what is believed to be true), and thus of ethics to science'.[67] Bérenger-Féraud fits this description to some extent, but exemplifies an additional tendency to let these abstract 'truths' inform all subsequent social observation.

The tragedy is that Bérenger-Féraud was not regarded as a quack. In fact, his work was regularly cited until as late as 1942, when Robert Cornevin, who was to become a highly respected historian of French colonialism, in his *mémoire* for the École Nationale de la France d'Outre-Mer treated Bérenger-Féraud's remarks on métis as points worth taking seriously rather than examples of a defunct line of reasoning.[68] Métis themselves were almost entirely excluded from the debate about their characteristics; those with whom Bérenger-Féraud was acquainted may well have been surprised to learn that, scientifically speaking, they were unable to procreate.

---

[65] Ibid. 32.    [66] Ibid. 56–7.    [67] Todorov, *On Human Diversity*, 121.
[68] Cornevin, 'Les Métis dans la colonisation française', 51–2. Bérenger-Féraud's work can also be found cited in, for example, d'Anfreville de la Salle, *Notre vieux Sénégal*, in particular 102, favourably quoting the passage on sterility.

## ADAPTING DEGENERATION

It would be wrong to suggest that all theories developed in the *métropole* were resilient enough to survive the journey to the colonies unchanged. The idea of degeneration, for example, is of particular interest in this regard.

As has been shown, the word 'degeneration' was liable to emerge in a range of different contexts in France. This was likewise the case in French West Africa. In 1905, for example, Commandant Edmond Ferry wrote that: 'The Moors and the Tuaregs appear as the degenerate descendants of ancient white races, from whom they have retained, in their wretchedness, a certain grandeur.'[69] This notion of degeneracy could claim a lineage stretching back to Buffon, based originally on the idea that 'the European was the original form of man from which the other races had degenerated through exposure to unsuitable conditions in certain parts of the world'.[70] Away from particular applications to evolutionary racial theory, however, numerous tensions emerged in theories of degeneration when they were transported to the colonies.

Dr Barot's *Guide pratique de l'européen dans l'Afrique occidentale* of 1902 once more helps to highlight many of these tensions. Barot picked out the symptoms of a form of degeneration which he claimed was especially liable to afflict Europeans in West Africa, a condition he called *soudanisme*. This morbid psychological affliction resulted, he wrote, from a weakening of discipline brought about by the material difficulties of living in West Africa and the 'permanent danger' posed by the climate and diseases such as malaria. Europeans suffering from *soudanisme*, a sort of overheated delirium, could be identified from a variety of antisocial behaviours. These ranged from foul moods and persecution complexes right through to sexual excess and alcoholism. Life in West Africa was turning Europeans soft in the head.[71]

In Barot's writing, however, degeneration then becomes confused with the progressive notion of the 'civilizing mission':

The fetishist peoples who have lived in contact with us for some time . . . have assumed all our vices, especially alcoholism with its accompanying defects: criminality, degeneration, madness, etc. . . .

[69] Commandant Edmond Ferry, *La France en Afrique* (Paris, 1905), 218.
[70] Bowler, *Evolution*, 88; also 70. See also John H. Eddy, Jr., 'Buffon's *Histoire Naturelle*: History? A Critique of Recent Interpretations', *Isis*, 85 (1994), 651–4.
[71] Barot, *Guide pratique*, 310. Barot's litany of degenerate traits will again appear familiar as faults to which métis were supposedly susceptible. For more on the dangers of degeneracy to colonists see Stoler, 'Carnal Knowledge', in particular 76–7; also Stepan, 'Biological Degeneration', 103.

It is necessary to consider and treat the fetishists as children; only a slow adaptation over three or four generations will lead them to a conception of social duties and moral laws.[72]

Barot sees no contradiction in this position, which presents the French as both the cause of and the cure for a range of social ills. Although his ideas concerning degeneration are never properly worked out, his belief that Africans could be 'improved' over a period of three or four generations provides a neat twist to classical degeneration theory, throwing the process more or less into reverse and offering a morally reassuring *ex post facto* justification for colonialism. (It is this latter point which particularly distinguishes Barot from the earlier work of Bérenger-Féraud.) The colonial enterprise nevertheless remains deeply coloured by self-doubt, an antithetical residue of morbid degenerationism skewing the entire ideology of the 'civilizing mission'. This is even more evident in the work of the anti-assimilationist Dr Corre, who writes that 'civilization contributes to the destruction of certain customs which are certainly detestable, but it replaces them with degenerative vices'.[73]

Barot was fundamentally more optimistic, and concerned to explore the possibilities by which Europeans might adapt to life in West Africa, thereby facilitating their rule. As Barot saw it, the problem of acclimatization held the key, particularly given the importance he attached to the West African climate as a cause of degeneration. Some theorists were concerned that degenerate traits acquired by whites in the tropics might be passed on to children born there.[74] Barot, however, in another departure from the more familiar lines of metropolitan thought, suggested miscegenation as a potential solution:

The whole problem of adapting our races to these climates lies there: it is by creating mulatto races that we will most easily Gallicize West Africa.... Initial cross-breeding between Europeans and Blacks, later successively attenuated by unions of whites and mulattoes, seems to us the essential condition of acclimatization.[75]

---

[72] Barot, *Guide pratique*, 317.    [73] Corre, *L'Ethnographie criminelle*, 506.

[74] See e.g. Comte de Hutten Czapski, Dr Hubrecht, and Dr Dryepondt, 'Rapport sur la question de l'acclimatement des populations de race blanche en pays tropicaux', in Institut Colonial International, *Compte rendu de la session tenue à Brunswick les 20, 21 et 22 avril 1911*, i (Brussels, 1911), in particular 349–51. By this time such questions were being used to cast doubt on the wisdom of encouraging European women to accompany their husbands to the colonies.

[75] Barot, *Guide pratique*, 331.

This plan does not appear quite so radical when it is placed in the context of a long-running debate over acclimatization and colonialism. In fact, this was a central theme in the argument between the polygenists and monogenists. The former generally tried to demonstrate that each race was adapted to the climate of a particular area; any move from these regions would end in degeneration or death. Monogenists such as Armand de Quatrefages and other members of the Société Zoologique d'Acclimatation, on the other hand, argued for the cosmopolitanism of man—the potential for each race to adapt to almost any climate.[76]

Without going too far into the complex arguments involved in the acclimatization debate, Barot's position is less clear-cut than it may at first appear. He does seem to follow the general monogenist line that all races, being of the same species, are perfectly able to procreate freely among themselves, and that if *métissage* has any harmful effects then social or environmental factors are to blame.[77] Contrarily, however, Barot's insistence on the need for miscegenation suggests a doubt in the potential for Europeans to adapt to the West African environment, and the colonial disease of *soudanisme* appears to be an example of the kind of degeneracy suffered by 'a race out of its proper place'.[78]

These inconsistencies result once more from the attempt to incorporate ideas devised in the *métropole* into a context which did not suit them. The notion that Europeans degenerated in the tropics, Stepan has remarked, 'was an expression of the ambivalence still felt by European physicians and biologists at the end of the nineteenth century about colonial settlement, rather than of new medical and biological knowledge'.[79] Barot was patently not ambivalent about colonial settlement, but he was unable to develop a consistent scientific philosophy of colonialism based on the theories available to him at the time. His guiding principle, the humanist position derived from Rousseau that 'to deny the perfectibility of a living soul is to deny life itself',[80] was not enough to sustain him. Humanism and colonialism were always uneasy bedfellows.

[76] The acclimatization debate is covered in detail in Michael A. Osborne, *Nature, the Exotic, and the Science of French Colonialism* (Bloomington, Ind., 1994), 62–97. See also Stepan, 'Biological Degeneration', 98–104; Stocking, *Race, Culture and Evolution*, 54.

[77] See Stocking, *Race, Culture and Evolution*, 49. In 1860 de Quatrefages claimed that '[racial] crossings are useful in the majority of cases, while admitting that, in many cases, they can be more or less harmful'. See *Bulletins de la Société d'Anthropologie de Paris* (1860), 190.

[78] Here I am paraphrasing the title of Stepan's article, 'Biological Degeneration: Races and Proper Places'.

[79] Stepan, 'Biological Degeneration', 104.          [80] Barot, *Guide pratique*, 331.

Such intellectual problems thrown up by colonialism often proved difficult to resolve. Likewise, the issue of whether people of mixed race were
better acclimatized to life in West Africa remained a matter for dispute.
In 1909 a French doctor based in Senegal, Dr d'Anfreville de la Salle,
asserted that, 'despite the legend', métis were no more adapted to tropical
climes than were the French.[81] Many more would have rejected Barot's
ideas simply because they involved miscegenation. D'Anfreville de la
Salle himself recapitulated Bérenger-Féraud and spoke of 'the necessity
for colonials to form a true elite'.[82] In the same year Joseph Chailley-Bert,
directeur-général of the Union Coloniale Française, attempted in a debate
at the Institut Colonial International to scotch any notion that Europeans
were incapable of reproducing indefinitely among themselves in the tropics
without recourse to *métissage*. His intervention, supported with examples
drawn from the Antilles and Réunion, was an open endorsement of the
merits of racial purity, further highlighting the dangers of caricaturing
French colonial policy as 'assimilationist' and somehow lacking in notions
of social and racial 'distance'.[83]

#### 'THEORY' CHALLENGED?

By this time it was becoming increasingly clear to some observers that
scientific theories of *métissage* rested on some highly dubious premisses.
In 1906 Georges Hervé, a lecturer at the École d'Anthropologie in Paris,
had used Bérenger-Féraud's work in an article on miscegenation.[84] He
was, however, becoming aware that the scientific study of race mixture had
barely progressed since the work of Broca in the 1850s, because 'instead
of pursuing and expanding objective research, we have hastened to make
generalizations and draw conclusions'.[85] As a result, 'practically nothing'
was known about the fertility and effects of interracial unions, while the
'physical, intellectual, and moral aptitudes' of métis remained equally
speculative. Some of Broca's conclusions—particularly those suggesting
that there was such a thing as 'dysgenic hybridity', wherein métis born of

---

[81] D'Anfreville de la Salle, *Notre vieux Sénégal*, 103.      [82] Ibid. 104.
[83] See 'Discussion de la question de l'acclimatisement de la race blanche dans les colonies
tropicales', in Institut Colonial International, *Compte rendu de la session tenue à La Haye le
2 juin 1909* (Brussels, 1909), 174–7.
[84] See Georges Hervé, 'Noirs et Blancs. Le Croisement des races aux États-Unis et la théorie
de la "Miscégénation"', *Revue Anthropologique* (1906), 353.
[85] See 'Enquête sur les croisements ethniques', *Revue Anthropologique* (1912), 337.

certain unions were alleged to be almost completely sterile—were now
recognized as simply wrong.[86]

Hervé regarded the issue as so important that nothing less than
anthropology's claim to be a serious scientific discipline was at stake. The
anthropological study of *métissage* and its consequences had been, as he saw
it, 'invaded and encumbered by a priori systems and premature theories'.[87]
Hervé's colleague at the École d'Anthropologie, Dr Georges Papillault,
noted that

> It is in the name of a humanitarianism often coloured by religion that one advises
> the mixture of all races [*la panmixie*]; and it is to defend aristocratic principles which
> have never been respected that one demands the absolute segregation of superior
> races. . . . Life is more flexible than our theories, it does not limit itself to these
> extreme solutions; it follows more complex processes. We will only be able to uncover
> these processes by pursuing disinterested, methodical observation over several years.[88]

In 1907, therefore, at the instigation of Hervé, Papillault, and others, the
Société d'Anthropologie de Paris set up a permanent commission, with
Hervé as its president, to 'wipe the slate clean of all theory' and tackle the
problem anew.[89]

The problem was addressed by means of a survey conducted in French
West Africa in 1910 with the help of the colonial authorities. A questionnaire drawn up by Papillault was sent via Governor-General William
Ponty to various local administrators, doctors, and so on, who were asked
to supply as much information as possible while refraining from any assessment of a general or theoretical nature.[90]

In practice, the project was beset by problems. The most common complaint made by those conducting the survey was that in many areas the
French presence was too recent for much information to be supplied. The
findings tended, therefore, to be sketchy. Even from Senegal, however,
there was only one response, compiled by none other than Dr d'Anfreville
de la Salle. His contribution carried details of four families who might almost
have been chosen to fit the remarks he himself had made on the subject
of métis in the book he had published the previous year, which claimed
that 'the facts' seemed to confirm the opinions of Bérenger-Féraud.[91] In his
reply to the questionnaire, d'Anfreville de la Salle portrayed the children
born of parents of 'pure race'—at least, those who survived childhood—as

[86] 'Enquête sur les croisements ethniques', *Revue Anthropologique* (1912), 337, 341.
[87] Ibid. 342.    [88] Ibid. 343.    [89] Ibid. 342.
[90] Ibid. 344. The questionnaire also appears in full in White, 'Miscegenation and Colonial
Society', 333–7.
[91] D'Anfreville de la Salle, *Notre vieux Sénégal*, 102.

relatively normal. Several of those born of mixed-race parents, on the other hand, were presented either as physically degenerate or with criminal tendencies. D'Anfreville de la Salle was not necessarily falsifying his evidence, but there is reason at least to suspect that his sample was selective.[92]

Researchers came across a further practical problem when they carried out their work. The acting Lieutenant-Governor of Dahomey, Raphaël Antonetti, explained that in Lower Dahomey métis (some of Portuguese descent) had refused to co-operate with the survey, regarding the questions as an affront to their personal dignity. This he put down to their 'pride', which led them only to want to consider their white ancestry. They had to be threatened with violence before agreeing to take part in the survey.[93]

Antonetti might have reflected that a little more than 'racial' pride was at stake for respondents to a questionnaire containing such headings as 'Criminality' and 'Sexual Morality'. One administrator in the Ivory Coast, who also happened to be a member of the Société d'Anthropologie de Paris, took the study a step further, enthusiastically drawing up an elaborate table of bodily measurements. Much to his disappointment, however, he was unable to measure three métis children, who were too frightened to co-operate. Instead, he had to content himself with measuring their mothers, and in one case a grandmother.[94]

Did this violation of human dignity serve the greater purpose of challenging some of the myths attached to people of mixed race? Certainly, those who paid heed to the request not to indulge in speculation tended to produce responses which suggested there was nothing particularly unusual about métis, either in terms of their 'fertility' or their general state of health. Moreover, few bothered to consider their 'moral qualities', albeit partly because the subjects of the enquiry were rarely older than their teens. Indeed, the respondent from the Korhogo district of the Ivory Coast— the only missionary involved in the survey—tentatively ventured to challenge one of the more pernicious stereotypes:

in my humble opinion, it is not very accurate to say that métis have all the faults of both whites and blacks. They have the faults and qualities of any human being, and intelligence and emotions open to development. A strict education can make of them worthy and creditable members of the family of man.[95]

---

[92] 'Enquête sur les croisements', 362–5; cf. d'Anfreville de la Salle, *Notre vieux Sénégal*, 102–4.

[93] 'Enquête sur les croisements', 366.

[94] Ibid. 351; the respondent from Tombouctou made a similar complaint at 396.

[95] Ibid. 361.

It is striking to compare the reply from Ségou, where much of the information had been supplied by those responsible for teaching and looking after the children of the local orphanage,[96] with one of the responses from Kayes, written by one Dr Marquis. The former made a straightforward attempt to answer the questionnaire in an impartial and informed fashion. None of the children's physical or personal characteristics were explained by reference to their 'race'. The answers to the question about their abilities in schoolwork, for example, would have given no support to the idea that people of mixed race showed no aptitude for the sciences (which required a rational turn of mind thought to be less pronounced among those with a degenerate 'artistic temperament'), as several of the children were said to be good at arithmetic.[97]

Dr Marquis, on the other hand, provides very little to suggest that he had much personal experience of these matters, despite the scientific veneer he gives his remarks. Unions between Europeans and African women are 'generally sterile'; the constitution of mixed-race children is 'weaker than that of black children'; métis are 'lacking in vigour', 'sickly', and 'never robust'; they are 'fragile bodies', generally afflicted with hereditary syphilis and malaria, who rarely live to see adolescence. What is more: 'The morality of métis is low. The girls are barely nubile when they abandon themselves to loose living.'[98]

In many ways the questionnaire itself shows what Hervé and his colleagues expected to find. Its emphasis on the health and morality of métis revealed, if anything, the racially deterministic mentality of its authors, rather than suggesting that it was designed to bury some socially ruinous stereotypes. As such, Dr Marquis's remarks do not seem out of keeping with the spirit of the enterprise. Hervé, for his part, found Dr d'Anfreville de la Salle's response to be particularly 'remarkable',[99] but the fact that the replies were only ever published unedited in the *Revue Anthropologique*, the journal of the École d'Anthropologie, suggests that neither he nor the Société d'Anthropologie de Paris got quite what they were looking for.

As a result, the survey did not in any way represent a 'fresh start'. In the *métropole*, Louis Vignon, a lecturer at the École Coloniale, cited the survey in 1919 yet still saw the métis as an infertile hybrid made psychologically

---

[96] Namely Mme Estève, the predecessor of Mme Pion-Roux at the Orphelinat de Ségou, and M Quilichini, head of the local *école régionale*. Several of the children whose letters were analysed in the previous chapter were subjects of the survey.

[97] See e.g. 'Enquête sur les croisements', 386–9.    [98] Ibid. 377–80.

[99] See ANS, 1G 340, a file containing many of the original responses to the questionnaire.

unstable by the 'conflict of heredities'—although he acknowledged that the whole question remained largely unexamined.[100] Another writer with colonial experience managed in 1922 to cram almost every unfavourable characteristic ever ascribed to people of mixed race into one brief passage:

How is one to defend these poor creatures who, almost invariably, come into the world with the defects of two races? Almost invariably, they arrive sickly and lethargic to excess. Almost invariably, one finds them very quick to begin their education, oversensitive to an excessive degree, then suddenly everything falls apart, usually about the age of puberty. In Africa, the girls become easy recruits to the army [of prostitutes]. Europeans and blacks seem to prefer them to pure blacks. But the man, the *mulâtre*, the Devil's *café au lait*, when he escapes the poison which threatens his early life, deprived as he is of the physical energy possessed by pure blacks, deprived likewise of the support of whites, usually languishes into a life of delinquency. Their sickly state makes them even more lazy and capricious than blacks. It is difficult to direct them towards manual occupations. This state of affairs leads one to note that these poor *mulots* [*sic*], raised in such unfavourable circumstances, combine too often the vices of both whites and blacks. . . .[101]

The author of the questionnaire himself, Georges Papillault, a prominent eugenicist, offered a judgement of the worth of *métissage* in work completed for the Colonial Exhibition of 1931. Papillault was not as frankly condemnatory as Louis Vignon, but argued nevertheless that miscegenation involved the elevation of a comparatively 'unevolved' people and the corresponding abasement of an 'evolved' people. Moreover, while 'negroid métis' could to some extent be educated, they were ultimately 'non-assimilable'.[102]

Such opinions were relatively easy to sustain in the *métropole*, even in an era when many French people seem to have convinced themselves that they were incapable of racial prejudice.[103] However, it cannot be assumed, as the response from Ségou might have suggested, that close contact with métis was all that was required to break down some of the tenacious myths which afflicted them.

---

[100] Vignon, *Un Programme de politique coloniale*, 367–9.

[101] Joseph Blache, *Vrais noirs et vrais blancs d'Afrique au vingtième siècle* (Orleans, 1922), 160–1. The word 'mulot' means 'field-mouse'; this may be a misprint or a corruption of 'mulet', meaning 'mule'. This passage is shortly followed by an equally excitable account of the author's relationship with a Gabonese woman.

[102] See Catherine Hodeir and Michel Pierre, *L'Exposition Coloniale* (Paris, 1991), 96–7, in which Papillault's name is wrongly cited as Papillant.

[103] e.g. Gossard, *Études sur le métissage*, 25: 'colour prejudice . . . is an eminently Anglo-Saxon attitude . . . colour prejudice is alien to metropolitan French people.'

### HEREDITY AND MILIEU

In 1907 the administrator in Ségou observed during an inspection of the local orphanage that métis children seemed particularly delicate. 'Born of the crossing of races—which, to judge by Ségou, certainly does not produce an improvement—[they] supply the doctor with a regular clientele, especially the boys.'[104]

Such a belief in the omnipotent power of 'race' to determine physiological characteristics was equally prevalent among those who worked with mixed-race children, such as teachers and those in charge of the *orphelinats de métis*. In 1916, for example, the head of the mixed orphanage at Porto-Novo, Madame Mougenot, requested that the children's dormitories be better protected from mosquitoes. As matters stood it was too easy for them to fly in through the gap between the walls and the roofing, with harmful consequences for children who were 'subject to frequent bouts of malaria, to which their weak constitutions, a consequence of their heredity, leave them exposed'. Her superiors wryly observed, however, that mosquitoes were everywhere in Porto-Novo, and could hardly be refused entry to European lodgings.[105]

A similar belief frequently determined the type of food given to métis children in the orphanages. A report on the Orphelinat des Métisses de Bamako in the 1930s partly justified its existence on the basis that, especially given the rigours of the climate, the 'delicacy' of métis demanded special attention in terms of hygiene, clothing, and diet—attention deemed to be lacking in African homes. As such, the predominantly African diet of the 'sensitive, weak' métisses in the establishment was 'complemented by dishes cooked in the European style', which, the report concluded, helped to explain the low mortality rate in the institution.[106] Likewise, the authorities at the Foyer des Métis in Bingerville decided in 1943 that 'a diet akin to that of Europeans, richer than a purely indigenous diet, would better suit the fragile constitution of métis'.[107]

The residual belief in the degenerate inheritance of people of mixed race was equally manifested in their supposed personality traits. Madame Mougenot was still in charge at Porto-Novo in 1918 when the children in her care were described as being generally 'apathetic, lazy, often mendacious, and all very proud'.[108] The teacher of a class made up predominantly of

[104] ANS, J 36.     [105] ANS, J 47.     [106] ANS, FM: 17G 219.
[107] ANS, FM: O 501, 'Procès-Verbal du Conseil de Perfectionnement du Foyer des Métis de Bingerville', 3 Apr. 1943.
[108] ANS, J 47.

mixed-race children in Bingerville found their characters 'capricious', but added that they were good talkers.[109]

This is not to deny that some of these children may well have lived up to their descriptions. It is simply worth pointing out how often these alleged flaws matched those ascribed to 'degenerates' in the theories described earlier. These characteristics were so often accompanied by pseudo-scientific speculation that the similarity cannot be easily dismissed as coincidence. Observations of métis were constantly coloured by confusion over their racial identity, an identity which was supposed to determine their personality traits.

These tendencies are visible in the comments made by Madame Nogue on the students in her midwifery class. Nogue contrasted the 'beaming' faces of her black African pupils with the 'solemn, meditative, and some-times anguished' faces of her mixed-race students.[110] She added that the métisses in her class seemed to have slower reflexes: 'Perhaps the conflict of two heredities so foreign to each other creates individuals physically more fragile and less readily adapted to the climate and the environment.' Even so, despite being gloomy, sullen, or excessively shy, some of them were occasionally capable of 'an exquisite sensitivity'. While she labelled her black African students impulsive and naturally idle 'big children', these faults did not carry quite the same implication of physical and mental (or racial) instability and degeneracy.[111]

Such ideas lingered throughout the inter-war period. The extent to which attitudes did or did not change can be gauged by studying another survey, this time from the 1930s. The Commission d'Enquête dans les Territoires d'Outre-Mer, also known as the Commission Guernut from the name of its president, the politician Henri Guernut, was set up by the Popular Front government in 1937 to look into a range of colonial problems. The inquiry into 'the métis problem' posed questions somewhat similar to those asked by the Société d'Anthropologie de Paris nearly thirty years earlier, includ-ing a renewed attempt to discover the 'Anthropological, moral, social, and linguistic characteristics of the populations born of *métissage*'. Some of the results from French West Africa, all compiled in 1938, do suggest, however, that certain attitudes were beginning to change.[112]

---

[109] ANS, J 41, report on the Groupe Scolaire de Bingerville, Cinquième Classe, 1918–19.

[110] This recalls the image of the spahi's serious, unsmiling infant son in Loti, *Le Roman d'un spahi*, 252.

[111] Nogue, 'Les Sages-Femmes auxiliaires', in particular 325, 328, 332, 335, 350.

[112] See ANS, FM: 17G 252. The project involved a number of politicians, colonial admin-istrators, and various 'experts', among them Lucien Lévy-Bruhl, André Gide, and Robert Delavignette. Funds for research were cut in September 1938, and as a result the survey never came to fruition in the manner envisaged; see CAOM, Commission Guernut 10, A VIII. For more details see Thobie *et al.*, *Histoire de la France Coloniale*, i, 259–60.

This cannot be said of many of the responses from Dahomey or from the mandated territory of Togo. Researchers in Togo provided a mass of anatomical detail—twenty-four métis had their skulls and various other parts of the body measured—despite apologies that Broca's scale had not been available to make the data more precise. Conclusions ranged from the commonplace idea that mixed-race children were weak and sickly, to rather less familiar notions: that when (or if) they reached maturity they tended to obesity, and that they were liable to go bald much more quickly than 'pure' whites or blacks. The belief in their intermediacy was sustained in the remark that their hair was 'less developed than that of whites' but 'much more developed than that of blacks'; the suspicion of biological instability was likewise preserved in the suggestion that their average life span was shorter than that of both blacks and whites.[113]

Many of the replies from Dahomey were equally unfavourable. The teacher who compiled the response from Segboroué claimed that after leaving school the males were more prone to drunkenness than 'pure Blacks', given that their constitution was weaker from a 'physical, moral, and psychological' point of view. Métisses turned 'almost to prostitution' for similar reasons. An administrator in Grand-Popo considered that in the future people of mixed race would constitute

a category of natives with a distant European ancestor whose name they will carry, dressing as Europeans but living as natives, refusing to perform manual labour and often unsuited to types of work which require more intelligence. *Métissage* is not to be encouraged unless it leads to a French race born in the colony and perfectly adapted to life in the tropics.

The response from Cotonou was even more damning and suggestive of the types of prejudice against which people of mixed race constantly had to battle. Intriguingly, though written up by a French schoolmaster, the reply was based on 'information' supplied by African teachers. This helps to explain why it emphasized the abilities and potential long-term political role of black Africans. People of mixed race, by contrast, were portrayed by means of a crude and familiar list of stigmata, some of which could have been taken straight from Gobineau. The métis was 'an unstable hybrid' of dubious morality, vain and prodigal:

Born of two very different races, these are mentally unstable people, apathetic (especially the girls) and of irresolute will-power; of a fairly lively imagination, they often succeed in the artistic field (music, drawing . . . ), [but] generally display very

---

[113] CAOM, Commission Guernut 101.

little aptitude for the exact sciences; their memory is worse than that of blacks. From the point of view of intelligence and comprehension, they are slower than their black schoolmates and are often classed behind them . . . *Métissage* is not to be encouraged.[114]

This deterministic line was not followed, however, by the respondent from Porto-Novo. He felt that the characteristics of métis were dependent on the milieu in which they were raised.[115] Other replies confirm the impression that this approach was gaining ground in the 1930s. The report covering Senegal, for example, concluded that 'The moral and social condition of métis in Senegal is . . . a function of the education and instruction they have received'.[116] The reply from the French Soudan was in fact compiled by a métis group, the Mutualité des Métis du Soudan. They referred their questioners to the work of Paul Moreau, a colonial administrator whose published doctoral thesis had argued that 'métis are what those who raise them make of them; like Europeans, Blacks, or Asiatics, they are shaped by the surrounding environment, and by the education they receive'.[117]

Such ideas spread gradually in the 1930s and early 1940s, and were evident in the efforts discussed in the previous chapter to reassess French policy towards métis around the time of the Brazzaville Conference. Robert Cornevin's ENFOM thesis on métis, written in 1942, is indicative of a period of transition. While generally accepting the argument that the human environment was the most important factor in shaping their characters, he nevertheless continued to believe that métis had no gift for the exact sciences.[118]

These developments ran parallel with doubts among scientists about the applicability of racial biology. As Stepan has shown, only in the 1930s and particularly during the Second World War did members of the scientific community begin in any concerted fashion to challenge existing notions of race and racial degeneration, in the attempt to distance themselves from the catastrophic uses to which the Nazis were turning racial science.

[114] Ibid. Compare, for example, this passage from Gobineau: 'to ensure a true victory in the arts, it would be necessary to obtain a mixture of black and white blood, thus creating a race gifted with immense imagination and sensitivity in addition to much intelligence.' Gobineau, *Essai sur l'inégalité*, ii. 99–100.
[115] CAOM, Commission Guernut 101.     [116] ANS, FM: O 715.
[117] Moreau, *Les Indigènes d'A.O.F.*, 72. For more on the Mutualité des Métis du Soudan, see Ch. 6 below.
[118] Cornevin, 'Les Métis dans la colonisation française', 57; see also 51, suggesting that the commercial strength of people of mixed race in pre-colonial Saint-Louis was due to their 'special resistance to the climate'.

In France itself, as one might expect, scientists of the old school thrived under the Vichy regime. An Institut d'Anthroposociologie was set up in December 1942, headed by none other than the son of Georges Vacher de Lapouge, whose work now found favour in a way he had never known before his death in 1936. Also involved in this project was Dr René Martial.[119] Martial was a popularizer of various racial theories whose ideas on immigration and eugenics were, as William H. Schneider has shown, of some influence in the inter-war period.[120] His standing peaked, however, in the Vichy era.

Martial's book *Les Métis*, published in 1942, synthesized his earlier work. Strongly advocating positive selection and obsessed with the 'Asiatization' of France and Jewish 'infiltration', he contended that Gobineau remained relevant: 'The rise and fall of civilizations is explained by racial mixture.'[121] For Martial, the characteristics of métis included 'vulgarity, facial asymmetry, badly proportioned limbs and torso, psychic instability or apathy, a perverse spontaneity or a morbid originality'.[122] Confirming the anti-democratic nature of much metropolitan writing on miscegenation, he claimed that the 'instability' of métis was contagious, leading to 'interminable and useless discussions which paralyze action'.[123]

The collaborator Martial stands at the end of an era of theorizing about miscegenation and its effects, his acknowledgement of Gobineau (and Lapouge) bringing this discussion almost full circle.[124] Stereotypical ideas concerning people of mixed race did not, however, automatically disappear with the Liberation, despite the fact that the notions of the non-cosmopolitan race and of the degenerate 'hybrid' were soon explicitly rejected by the scientific community.[125] In 1948, for example, one ENFOM student wrote in his thesis that 'The métis is a white man lost in black blood', and spoke of 'his sensitiveness', 'his aversion to manual labour',

---

[119] Schneider, *Quality and Quantity*, 261.     [120] Ibid., in particular 230–55.

[121] René Martial, *Les Métis* (Paris, 1942), 45, 53, 80.

[122] Ibid. 44. Martial obtained statistical information on West African métis directly from the colonial authorities in 1939, although a questionnaire he sent seeking biological details met with little response; see ANS, FM: 2H 17. The text of *Les Métis* at 55 suggests that his enquiries in French Equatorial Africa were more fruitful.

[123] Martial, *Les Métis*, 58. For a more detailed analysis of this and other aspects of Martial's work, see Pierre-André Taguieff, 'La Bataille des sangs', in Blanckaert (ed.), *Des sciences contre l'homme*, i. 144–67.

[124] Already in his seventies by the time of the Liberation, Martial appears to have spent the remaining years of his life in Madagascar. See Schneider, *Quality and Quantity*, 286, 350.

[125] Particularly in the first UNESCO *Statement on Race* in 1950. See Stepan, 'Biological Degeneration', 115; William B. Provine, 'Geneticists and the Biology of Race Crossing', *Science*, 23 Nov. 1973, 795–6.

and so on.[126] Clearly, such long-established attitudes died hard. Moreover, as the student's examiners noted, the status of métis in colonial society was hardly improving; that particular paradigm, at least, had not yet shifted.

The realignment of scientific opinion over the question of miscegenation did not result from any significant new scientific discovery; the changes stemmed more from shifting social and political attitudes in the aftermath of the Second World War and the Holocaust.[127] If scientific ideas owed much to their social context, it is similarly difficult to resist the conclusion that the range of stereotypes described above were often of some use to the colonial authorities in French West Africa. The supposedly pathological 'intermediacy' of métis led neatly, as the previous chapter demonstrated, to their employment as petty bourgeois functionaries. Such a development equally represented the reification of the idea that their lack of physical vigour made them unsuited to perform manual labour. The line between 'scientific' speculation and self-fulfilling prophecy could be very fine.

[126] Claude Pauchet, 'Le Problème des métis en Afrique', college thesis (École Nationale de la France d'Outre-Mer, 1947–8), 3, 10.

[127] See especially Provine, 'Geneticists', 796; Stepan, 'Biological Degeneration', 115; Steve Jones, *The Language of the Genes* (London, 1993), p. x.

# 5
## Paternity and the Mother Country

Though French West African métis were deeply affected by serving as the focus for a slew of racial theories, their lives were determined even more by the social relations which emerged under colonial rule. If métis were thought in any way to be 'dangerous', it was primarily because they did not fit neatly into any social category, blurring the racial boundaries which, broadly speaking, served to distinguish the rulers from the ruled. The fear was that, as a speaker at the Institut Colonial International put it in 1921, 'if there were no difference in the colonies between the dominant race and the natives, there would not be any colonies in the true sense of the word'.[1]

The distinguished ethnographer and administrator Maurice Delafosse was under no illusions about the nature of colonial society in French West Africa. In 1923 he observed that white society only ever accepted métis with a barely concealed reluctance. Whites in West Africa were also, he continued, quick to accuse métis of combining the faults of both the races of which they were born.[2] Elsewhere, however, Delafosse seemed to suggest that social exclusion was a necessary process. Métis, he argued, should be left to return to 'the native race', because:

In relation to the coloured races, the white race is too small in number for one to hope for the integration in its midst of the mixed-race children produced by it. Little by little this operation would transform European society into a society dominated by the métis element, and there would no longer be a métis race interposed between the whites and the coloured races who would absorb them.[3]

Such fears for the integrity of social and racial boundaries emerged particularly strongly when the colonial authorities considered the claims of métis to French citizenship, and the possibility of applying metropolitan legislation giving greater scope to pursue paternity suits. These were ongoing subjects of debate throughout the period in question. This chapter will

---

[1] Quoted in Knibiehler and Goutalier, *La Femme au temps des colonies*, 72.
[2] Maurice Delafosse, 'Note relative à la condition des métis en Afrique Occidentale Française', in Institut Colonial International, *Rapports préliminaires* (Brussels, 1923), 87.
[3] Cited in the article 'A l'Institut colonial', *La Presse Coloniale*, 17 Nov. 1926.

explore how the colonial power addressed the problem of the legal status
of métis, paying attention to the consistency of French actions with the
principles by which they claimed to operate. It will also begin to consider why many métis sought French citizenship, a question which will
be developed more fully in Chapter 6.

REWARDING THE FAITHFUL

Attempts to clarify the legal status of métis began to receive serious attention in the early 1900s. In 1902 the colonial minister, Gaston Doumergue,
raised the issue in relation to 'certain mixed-race populations of Dahomey',
many of whom were of part-Portuguese descent. This fact did not deter
Doumergue from wondering whether French citizenship might be extended
at least to the most worthy of these people, who he felt in any case ought
not to be 'completely assimilated to the native population'. The Governor-
General was asked to look in more detail at the problem of defining their
nationality.[4]

Doumergue's request was at least partly inspired by a contemporary *cause
célèbre* involving two mixed-race brothers, Xavier and Achille Béraud. The
Béraud brothers had been born in Ouidah of an unknown father and
a Dahomean woman. The French authorities offered rich praise for the
brothers' decision to leave lucrative posts with the English in Lagos to assist
with the French conquest of Dahomey. Members of their family who had
remained in Ouidah had suffered execution at the hands of King Behanzin
as punishment for this assistance. The brothers' claim for naturalization was
entered as early as 1896. However, no legislation empowered Doumergue
to fulfil their desire, despite general agreement among all the relevant authorities that they entirely merited it. The path of naturalization in the colonies
was open only to non-French nationals, via a decree of 1897. As French
subjects, the brothers were already deemed to hold French nationality; the
possibility of acquiring French citizenship, carrying advantages which will
be outlined later, did not yet exist for colonial subjects.[5]

In response to Doumergue's request for suggestions on the question of
métis nationality, acting Lieutenant-Governor Decazes of Dahomey pointed
out the dangers of any kind of favouritism. To create an intermediate status
for métis between the two existing colonial categories of French subject

[4] CAOM, SG, Dahomey VII dossier 7 bis, Doumergue to GG, Paris, 26 Nov. 1902; also
ANS, 23G 34.
[5] ANS, 23G 30; 23G 34. They were finally granted French citizenship in 1914.

and French citizen—regulated respectively by customary and French law—
would, he felt, be socially divisive as well as legally complicated. Moreover,
he foresaw difficulties in defining individuals as 'métis', particularly as
French law did not at this time allow for paternity suits. Thinking it safest
not to distinguish between black Africans and métis, Decazes went on to
draft legislation which proposed to offer citizenship to colonial subjects
who rendered 'exceptional service' to France or the colony. Non-military
applicants would be expected to read and write French, while the morality
and marital status of all candidates—polygamy being a cause of particular
concern—would also be considered.[6]

Though internal correspondence in the Governor-General's office suggests that these ideas were sympathetically received, nothing immediate
came of Decazes's proposals. A successor of Decazes, Lieutenant-Governor
Marchal, noted as much in 1907 when he raised the issue anew. In reiter-
ating the points made by his predecessor, Marchal added that:

Doubtless our efforts are aiming to bring as many natives as possible to our level
of civilization, but however great that number might one day be, it seems to me
necessary strictly to limit the numbers to be granted the status of French citizen.
Naturalization must preserve the character of an absolutely exceptional reward.
By proceeding in this way, we will win the loyalty of the elite of the population
without alienating the masses, who will retain the hope of an identical reward.
Naturalizations awarded *en masse* or in too large numbers would not achieve the
goal we are setting ourselves. On the contrary, in placing the colony in the hands
of people of rudimentary intellect and morality, we would risk irrevocably compromising the civilizing task which we have taken up.[7]

This passage is typical of its time. Marchal was expressing a firm belief
in the 'civilizing mission', complete with its paternalistic, assimilatory gloss.
His strictures that citizenship should only be granted in exceptional circumstances carried with them the conviction that French citizenship was indeed
an exceptional honour, one to which he imagined large numbers would aspire.
This grand talk, however, barely concealed the serious business of isolating
an indigenous elite to assist in the colonial project without antagonizing the
rude masses who, in certain circumstances, might threaten the refined aims
of the colonial power.[8] Marchal thus presented colonial government as a
delicate balancing act, where the fear of rebellion acted as a spur to consider
new legislation; he worried aloud about 'good servants, descended for the

[6] ANS, 23G 34, acting Lt.-G. Decazes to GG, Porto-Novo, 13 Nov. 1903.
[7] Ibid., Lt.-G. Marchal to GG, Porto-Novo, 12 Jan. 1907.
[8] Compare the later guiding principle of colonial education in West Africa: 'Instruct the
masses and extract the elite' (see Ch. 3 above).

most part from French men' who might 'turn their intelligence and activity against us' if they felt themselves disowned by France.

This fear was perhaps not without foundation. In 1908 Porto-Novo witnessed demonstrations which, in the language of a report from the time, necessitated the intervention of the forces of law and order. Though these protests were ostensibly concerned with a new tax on traders, subsequent investigation concluded that the movement was the work of a group of métis with political motives, their central objective being the acquisition *en bloc* of naturalization.[9] This suggests that there was already a degree of social awareness and organization among métis, at least in some of France's older possessions. In this particular instance, however, the trading community of Porto-Novo, which had become a French protectorate as early as 1882, was dominated by mixed-race 'Afro-Brazilians', a testimony to the Portuguese presence which preceded the French. It seems likely that this community, which tended to welcome the European presence, played a significant role in this incident, but their reasons for wanting French citizenship at this point can be no more than guessed at.[10]

The Dahomean initiative to expand the possibility to acquire French citizenship was not successful, at least in the short term. Governor-General Roume understood Marchal's concern, but insisted that any legislation would have to be applicable to the whole of French West Africa rather than to one particular colony.[11] Nevertheless, five years later such a piece of legislation was passed, which seemed to satisfy many of the suggestions made by Decazes and Marchal.

The 1912 naturalization decree offered French citizenship to native-born French West African subjects who 'approach us in education, adopt our civilization and our customs, or distinguish themselves by their service.' Citizens held certain privileges in colonial society. They were listed as taxpayers and given a receipt upon payment, rather than left to the vagaries of the system wherein local administrators levied a fixed amount of tax for their region in whichever way they chose. (This may or may not have been to the benefit of citizens; it might be argued that it made payment of tax almost impossible to avoid.) Citizens were also able to forgo their annual due of unpaid forced labour on payment of a fixed sum. They were not at the mercy of the *indigénat*, the barely regulated system of justice which allowed administrators to send subjects to jail without appeal for up to two weeks for a variety of offences, including 'any act of a nature to

[9] ANS, 17G 37.
[10] Coquery-Vidrovitch (ed.), *L'Afrique occidentale au temps des français*, 373.
[11] ANS, 23G 34, GG to Lt.-G. du Dahomey, Gorée, 20 Mar. 1907.

weaken respect for French authority'. Finally, the rules governing citizens' military service were different, as will be detailed later.[12]

The decree stipulated several conditions that had to be satisfied before citizenship would be granted. The applicant, aged at least 21, had to have demonstrated (in some unspecified manner) his or her devotion to French interests, or worked for ten years for a public or private French concern. He or she had to be able to read and write French, and provide evidence of a secure means of support and good character ('bonne vie et moeurs').[13]

These conditions of acceptance ensured that, in line with Marchal's desire, citizenship was indeed an 'absolutely exceptional reward'. So much so, in fact, that between 1914 and 1922 only ninety-four French subjects in West Africa gained citizenship in this way.[14] A reading of rejected applications reveals that the authorities were quick to brand candidates as insufficiently assimilated to French ways. Polygamy was one of the more obvious sticking-points, given that any successful applicant had to agree to abide by French law; but the morality of each candidate was also held up to close scrutiny.

The morals of one rejected Guinean applicant, Étienne Gaëtan, were deemed in 1914 to be 'easily won over'. Accused of participating in various intrigues, the mayor of Conakry further charged him with 'allowing and perhaps encouraging the loose behaviour of his wife'.[15] Immorality and nationalist feeling, as Stoler has pointed out, seem to have been regarded as somehow incompatible; the norms of 'respectable' sexuality were inextricably integrated within the idealized vision of civic virtue which was demanded from the would-be citizen.[16] As a result of his alleged personal defects, those signs of 'Frenchness' exhibited by Étienne Gaëtan were thought to be superficial; they were and could only be imitative, rather than 'felt'. In this context, the supposedly more inclusive ideal type of French nationhood, with its voluntaristic concept of citizenship, looks as remote to the outsider as the ethnic and cultural conception of the nation held to be characteristically 'Germanic'.[17]

---

[12] L. P. Mair, *Native Policies in Africa* (London, 1936), 192–3; also Conklin, *A Mission to Civilize*, 121. On the *indigénat*, see Buell, *The Native Problem*, i. 1,016–20.

[13] Decree of 25 May 1912. See ANS, 23G 31; Buell, *The Native Problem*, i. 946.

[14] Buell, *The Native Problem*, i. 947; see also Michael Crowder, *Senegal: A Study of French Assimilation Policy* (London, 1962), 26. Buell notes that more liberal legislation to provide citizenship to decorated war veterans after the First World War similarly failed to open the floodgates, just fourteen soldiers apparently taking advantage of it.

[15] ANS, 23G 31.          [16] Stoler, 'Sexual Affronts', 523–4.

[17] See e.g. Dominique Schnapper, *La France de l'intégration. Sociologie de la nation en 1990* (Paris, 1991), in particular 33–40.

On the one hand, therefore, it is easy to highlight the limited para-
meters of what might have been seen as a particularly 'assimilative' piece
of legislation. For administrators like Lieutenant-Governor Noufflard of
Dahomey it was primarily, if used sparingly, a valuable tool of government
which could keep an aspiring elite safely in the pocket of the colonial power.
Yet it is hard to imagine any more than a tiny minority of Africans shar-
ing Noufflard's additional conviction that French citizenship would be the
'dazzling consecration' of a long period of service.[18] Although the motives of
those who did apply often remain obscure, the benefits of French citizenship,
as Lucy Mair noted in 1936, were hardly enticing enough to encourage
many to go through the lengthy, bureaucratic, and more often than not
unsuccessful process which it entailed.[19]

The decree of May 1912 by no means put an end to the debate about
whether métis should be treated as a special case in the matter of French
citizenship. As early as 1913 a report complained that the decree failed
to acknowledge the situation of *assimilés* in general, who were 'French in
their hearts', and métis in particular, who were also French by blood.
'These people do not regard themselves as natives', the report stated; 'they
would find it distasteful to follow the same formalities as a native from
the depths of the Soudan.' The report concluded that, rather than an act
of naturalization, 'a simple act of recognition' was required for this group
of people.[20] As will be shown later, this argument did not receive practical
consideration from the authorities until the 1920s. Before looking at this in
more detail, however, the ambivalence of official colonial attitudes towards
métis citizenship can be highlighted further by studying reactions to a
proposed change in the paternity laws.

### FATHERS IN LAW

For some time, feminist groups in France had been lobbying for modifications to the law recognizing paternity outside marriage.[21] However, it was not
until June 1910 that the Senate adopted a private bill to overhaul Article 340
of the Civil Code. This bill called for the legal declaration of extramarital

[18] ANS, 23G 31, Lt.-G. Noufflard to GG, 18 Oct. 1913.
[19] Mair, *Native Policies*, 191.
[20] ANS, 23G 35, 'Rapport sur l'état juridique des habitants des territoires d'administration directe du Sénégal', May 1913.
[21] See e.g. Laurence Klejman and Florence Rochefort, *L'Égalité en marche. Le Féminisme
sous la Troisième République* (Paris, 1989), 146.

paternity in a range of circumstances, including rape, abduction, various types of deception, and, perhaps most significantly in the colonial case, 'where the alleged father and the mother are known to have lived in a state of concubinage during the period of conception'.[22] Article Four of the bill was to make the new law applicable in Algeria and the colonies. Pressurized by the colonial press, the Minister for Colonies called upon all colonial governors to pronounce on the wisdom of allowing this article to stand.

Of the West African governors, only Lieutenant-Governor Poulet of Guinea spoke unequivocally in favour of the change, viewing the matter as a simple question of moral justice.[23] It is worth noting, in fact, that all the governors of West Africa seem to have been in favour of the bill in so far as it related to France itself. Lieutenant-Governor Clozel of Upper Senegal and Niger, for example, acknowledged that the Civil Code as it stood allowed for many injustices.[24] Unlike Poulet, however, Clozel and the other governors went on to warn that the laudable aims of metropolitan legislators could not be applied in West Africa without running a number of risks, or at least without encountering insurmountable legal obstacles.

This last line of reasoning formed the basis for the Governor of Mauritania's contention that the proposed new law could apply only in cases involving Europeans. The argument ran that if an African woman with a child by a European man were to issue a paternity suit, it would be dealt with by a European tribunal. The European would be covered by the French Civil Code, the African woman by Islamic or customary law. The defendant could then question the admissibility of the claim, as it was not possible for a plaintiff to be regulated by two different legal codes. Again, métis seemed to fall into some non-existent intermediate category.[25]

Both Clozel and Lieutenant-Governor Angoulvant of the Ivory Coast reached the same conclusion as their Mauritanian counterpart, but by a rather different route. Clozel claimed that the sexual habits of African women, over whom temporary European husbands could only maintain 'a superficial surveillance', would make paternity hard to prove. In a similarly disparaging tone he raised the spectre of blackmail by women who would see 'an easy way of obtaining numerous and abundant subsidies for their personal upkeep, and very subsidiarily for that of their offspring'. If

---

[22] ANS, M 45. Again, the African women involved may well not have chosen the word 'concubinage' to describe such relationships.

[23] Ibid., Lt.-G. de la Guinée française to GG, Conakry, 29 Sept. 1910.

[24] Ibid., Lt.-G. Clozel to GG, Bamako, 11 Nov. 1910.

[25] Ibid., Lt.-Col. Patey, Commandant militaire en Mauritanie, to GG, Saint-Louis, 20 Oct. 1910.

certain feminist arguments were becoming more palatable in France itself, they were not yet sufficiently compelling to overcome the basic mistrust felt by men like Clozel towards African women. As for métis children, Clozel feared that the new legislation would lead them to try to acquire 'a name and a fortune'.[26] The potential threat to the reputations of many of Clozel's colleagues is implicit in his remarks, which highlight once again the insistent relativism which saw the colonies and the *métropole* as separate moral domains. In this case, too, the possibility of a personal interest in the preservation of the status quo should not be ruled out.

Angoulvant also focused on female rather than male morality, concluding somewhat sanctimoniously that: 'Until civilization is further advanced and the morals of the natives more refined, we cannot do more for illegitimate children.' In the meantime, he felt that special homes for métis children represented the most that could be done in their favour.[27] The deflection of attention away from the behaviour of French men by long-serving colonials like Clozel and Angoulvant reflected their desire to preserve the prevailing moral climate, within which they had operated for upwards of a decade. Bearing in mind that the abandonment of illegitimate children was soon to be condemned by colonial minister Lebrun,[28] however, this climate was clearly beginning to shift, with metropolitan conceptions of morality encroaching ever more closely on the colonies.

Lieutenant-Governor Malan of Dahomey raised a different set of objections to the proposals. Legislation drawn up with French society specifically in mind could, he felt, ramify unpredictably and even dangerously in the colonies. Malan was particularly concerned that a recognition of paternity would mean the creation of another mixed-race French citizen. 'Should we make the *mulâtre* a citizen, a voter, give him our rights, make him subject to our laws, which might conform neither to his temperament nor his customs, and which might for example lead to his sentence for polygamy?'

Of all the West African governors, Malan seems to have been the most troubled by the implications of rejecting the full application of the law. The problem stemmed, as he saw it, from the contact of 'two races and two civilizations, which have evolved separately for countless centuries [and] suddenly . . . find themselves face to face today'. Metropolitan legislators had, in effect, inadvertently called into question the problem of 'assimilability' and the ideology of the 'mission to civilize', which was still a motivation

---

[26] Ibid., Lt.-G. Clozel to GG, Bamako, 11 Nov. 1910.
[27] Ibid., Lt.-G. Angoulvant to GG, Bingerville, 22 Dec. 1910.
[28] In his circular of May 1912. See above, Ch. 2.

for many French colonial administrators. The First World War is generally seen as a watershed after which this ideology was permanently altered,
but the more astute colonialists were well aware of its ambiguities before
then. Malan was entirely correct to see the problem of métis citizenship
as being in a sense 'fundamental to all colonial questions'.[29]

Nevertheless, as a result of the reservations expressed by Malan and
his colleagues, and despite continued pleas in the Senate to let the bill
stand in its original form, Article Four of the bill was amended to allow the
authorities in each of France's possessions to promulgate the law in such
a way that it only applied 'where the mother and the alleged father are of
French nationality or belong to the category of foreigners assimilated to
French nationals'.[30]

This amendment met with strong criticism in the feminist weekly *La
Française*. An article written by one L. Frappier, a creole from Guadeloupe,
argued forcefully that it was an escape clause which absolved French men
of responsibility for any mixed-race children they might have in the colonies.
Frappier viewed the tendency to pick and choose which legislation to
apply in the colonies as an affront to Republican principles. Moreover, she
described the potentially revolutionary effects of a measure which would
force French men to consider their actions more carefully. She envisaged
more French women going to the colonies and a decline in the 'shameful
traffic in flesh'. Most of all, however, the benefit would be to 'our race,
our country, our influence, to which the free multiplication of métis is
a danger from all points of view'. This was not just because the task of
caring for abandoned métis children was becoming increasingly costly; it
was a particular danger because it created a pool of potential rebels and
generated racial disharmony.[31]

Frappier called on the socialist spokesman for the law in the Chambre
des Députés, Maurice Viollette, whom she described as a proven supporter
of feminist causes, to resist the amendment. Her arguments were to no
avail, however, and the new version of Article Four remained when the
law was finally passed on 16 November 1912. Colonial administrators now
had to decide how liberal they ought to be in promulgating the law in the
territories under their control.

---

[29] ANS, M 45, Lt.-G. Malan to GG, Porto-Novo, 24 Nov. 1910. On the evolution of the
'mission to civilize', see Conklin, *A Mission to Civilize*, for example 142–3.

[30] ANS, M 45. The text did not define the meaning of 'foreigners assimilated to French
nationals'.

[31] L. Frappier, 'Contre l'article 4 de la Loi sur la Recherche de la Paternité', *La
Française*, 18 Feb. 1912.

In the meantime, Maurice Viollette admitted that it was with West and Equatorial Africa in mind that he had returned the bill to the Senate for the amendment. His lack of confidence in African witnesses was a key influence on this decision. Even in France, of course, there was a certain suspicion felt towards witnesses in these cases. Here, however, the racial angle should not be played down. In cases where proof was needed that a child had been conceived during a period of 'concubinage', Viollette felt that 'certain African peoples do not offer the intellectual guarantees that would allow one to place faith in a testimony which would risk seeming to them a formality of no importance'.[32]

The 'assimilability' of Africans was once again at issue here. Étienne Balibar has suggested that the counterpart to the French idea of a 'universal mission to educate the human race' was a need to 'differentiate and rank individuals or groups in terms of their greater or lesser aptitude for—or resistance to—assimilation'.[33] This helps to explain Viollette's racist appraisal of African aptitudes in a European legal environment. Even Viollette, however, went on to reflect that racial considerations should not obscure the primary concern of the legislation, which was the welfare of the child. Though the naturalization *en bloc* of métis would be 'an injustice' and 'a folly', he now wondered if the law should be introduced without restriction even in Africa.[34]

In practice, only the governments of Indochina, New Caledonia, and the New Hebrides adopted the law as it applied in France. The government of French West Africa finally promulgated the law in November 1916, but, unsurprisingly in view of earlier objections, opted to restrict its application to cases involving only French nationals or 'assimilated foreigners'.[35] In fact, Africans might have argued that technically speaking they held French nationality anyway, and were therefore eligible; the legislators presumably intended only to allow French citizens the possibility of profiting from the law. Words such as nationality, naturalization, and citizenship were constantly used with imprecision. However, this particular loophole does not appear to have been exploited.

In any case, even in Indochina, the more liberal interpretation of the law did not have the far-reaching effects envisaged by some. As one

[32] Maurice Viollette, 'La promulgation de la loi sur la recherche de la paternité aux colonies', *Les Annales Coloniales*, Jan. 1913.

[33] See Étienne Balibar and Immanuel Wallerstein, *Race, Nation, Class: Ambiguous Identities* (London, 1991), 24.

[34] Viollette, 'La Promulgation de la loi'.

[35] See P. Dareste, *Traité de Droit Colonial*, ii (Paris, 1931), 361–2. For the text passing the law in Indochina, see CAOM, AP 1194.

administrator in Tonkin was to note in the 1930s, the vast majority of métis there were unable to benefit due to the time and expense required to bring accusations of paternity to court—particularly as the hearings were held in the town of residence of the defendant, who in most cases had returned to France. The legislation was, in the view of this administrator, no more than an 'ineffectual palliative'.[36] This was not enough, as will be shown, to discourage West African métis from attempting to change the law. In the meantime, some métis explored other avenues in their desire to be treated on the same footing as ordinary French people.

### FIGHTING FOR FRANCE

In February 1918 a group styling itself 'The *mulâtres* of Upper Senegal and Niger' sent the following letter to the Governor of that colony.

Bamako, 16 February 1918

Monsieur le Gouverneur,

We have the honour of addressing you the following request:

From the outbreak of hostilities until the present day, we have continually manifested our desire to perform military service just like all citizens who love France and defend its *cause sacrée*.

'You have not been recognized by your fathers, you do not have birth certificates, it is impossible to draft you.' These are the only responses we have drawn.

It is evident that we have not been recognized by our fathers, but it is no less evident that it is their blood, French blood, which flows in our veins.

Also, at the time of our birth, the register of births, marriages, and deaths [the *état civil*] was not organized; only the Catholic missions registered baptisms, the records of which are not valid and cannot stand in place of [official] birth certificates.

Accordingly, Monsieur le Gouverneur, we are writing to request that you inscribe our births 'with unknown father' (since our fathers did not recognize us) on the *ad hoc* lists of the *état civil*, to allow us to perform our military service or to be drafted to the Foreign Legion.

We are choosing just the right moment to offer up our blood to France, whose children we are.

In the hope of a favourable response to our request, yours sincerely,

Faithful and devoted servants of France:

[36] CAOM, Commission Guernut 97, 'Le Problème Eurasien au Tonkin', Anon to GG/Indochine, 19 June 1938, 67. See also Mazet, *La Condition juridique des métis*, 68; A. Girault, *Principes de colonisation et de législation coloniale*, ii. 524.

Louis Pierre Jacques *dit* Marteilly
Édouard Bêchet
Pierre Kamara *dit* Delassus
Louis Valentin
Eugène Bardot
Jean Joseph Marie *dit* Nègre
Jean Antoine Marie *dit* Lambert
Paul Diarra *dit* Villemot
Étienne Kanté *dit* Mourkou[37]

As French subjects, these métis, most still in their teens, were eligible only to serve in the *tirailleurs sénégalais* rather than the regular French army. The latter course was open only to citizens; in the wake of the Diagne Laws of 1915 and 1916 these included those born in the Four Communes of Senegal (Dakar, Gorée, Rufisque, Saint-Louis) and their descendants. Partial conscription of French West African males to perform military service had been introduced in 1912, but the First World War ensured that there would be no turning back in the increased use of African troops by France. In 1919 universal peacetime conscription was introduced in French West Africa.[38] Subjects were based in France for their three years of military service, while citizens served the same period as their metropolitan counterparts and did not have to leave the colony.[39]

Peggy Sabatier has noted the reluctance of the comparatively Gallicized graduates of the elite École William Ponty to serve with the *tirailleurs sénégalais*:

Much to their dismay [those Ponty graduates who were not French citizens] were expected to wear the clearly non-European uniform of the *tirailleurs sénégalais*, sleep on mats instead of beds and eat the simplest African fare (such as boiled corn gruel or manioc with sauce) instead of the meat and bread they were used to at Ponty. However, perhaps the greatest indignity was that, like the *tirailleurs*, they were often expected to go barefoot.[40]

Similar cultural attitudes seem to have been at work in the letter reproduced above, along with other letters sent independently by some of the signatories. At a time when Clemenceau had just increased the

[37] ANS, H 25.
[38] See Myron Echenberg, *Colonial Conscripts: The Tirailleurs Sénégalais in French West Africa, 1857–1960* (Portsmouth, NH, 1991), 25–46. On the Citizenship Law secured by Blaise Diagne, see Buell, *The Native Problem*, i. 951–2; also Conklin, *A Mission to Civilize*, 154–6.
[39] Mair, *Native Policies*, 192.
[40] Peggy Sabatier, 'Did Africans Really Learn To Be French? The Francophone Élite of the École William Ponty', in G. Wesley Johnson (ed.), *Double Impact*, 181. See also ANS, FM: 17G 381, Savineau report 1: Bamako, 13–14.

recruitment of West Africans to fight in Europe to unprecedented levels,[41] Pierre Kamara *dit* Delassus—or Delassus *dit* Kamara, as he preferred to style it—proclaimed 'I consider myself better than a *tirailleur* and if I am not allowed to do otherwise, I will abstain from military service'.[42]

Other letters sent by members of this group of métis confirm the impression that they keenly cultivated a sense of 'Frenchness'.[43] Although he did not meet the conditions necessary to become a French citizen, Jean Joseph *dit* Nègre stated that his outlook and way of life were those of a 'bon français', and that his request was motivated by pride in his French birth. All expressed their willingness or even their desire to die for the French cause. 'Despite my young age', wrote Jean Lambert *dit* Traoré, 'I wish to shed my purely French blood for the mother country.'[44]

This was not the first request for métis to be treated as French with respect to military matters. Lieutenant-Colonel Bonifacy, who wrote several articles on the subject of Indochinese métis, found it unacceptable that so many children of French soldiers should be excluded from the French army. The Ligue pour la Défense des Droits de l'Homme complained to the Colonial Minister in 1915 that the Foreign Legion admitted foreigners and criminals but not people of mixed race.[45] Upon receiving the petition from his métis subjects, Lieutenant-Governor Brunet of Upper Senegal and Niger showed himself similarly sympathetic to their demands. While acknowledging that these demands could not be met under existing legislation, he raised the general problem of their social and legal condition, pointing out that

this condition does not correspond to the education which many of them have received, either from their father or in the orphanages created for their benefit in French West Africa. Their childhood has passed most often in a much more refined environment than that of the mass of our subjects, and the social habits that they have generally retained from this [upbringing] do not in any way prepare them

[41] Echenberg, *Colonial Conscripts*, 44.

[42] ANS, H 25. The legitimacy of the common use of the word 'dit' followed by the name of the presumed French father was questioned by French administrators from time to time; see e.g. ANS, FM: O 685, Lt.-G. du Haut-Sénégal-Niger to GG, 20 Nov. 1907.

[43] It is perhaps worth noting that at least three of the signatories to the group letter (namely Pierre Kamara *dit* Delassus, Paul Diarra *dit* Villemot, and Étienne Kanté *dit* Mourkou), along with another who made a similar request independently (Alexandre Diallo *dit* Gauthier), had spent time in the *orphelinats de métis* at Ségou or Kayes. See IF, 5940 vol. 2; 'Enquête sur les croisements ethniques', 390–1, 395–6.

[44] ANS, H 25.

[45] Lt.-Col. Bonifacy, 'Les Métis Franco-Tonkinois', *Revue Anthropologique* (1911), 265; CAOM, AP 1194, Ligue Française pour la Défense des Droits de l'Homme et du Citoyen to Ministre des Colonies, 1 Feb. 1915.

for the return to the primitive way of life of the native family. Keeping them there inevitably results in a tendency among these '*déclassés* in spite of themselves' to lose their affection for their original educators; far from having done what we wanted to do, namely to raise them to our level in order to create auxiliaries for our political ends, we risk alienating them for good.

Easy access to French citizenship was, in Brunet's view, the only sensible way of completing the cycle of colonial assistance given to métis children; otherwise, this assistance might itself become dangerous. Brunet saw the case for helping more métis to become citizens as even more compelling in the light of recent moves to favour decorated African soldiers in this way.[46] 'It would not be very logical', he concluded, 'to leave behind individuals who are closely related to us as much by their blood as by their education and whose moral tutelage we have assumed.'[47]

A telegram from acting Governor-General Gabriel Angoulvant confirmed that the request made by the *mulâtres* of Upper Senegal and Niger could not be met, and that the 'delicate question' of the legal status of métis should not be tackled piecemeal.[48] But the issue refused to go away. An article published in May 1918 by François de Coutouly, a colonial administrator of several years' experience who had métis children of his own by his marriage to a Fulani woman, argued that citizenship should be granted to métis *en bloc*. Raising once more the dangers of creating an intermediate caste, he added that 'there is no advantage in us raising métis above the level of the race said to be inferior, if we do not raise them at the same time to the level of the race said to be superior'.[49] The arguments against denying citizenship to people of French blood gained extra potency in the context of the declining birth rate in France and the crippling losses sustained in the war, along with the recent decision finally to confirm the citizen status of the *originaires* of the Four Communes of Senegal. The struggle between what Stoler has termed 'inclusionary impulses and exclusionary practices'[50] was set to continue.

---

[46] In a decree passed on 14 Jan. 1918.

[47] ANS, H 25, Lt.-G. Brunet to GG, 6 Mar. 1918.

[48] Ibid., GG to Brunet, 11 Apr. 1918.

[49] François de Coutouly, 'Note sur les métis en A.O.F.', *Bulletin de la Société des Anciens Élèves de l'École Coloniale* (May 1918), 10–11; see also id., 'La Question des métis en Afrique Occidentale Française', *Revue Indigène* (1912), 548. De Coutouly was one of the very few French administrators to marry a West African woman according to French law; see Amadou Hampâté Bâ, *Oui mon commandant!* (Arles, 1994), 194, 210. De Coutouly's father had manifested a similar interest in métis during his time as French consul in Batavia in South-East Asia at about the turn of the century; see ANS, FM: O 685.

[50] Stoler, 'Sexual Affronts', 514.

## RECOGNIZING *MÉTIS NON RECONNUS*

In the decade following the end of the First World War there was a
growing lobby in favour of legislation which would allow the category of
unrecognized métis (*métis non reconnus*) to have their Frenchness (*qualité
de français*) recognized solely by means of proving their French heredity.
The fourth congress of the Mutualité Coloniale et des Pays de Protectorat
passed a motion to this effect in Tunis in 1923. The Institut Colonial
Français made a similar request in 1926. That same year Governor-General
Varenne of Indochina drafted a decree to put these calls into practice.
Varenne's proposals were put before the Conseil Supérieur des Colonies,
a metropolitan advisory body, where they came under the scrutiny of Arthur
Girault, France's most prominent expert in the field of colonial law.[51]

It is not clear why these developments should have occurred at this particular moment. Most of the reasons given at the time were vague and will
already appear familiar. The motion passed in Tunis was typically general,
stating that: 'whether on the grounds of equity, and in the particular interest
of these children, or for political considerations and in a general interest,
it is important that these children, because of the French blood which flows
in their veins, should enjoy the status of French citizen.'[52]

By this time there was, it is true, the precedent of a court case in Cambodia
in 1921 which had pointed towards the possibility that a Eurasian might
be recognized as the child of an unnamed French father. However, other
French courts had ruled to the contrary in the past, and might have done
so again.[53] After all, it was only a few years earlier that the authorities
in Indochina had expressed a fear of increasing the number of 'native'
French citizens there as cases came to light of French men falsely recognizing Eurasian children as their own, whether for philanthropic or financial
motives. (The recognition procedure was subsequently tightened up in a
decree of March 1918.)[54]

In searching for alternative explanations, it could be argued that the usual
fears of *déclassement* (along with the related desire to make use of potential
*auxiliaires*) may have been sharpened in the 1920s as growing numbers of

---

[51] See Moreau, *Les Indigènes d'AOF*, 76; 'A l'Institut colonial: Le Statut des métis non
reconnus', *La Presse Coloniale*, 17 Nov. 1926; CAOM, AP 1194; 'Position Juridique des Métis',
*L'Eurafricain*, Dec. 1949.

[52] See Moreau, *Les Indigènes d'AOF*, 76.

[53] See the article 'Position Juridique des Métis', *L'Eurafricain*, Dec. 1949, 12–14.

[54] See Raoul Abor, *Des reconnaissances frauduleuses d'enfants naturels en Indochine* (Hanoi,
1917); CAOM, AP 1194; Stoler, 'Sexual Affronts', 523, 531.

métis reached maturity. The potential threat posed by proto-nationalist movements in the colonies cannot be ruled out as a connected cause, although, as Stoler points out, métis were never really prominent in such movements in Indochina.[55] It does seem, however, that about this time the French were becoming increasingly sensitive about the image their colonial activities conveyed to the world at large. This is evident in the affronted response to the publication in 1928 of *The Native Problem in Africa*, a compendious and, to modern eyes, relatively innocuous survey of colonial matters by a Harvard Professor, Raymond Buell. Though the colonial press accused him somewhat illogically of jealousy as well as Francophobia, the colonial authorities felt that if the British had been portrayed in a more favourable light it was because they had taken the simple precaution of ensuring that Buell was accompanied on his tour of their possessions.[56]

In the *métropole*, too, literature critical of aspects of French colonialism (though not, strictly speaking, anti-colonial) was beginning to find a much wider audience. In 1921 René Maran won the prestigious Prix Goncourt with his novel *Batouala*, which painted the colonial regime in less than favourable colours. Evidence of a growing struggle for the hearts and minds of the French public is suggested by the editor's note in a book published the following year, *Vrais noirs et vrais blancs d'Afrique au vingtième siècle* by Joseph Blache, which claimed it to be 'a refutation of *Batouala*'. (In fact, it is difficult to imagine this particular book doing much more than to furnish colonial critics with further ammunition.)[57] Later in the decade André Gide famously denounced abuses in French Equatorial Africa in two works of non-fiction, *Voyage au Congo* and *Le Retour du Tchad*. In 1928, moreover, one only had to purchase *Le Petit Parisien* to find criticisms much more damning than those made by Buell, as it serialized the well-known journalist Albert Londres's account of his travels in French Africa.

One such article was a pathos-charged exposé of what Londres described as the métis 'tragedy'. This piece mentioned the legislation then under consideration to accord citizenship to *métis non reconnus*, and found strongly in its favour. Londres claimed that individual métis were not interested in pursuing paternity suits against their errant fathers. Nevertheless, Londres continued, they knew that the 'vrai blanc'—the 'real' white man—was worthy of respect. As such they coveted their father's nationality, rather than his name.[58]

[55] Stoler, 'Sexual Affronts', 517.
[56] CAOM, AP 28; *La Dépêche Coloniale*, 15–16 Apr. 1928.
[57] Blache, *Vrais noirs et vrais blancs*, 435.     [58] Londres, *Terre d'ébène*, 71–2.

Londres's use of the phrase 'vrai blanc', echoing the title of Joseph Blache's book mentioned earlier, is of particular interest here. The 'vrai blanc' Londres had in mind was evidently a different creature to the 'vrai homme' ('real man') who may have fathered the young métis encountered by Londres in the French Soudan. But this 'vrai blanc', a model citizen and standard-bearer of French Republican values, did not exist in reality. He was an abstract paragon of French virtues rather than a particular individual. Despite speaking in favour of citizenship legislation for métis, Londres does not appear to have considered whether they could ever qualify as 'vrais blancs'. For all his belief in the inclusive potential of French nationality, Londres's answer would have had to be in the negative because, as he wrote in the same article: 'They are neither black nor white, neither French nor African. . . . The misfortune is that they should all the same be *something*.'[59] Once again, inclusive impulses were not sufficient to resolve the dilemmas posed by the existence of métis, whose identity was so indeterminate.

Whether the special pleading of the kind made by Londres contributed to the creation of a legislative climate more 'generous' to métis remains unclear, although Arthur Girault did suggest later that 'the public conscience' had played its part.[60] It is less difficult to explain the relative timing of this legislation from colony to colony. For in the eyes of many French observers, there were degrees of civilization in much the same way there were degrees of 'whiteness'. In 1928, for example, the president of the influential pressure group the Union Coloniale Française wrote to the colonial minister that reform in Indochina was especially desirable, given that 'the peoples of Indochina belong to an ancient and very evolved civilization, and . . . the mentality of Franco-Indochinese children should not be considered inferior'.[61] In addition, the métis population of Indochina was simply greater in number than in France's African possessions.[62]

With such considerations in mind, the decree allowing *métis non reconnus* in Indochina to seek recognition of their status as French citizens (or, if they were still minors, to have it sought on their behalf) was passed on 4 November 1928.[63] The principal proofs that the applicant 'presumed to be of French race' had a French parent were to be 'the name carried by

[59] Londres, *Terre d'ébène*, 70.        [60] Girault, *Principes de colonisation*, ii. 526.

[61] CAOM, AP 1194, letter from 22 May 1928.

[62] See the statistical detail in CAOM, Commission Guernut 97.

[63] For the full text of this and similar decrees passed in other French colonies, see Charles Poirier, *Manuel-formulaire théorique et pratique sur l'état civil et la nationalité*, ii (Tananarive, 1936).

the child, the fact that he has received a French formation, education, and culture' and 'his position in society'. In practice, the courts tended also to require that Eurasians undergo a medical examination to establish their mixed heredity.[64] These terms gave the courts in Indochina a certain amount of leeway in such cases, whereas some observers felt that the only duty of the court in fulfilling the decree should be to establish that the applicant was 'non-indigenous'.[65]

The ability to exclude 'undesirables' from the French citizenry was still more at issue when the authorities in West Africa came to consider similar legislation. Governor-General Jules Carde took a racially deterministic line in claiming of métis that the fact that they had a white parent 'establishes in their favour a presumption of a mentality closer to our own, [and] a greater capacity for assimilation'. However, their African ancestry and the milieu in which they generally lived led Carde to doubt that they could be entirely separated from indigenous society. Hence he asserted that, in principle, unrecognized métis began as French subjects.[66]

This view was shared by the governors of several of the individual West African colonies. Lieutenant-Governor Fourn of Dahomey—who had more than one métis child of his own[67]—was particularly concerned that there should be a selection procedure which would enable the authorities to choose only those métis whose 'effort, perseverance, and intelligence' had earned them the honour of French citizenship. Moreover, he felt that only those who had reached manhood—he does not appear to have considered mixed-race women—should be able to acquire citizenship.[68] This was the same type of wait-and-see policy which, as shown in Chapter 3, influenced the treatment of métis children in the orphanages of Dahomey—institutions for which Fourn held responsibility.

The legislator Arthur Girault was critical of this line of reasoning, contending that it was much better for children to be certain of their legal status as they grew up.[69] Nevertheless, he was sufficiently swayed by the arguments made by Carde and the other governors for a significant addition to appear in the West African version of the legislation for *métis non reconnus*, which was passed on 5 September 1930. The final judgement on citizenship was to be made by the court of appeal in Dakar. Before reaching

---

[64] See CAOM, Commission Guernut 97.
[65] Mazet, *La Condition juridique des métis*, 98.
[66] ANS, FM: M 17, GG to Ministre des Colonies, Dakar, 18 Jan. 1928.
[67] ANS, FM: 23G 40. I am grateful to Ruth Dickens for this piece of information.
[68] ANS, FM: M 17.
[69] CAOM, Conseil Supérieur des Colonies (CSC) 25, Séance du 25 janvier 1928.

this stage, however, the claimant was obliged to obtain from the authorities a certificate confirming what was called 'possession d'état'. To receive this, the claimant had to provide proof of an upbringing that was observably 'French' in style. It was not a question of proving the biological fact of French paternity or maternity, nor was any attempt made to establish the actual identity of the unknown parent. The certificate was only granted after the colonial bureaucracy had conducted an inquiry into the personal history of the applicant. Administrators in the successive places of residence of each métis claimant were asked not only to check up on the details contained in their application forms, but also to pronounce on 'the way in which the applicant has been raised by those who took him in; on the way he is or has been treated by society; on his formation, his education, his culture, his mentality, his tendencies'.[70]

These requirements set the decree of September 1930 somewhat at odds with itself. In framing the decree, Girault had been at pains to insist that its main aim was to facilitate the *recognition* of citizen status. As such, it was supposed to establish the principle that *métis non reconnus* were French citizens by birth. However, as several critics pointed out, the Governor-General had effectively been given a right of veto, making the decree *attributive* of citizen status.[71]

Indeed, Girault himself practically cast the Governor-General of French West Africa in the role of Saint Peter holding the keys to the gates of heaven when he commented that: 'No one may enter the French City without his assent.'[72] *Le Petit Parisien*, having applauded its own role in the legislation by commissioning Londres's reports, likewise now praised the fact that 'the undesirables' could safely be shut out.[73] The decree therefore depended not so much on the presence of 'French blood' as on the satisfaction of a more abstract notion of 'Frenchness'. At least one contemporary observer was left in no doubt that this was a direct result of the fear of according French citizenship to 'individuals whose evolution does not appear sufficient to allow their assimilation to the colonizing race'.[74] Doubt had once again been cast on the 'assimilability' of Africans.

---

[70] From the *arrêté* of 14 Nov. 1930 laying down the procedure to obtain the certificate for *possession d'état*; text in *L'Eurafricain*, 8 (1950), 21–4. See also CAOM, AP 1637.
[71] Moreau, *Les Indigènes d'AOF*, 81–2; Mazet, *La Condition juridique des métis*, 105; ANS, FM: 23G 22.
[72] CAOM, CSC 25, report from 9 June 1928.     [73] *Le Petit Parisien*, 6 Oct. 1930.
[74] Mazet, *La Condition juridique des métis*, 107. For more on ideas of African 'assimilability', see Conklin, *A Mission to Civilize*, 167–8.

## APPLYING THE DECREE OF 5 SEPTEMBER 1930

Unsurprisingly, the contradictory nature of the decree of September 1930 caused a certain amount of confusion among those responsible for its application. This was evident in the case of Albert Taraoré *dit* Delanne, a 24-year-old official in the topographical department in the French Soudan. The Governor of Niger, the colony of his birth, rejected his demand for *possession d'état* in 1934 for three main reasons. First, it was claimed that Taraoré *dit* Delanne had been raised 'more as a native than as a European' for the first seven years of his life. Secondly, he had scored low marks in school. Finally, the Governor wrote that he did not yet appear worthy of the 'favour' of citizen status; as such, the authorities should wait until they could take account of his conscience and 'professional worth'. The *commandant de cercle* in Bamako, where Taraoré *dit* Delanne had been a pupil at the *école primaire supérieure*, took a similar line, claiming that he was not yet sufficiently 'evolved' or 'close to us' to merit French citizenship.

This interpretation was rejected by the head of the judiciary in French West Africa, *procureur général* Lanes. Lanes pointed out that Taraoré *dit* Delanne had been raised at the orphanage for métis in Kayes between 1917 and 1927, which indicated that his European ancestry had been generally recognized by colonial society. His school marks were irrelevant, and in any case the head of the mission in Kayes had praised his character. Furthermore, his career was progressing in a manner which suggested he was a respectable member of society. As such he deserved to receive the necessary certificate; it seemed probable that the court of appeal in Dakar would confirm his French citizenship.[75]

The case of Albert Taraoré *dit* Delanne is one of several which highlight the inconsistent application of the decree of September 1930. Even a person like Taraoré *dit* Delanne, whose behaviour could hardly have merited particular concern, was liable to have his initial application rejected. Such rejections often stemmed from seemingly trivial personal matters. For example, the Lieutenant-Governor of Dahomey at first tried to refuse a claim made by Étienne Loisel on the basis that he had once sent 'insolent letters' to one of his teachers.[76] Local administrators often seem to have been somewhat surprised to discover that such legislation even existed; in cases such as that of Loisel, the claimant was likely to succeed only if someone was able to explain the terms of the decree to the uninitiated

[75] ANS, FM: 23G 23, note from Lanes to Directeur des Affaires Politiques, 27 Mar. 1934.
[76] ANS, FM: 23G 23, Lt.-G. du Dahomey to GG, 17 Oct. 1931.

administrator. In this instance, however, Loisel was eventually declared to be a French citizen in January 1933.

Two further case studies from the French Soudan serve to emphasize the vagaries of this decree. In 1932 the *commandant de cercle* in Bamako opposed the granting of the certificate for *possession d'état* to André N'Diaye, who had been raised in the orphanage at Ségou,[77] on the basis that he had received a one-year suspended jail sentence for fraud. Governor-General Brévié pointed out that this was insufficient reason to refuse the certificate, but promised to bring the matter to the attention of the *procureur général*. Despite this, the court of appeal in Dakar recognized N'Diaye as a French citizen later that year.[78]

Two years later, however, a similar case had a different outcome. Robert Nomoko had spent nine years in the orphanage at Kayes, but failed upon leaving to realize his ambition of becoming an electrician. He was sacked from successive jobs with the public works department and the railway for 'laziness and professional incompetence'. At the time of his application to be recognized as a French citizen he had just been sentenced to a year's imprisonment for theft. Though it could not be denied that he had received a French education, Lieutenant-Governor Fousset of the French Soudan felt that 'his natural indolence and his unscrupulous character have prevented him from taking advantage [of his upbringing] from the point of view of his moral and social improvement'. Governor-General Brévié ought to have argued that, just as in the case of N'Diaye, this should not prevent him from obtaining his certificate for *possession d'état*. On this occasion, however, Brévié thought it best to file Nomoko's claim. Such rejections did not have to be justified to the applicant, and no new claim was possible without the production of new evidence.[79] Administrators were not just demanding proof of mixed heredity, therefore; they were also, in many cases, demanding irreproachable morals and seamless social skills.

Some métis were recognized as French citizens without any trouble at all. One of the first to be accepted was Paul Marcel Philippe *dit* Leblond, a medical worker in the French Soudan with a successful educational background. He received glowing character references and was welcomed as an 'excellent recruit for greater France'.[80] George Jeanson, a teacher at the Foyer des Métis de Bingerville, was another whose credentials impressed the authorities. One official wrote that: 'His degree of assmilation to French

[77] IF, 5940 vol. 2.     [78] ANS, FM: 23G 23.
[79] Ibid.; also CAOM, Direction du Contrôle 941 dossier 17.
[80] ANS, FM: 23G 23.

civilization is remarkable.'[81] Others, however, were thought to be insufficiently Gallicized. Jean Robert Vital *dit* Hamouille was deemed to be too
close to indigenous society. Despite receiving his certificate for *possession
d'état*, he does not appear from surviving lists to have been recognized by
the Dakar court of appeal.[82] Joseph Cartier met with a similar rebuttal. In
the words of one official, '[he] is being progressively influenced by the
African milieu he inhabits'. As such, his loyalty was also found questionable, and his application was thought unlikely to succeed.[83]

Mixed-race women were also subject to particular scrutiny. It ought first
to be pointed out that they seem to have been far less likely to make use
of the decree of September 1930. Indeed, women accounted for just four
of the eighty successful applications made before the end of 1934.[84] This
fact perhaps gives some weight to Robert Delavignette's contention that
mixed-race women were more likely than the men to remain within the
social milieu of their mothers.[85] The following example suggests that the
reality was more complicated. In 1938 two métisses from Niger, Lucienne
Koram and Denise Rhama, applied for the certificate for *possession d'état*.
Both had been raised in a state-run orphanage for métis. Yet Governor
Court of Niger chose not to accept their claims, on the basis that they had
each married black African men. Court was concerned that their husbands,
both of whom were native civil servants, would themselves press for a change
in status if Koram and Rhama were to be granted French citizenship. Acting
Governor-General Geismar rejected this interpretation as it was not in doubt
that they were of mixed race, but he added that the fact that they had both
married French subjects would eventually be taken into consideration.[86]

Men do not appear to have had the same problem. A precedent was set
by a métis in Guinea who, having been declared a French citizen, was able
to regularize according to French law the marriage he had previously contracted to a black African woman. Both she and their children thereby also
became French citizens. His choice of spouse had evidently not been at
issue in the way it had in the cases of Koram and Rhama. The implication
to be drawn from this is that the cultural background of the husband was
assumed to determine the way in which the married couple lived.[87]

---

[81] ANS, FM: 23G 97.     [82] ANS, FM: 23G 23.
[83] ANS, FM: 23G 97.     [84] ANS, FM: 23G 23.
[85] Delavignette, *Freedom and Authority in French West Africa*, 29–30.
[86] ANS, FM: 23G 23.
[87] See ibid., *cas* Guichard, and the similarly instructive case of Henri Goudard from the
Ivory Coast. On the question of citizenship for the families of black African applicants in
the 1930s, see Conklin, *A Mission to Civilize*, 168.

In many of the examples cited above there was a clear feeling among administrators that citizenship was being sought less through a sense of attachment to France than for selfish reasons. In fact, the true motives of métis applicants are often difficult to discern. It seems likely, however, that for every métis who applied there were others who were discouraged by the clumsy and somewhat demeaning bureaucratic process which it entailed, and the difficulty in providing proof of mixed ascendance. Others simply preferred to retain their local legal status for whatever reason.[88] It would be wrong to assume that this was the piece of legislation for which all métis had been waiting.

Between September 1930 and 1 January 1944 372 *métis non reconnus* were recognized as French citizens in West Africa. The procureur général, Robert Attuly, observed in 1944 that the vast majority of these were morally respectable and socially well placed: in short, part of a 'native "bourgeoisie"'. He acknowledged the importance of social considerations in the application of the decree, and went on to speak of 'the *mise en valeur* of métis'. In this he envisaged métis and black African 'évolués' playing a more active role in colonial society than had hitherto been the case, forming what he called a kind of petty officer class.[89]

In fact, many métis already fulfilled this description. For their part, they were often more concerned to be treated in a fashion commensurate with their status as French citizens. In 1937 Governor-General de Coppet had revealed plans to allow métis to rise to the same high levels in public administration as Europeans.[90] What métis civil servants particularly demanded, however, was to receive the 'colonial supplement' paid to those classified as civil servants of European origin. This supplement and various other allowances put civil servants from France in a completely different financial bracket from their indigenous colleagues. In 1945, for example, a midwife from the *métropole* working in Dahomey would receive a monthly colonial supplement of 1,462 francs, on top of a basic salary of 1,625 francs and a dependents allowance of 2,374 francs. A midwife from Dahomey itself would earn 1,578 francs per month.[91] A European lifestyle was very

---

[88]  See e.g. CAOM, Commission Guernut 101, reports from Cotonou and Porto-Novo.

[89]  ANS, FM: 17G 187, Attuly to GG, 11 Jan. 1944; ANS, FM: 23G 22, 'Note pour le Directeur-Général des Affaires Politiques', 11 Apr. 1944.

[90]  CAOM, Commission Guernut 101, GG to Gvr. du Soudan, 18 Sept. 1937. At about the same time, de Coppet (at the suggestion of the socialist Colonial Minister, Marius Moutet) planned to simplify the decree of 5 September 1930, placing full responsibility in the hands of the courts. These plans never came to fruition, despite resurfacing in the 1940s. See ANS, FM: M 17; FM: 23G 22.

[91]  See Coquery-Vidrovitch (ed.), *L'Afrique occidentale au temps des français*, 392, 453; also Sabatier, 'Did Africans Really Learn To Be French?', 182, 186.

difficult to sustain on this level of pay, as métis households were only too keenly aware.[92] Despite repeated requests for change, however, the unequal salary structure remained in place until 1950, when the second *loi Lamine Guèye* brought family allowances and additional perks, such as paid leave in France, to higher-ranking African civil servants.[93] What is clear, however, is that before this time a formal recognition of French citizenship did not, even at an official level, hold the key to being treated as French.

### MÉTIS UNDER THE FOURTH REPUBLIC

With the creation of the Fourth Republic came a new conception of citizenship for Africans. In May 1946 the first *loi Lamine Guèye* bestowed citizenship on every inhabitant of France's colonies, thereby eradicating the concept of 'French subject', and with it the arbitrary *indigénat* system of justice. (Forced labour, another scourge of the *sujet*, had been abolished the previous month.) A difference remained between citizens of common status, who had gained French citizenship prior to 1946, and citizens of local status. For those in the latter category, which included most of the indigenous inhabitants of French West Africa, customary law continued to apply in civil matters, such as marriage and inheritance. The first *loi Lamine Guèye* was later enshrined in the constitution of October 1946.[94]

The constitution left some doubt as to whether the citizenship extended to former French subjects related to France or to the newly founded French Union. For this reason Pierre Rosanvallon has described it as a 'purely formal' notion of citizenship, which did not correspond to any particular nationality.[95] Certainly, many métis seem to have regarded this as the case as they continued to apply to be recognized as French citizens under the terms of the decree of 5 September 1930, despite its apparent obsolescence

---

[92] See e.g. ANS, FM: 17G 381, Savineau report 1 (Nov. 1937): Bamako, 14. Savineau detailed the expenses of a 'typical' métis couple—he a teacher, she a midwife—whose pay also had to feed and accommodate four children, both their mothers, and an uncle.

[93] ANS, FM: 23G 22; Ruth Schachter Morgenthau, *Political Parties in French-Speaking West Africa* (Oxford, 1964), 58. Lamine Guèye, a socialist deputy from Senegal and a doctor of law, sponsored the bill in the Assemblée Nationale.

[94] See Morgenthau, *Political Parties*, 43, 49–50; Lord Hailey, *An African Survey* (London, 1956), 213–4, 339, 341, 616–7; John D. Hargreaves, *Decolonization in Africa* (Harlow, 1988), 82.

[95] Pierre Rosanvallon, *Le Sacré du citoyen. Histoire du suffrage universel en France* (Paris, 1992), 434–5.

under the new constitution.[96] In 1957 Gaston Cusin, Haut-Commissaire
de la République en AOF (the new title for the Governor-General), noted
that there were two possible cases which favoured the retention of the decree
of September 1930. First, it might serve some purpose in according the
status of common law citizen to a métis not yet at the age of majority, placing him or her under the regime of French civil law, even though there were
easier ways of attaining this status. Secondly, Cusin acknowledged the continued worth of the decree to métis who, 'for sentimental reasons', might
want to obtain recognition of their European heritage.[97] Judging by the number of métis who continued to go through the whole cumbersome process
in the late 1940s and 1950s, there was some truth in this latter suggestion.

This might seem to support Albert Londres's contention, restated by a
métis civil servant at the time of the Brazzaville Conference, that people
of mixed race coveted their fathers' nationality, rather than their name
or their inheritance.[98] This, however, ignores the fact that métis groups,
particularly towards the end of the 1940s, pressed strongly for the full
application of Article 340 of the Civil Code regulating paternity suits. Louis
Patterson, president of the Association Philanthropique des Métis Français
en AOF, hoped that this would put an end to the easy abandonment of
métis children by French men.[99] On this occasion the authorities in West
Africa were receptive to the idea. Governor Louveau of the French Soudan
felt that the colonial state should not be obliged as a matter of course to
assume the burden of caring for 'artificial orphans'. This recognition of individual responsibility was echoed by the Conseil Général du Dahomey, which
in September 1947 unanimously endorsed a call for a more liberal interpretation of Article 340 in West Africa. High Commissioner Barthes added
his support, with the observation that this 'moral obligation' might also
save the colonial authorities money.[100]

---

[96] See CAOM, AP 2125 dossier 2, GG/AEF to Ministre des Colonies, 17 Oct. 1947.
See also CAOM, AP 1194, for details of a bill of December 1946 which proposed to make
*métis non reconnus* French citizens from birth, apparently oblivious to the fact that they already
held this status via Article 80 of the constitution.

[97] ANS, FM: 23G 97, HC/AOF to all West African governors, Dakar, 12 Feb. 1957.
On the effect of independence on the legal status of métis, see Jean-Pierre Dumas, 'Effets
de la décolonisation sur la nationalité française des métis', *Revue Juridique et Politique,
Indépendance et Coopération*, Jan.–Mar. 1970, 44–7.

[98] Londres, *Terre d'ébène*, 72; ANS, FM: 17G 187, 'Le Point de vue des métis', by M
Bresson, a clerk in the service of the Governor of Soudan. Bresson was also president of the
Mutualité des Métis du Soudan Français, which will reappear in Ch. 6 below.

[99] CAOM, AP 1194, Patterson to Ministre de la France d'Outre-Mer, Dakar, 6 Nov. 1946.
See also *L'Eurafricain*, Dec. 1949, 11, 16.

[100] All quotations from ANS, FM: 2H 22.

Thus it was that in December 1949 a local decree was passed which gave West Africans the right to pursue paternity suits via French law. (In fact, in an oddly representative demonstration of the haphazard nature of the administration in French West Africa, it was realized the following year that such a decree had already been passed in 1938. Métis, the people most likely to gain from the decree, had been unaware of its existence. The decree of December 1949 was therefore itself abrogated in September 1950.[101]) The Union des Eurafricains de l'AOF welcomed this development, although for many of its number the value of the decree was likely to remain more symbolic than practical. Nevertheless, in the words of the society's president, Nicolas Rigonaux, it was 'the first stopping-off point on the long road we have to travel to attain our complete emancipation'.[102]

Such a statement indicates that by 1950 the position of métis continued to leave much to be desired. In this chapter we have seen how wary the colonial authorities were of acknowledging the heredity of people of mixed race. In the words of Stoler: 'Métis children undermined the inherent principles upon which national identity thrived—those *liens invisibles* that all men shared and that so clearly and comfortably marked off *pur-sang* French from those of the generic colonized.'[103] Africans who became French citizens could by no means expect to be welcomed as such by the expatriate French community. Their perceived pretensions were liable to ridicule in print, and their legal status was often irrelevant when, in French eyes, their colour tended to be taken as an indicator of their legal position.[104] The same was essentially true of métis. Governors came and went with alarming rapidity, some, notably those appointed by the Popular Front in the 1930s, more liberal than others. But the desire to pass liberal legislation for métis was consistently tempered by an underlying suspicion as to their true nature. This apprehension could work along racial lines, or be founded on mistrust of their links with African society. The example of the decree of 5 September 1930 clearly illustrates these concerns. It also

[101] Ibid.; *Journal Officiel de l'Afrique Occidentale Française*, 17 Dec. 1938, 1477.

[102] *L'Eurafricain*, 7 (1950), 1. Rigonaux also called for Article 340 of the Civil Code itself to be amended, as it continued to allow the government of each colony the possibility of applying the law restrictively. His desires were met via a law of 10 July 1951. See *L'Eurafricain*, 11 (1951).

[103] Stoler, 'Sexual Affronts', 532.

[104] See e.g. Morgenthau, *Political Parties*, 175–6, which describes what happened when two prominent Africans with French citizenship entered an Abidjan restaurant frequented exclusively by Europeans at the end of the war; also Martinkus-Zemp, *Le Blanc et le Noir*, 163–6; Cruise O'Brien, *White Society in Black Africa*.

shows how careful the authorities were to keep control over the ways in which métis could accede to French citizenship.

In the end, the problem of métis citizenship reveals the extent to which French colonialism in West Africa, for all its assimilatory pretensions, was founded on the racial differences believed to separate Europeans and Africans. The intensity of feeling working for or against métis may have varied through time, and some were clearly more acceptable to French society than others. Nevertheless, Maurice Delafosse's observation that 'White society, which . . . often only grudgingly accepts métis of European legal status, holds métis of local status fully at arm's length', seems to have contained a fundamental truth about colonial society.[105]

---

[105] Delafosse, 'Note relative à la condition des métis', 90.

# 6

# *Métis and the Search for Social Identity*

One image of métis, propagated by a variety of French individuals and organizations, was of a passive social group, the mute beneficiary of French largesse. This image, however, increasingly failed to reflect reality as growing numbers of métis reached maturity across French West Africa. Both individually and collectively, métis adopted a number of different strategies for making sense of the society in which they lived. Some of these strategies, of course, were more successful than others; the quest for some viable form of social identity was undoubtedly fraught with difficulties, and it was easy for individuals to feel socially marginalized. Gradually, however, sections of the métis population began to address the ambiguities and complexities which were part of their inheritance. From the 1930s in particular, when they began to organize themselves in mutual self-help groups known as *mutualités de métis*, West African métis set about defining the boundaries of their own community, and the relationship of this community with the French and other Africans. These issues will be explored in depth later in this chapter. While this chapter will be concerned primarily with the perspective of métis themselves, however, it will begin by addressing the question, somewhat neglected until now, of how they were perceived by black Africans.

## BLACK AFRICANS AND MÉTIS

It goes without saying that it is problematic, to say the least, to talk of a 'black African perspective' on anything at all, let alone the comparatively limited question under consideration here. To generalize about the attitudes of such a vast and diverse group of people risks rapidly becoming a futile exercise. It should be added that, until the 1930s at the earliest, it is difficult for the historian to find any written evidence on this subject from black Africans themselves: such opinions as do survive are often filtered through the accounts of French writers, whose own interests do not always make them trustworthy witnesses. This was demonstrated perhaps most clearly in Chapter 2, when it was suggested that the French notion of 'abandonment' as it related to métis children did not always correspond to that of their African mothers. Evidence on this subject cannot, therefore, always be taken at face value. With these reservations in mind, however, it is worth sketching in some of the more familiar lines of thought which emerge from the written sources available.

Métis children, of course, were living proof of sexual contact between French men and African women. Black African attitudes towards métis may well have been bound up with the degree of acceptance accorded to such unions. This was susceptible to change through time, and different ethnic groups addressed the matter in different ways. A lack of research conducted at the local level, however, means that useful conclusions are at present difficult to draw. One is left with a scattering of more or less impressionistic observations made by French administrators. At one extreme, Governor-General Ernest Roume suggested in 1904 that local antipathy towards métis was so great that they were at risk of being put to death.[1] Others portrayed them as objects of mistrust in indigenous society; 'even in their native family', stated an administrator in southeast Guinea in 1910, 'they are whipping-boys'.[2] At the other end of the spectrum, Maurice Delafosse contended that, despite the occasional and usually unsubstantiated rumour of the type perpetuated by Roume, métis raised by their mothers in indigenous society were generally welcomed 'with open arms' by Africans.[3]

Only infrequently does a black African voice come through before the late 1930s to help assess the validity of these claims. One basic point which does seem to emerge, however, is that métis were associated with the colonial power, or rather with colonialism itself. This may have been one of the most important factors in determining their treatment by black Africans, making them more vulnerable within indigenous society at certain times than at others. In 1910, for example, a respondent to the survey on *métissage* conducted by the Société d'Anthropologie de Paris mentioned that the local name of a métis child in Korhogo in the Ivory Coast was 'Nah Fighe', meaning 'White Man' in the Senoufo language.[4] It does not necessarily follow that this child was the target of prejudice, but the name did establish the colour of the child's skin as a symbolic marker of

---

[1] CAOM, SG, Sénégal X dossier 26, GG to Ministre des Colonies, 14 June 1904. Also see Blache, *Vrais noirs et vrais blancs*, 161.

[2] ANS, 1G 338.       [3] Delafosse, 'Note relative à la condition des métis', 90.

[4] 'Enquête sur les croisements ethniques', 360.

difference. In a comparable vein, a group of métis from the French Soudan complained in the 1930s that elders in the region told them that nature had not intended their existence: 'Dieu a fait le café, il a fait le lait, mais il n'a pas fait le café au lait' (God made coffee, he made milk, but he did not make *café au lait*). This saying was also current in Senegal, and had been so for some time.[5]

The recently collected oral testimony of a peasant woman from Lobi country in what was Upper Volta suggests that, in certain areas, métis children were far from welcome. The woman in question, named Waal-Hirèna, was in 1945 forced into a temporary union with a member of the local French administration, against whose presence the Lobi people had long struggled. When Waal-Hirèna fell pregnant she was sent back home, where her mother took the decision to allow the pregnancy to run its course—a rare step in Lobi country, where to give birth to a métis child was thought to lead to damnation.

The birth, attests Waal-Hirèna, transformed her life into an endless nightmare. She became an object of curiosity, visited by people in the area who wanted to see the woman who had dared to give birth to a 'white' child. Her mother refused to allow her to make use of the small allowance paid her every quarter by the colonial administration, arguing that this was 'bad money' which would lose her the child. Her husband and his family rejected her, refusing to feed a child of white people, who had killed so many of their clan. Fearing for the safety of her child, Waal-Hirèna decided to divorce, setting off a chain of events which led to the suicide of her husband and her flight from her place of birth.[6]

The *hauka* movement, which flourished briefly in parts of Niger in the late 1920s, provides a further illustration of a tendency socially to marginalize métis. This spirit cult first appeared in the northern Arewa region in 1925. The movement, which rejected the authority of French-backed local rulers, was structured around the imitation of aspects of colonial authority and society. Around Dogondoutchi and Filingué, villages were set up which paralleled yet stood beyond the system put in place by the

[5] 'Contre la fusion des races!', *Le Monde Colonial Illustré*, Aug. 1937, 205; ANS, FM: O 715; Hardy, *Une Conquête morale*, 74. The earliest reference I have found to this saying is in Alfred Fouillée, 'Le Caractère des races humaines et l'avenir de la race blanche', *Revue des Deux Mondes* (July 1894), 96, where it is cited as an Arab proverb, with the variation 'the devil created the métis'.

[6] Kambou-Ferrand, 'Souffre, gémis, mais marche!', 153–6. The name 'Waal-Hirèna'—of which the title of Kambou-Ferrand's article is a translation—was given in an initiation ritual, and refers to the suffering she had experienced in her life. Waal-Hirèna gave her own child the initiate's name 'Konnapounèna', meaning 'the birth that despoils'.

French. Representatives of authority who entered such places ran a serious risk of being captured and beaten.

The cult functioned through the spiritual 'possession' of certain recognizable figures in colonial society. During the performance of *hauka* rites, therefore, one member of the cult would adopt the person of the governor of the colony. Horace Croccichia, commandant of the administrative district of Niamey in which the movement emerged, was accorded semi-divine status as Komandan Krosisya, the bad administrator. Every rank in the colonial army was represented, right down to the infantry, whose role was played by young men carrying imitation rifles made of wood. Whistles and riding-crops were used to illustrate the militarized nature of the regime in Niger, but civil society was also represented in imitations of the colonial doctor, the clerk, the chauffeur, and so on.[7]

Of particular interest here, however, is the fact that the métis (given the name André) was another of the typically colonial characters incarnated in *hauka* rites. Métis were identified as constituting a distinct category, separate from yet inextricably linked to the French presence in Niger. Given the hostility which the cult manifested towards French rule in the area at this time, the position of métis may well have been compromised within local society to a dangerous degree by their association with the colonial power. The authorities gradually brought the areas under *hauka* influence back under French control, but the example serves to highlight the social differentiation of métis by other Africans.

Despite their French connections, there are grounds for arguing, as did Maurice Delafosse, that the manner in which the individual métis lived did most to determine the way in which he or she was treated by black Africans.[8] The implication is that the majority of Africans did not judge métis according to the same prejudiced criteria which Europeans so frequently employed. Delafosse went so far as to claim that '[the coloured races] do not have these colour prejudices which cause us to consider métis as inferior beings'.[9]

The problem here lies in the fact that to assess any given response by black Africans to métis, one first has to know the behaviour to which they

---

[7] On the *hauka*, see Coquery-Vidrovitch (ed.), *L'Afrique occidentale au temps des français*, 243–4; Finn Fuglestad, 'Les Hauka: une interprétation historique', *Cahiers d'Études Africaines*, 15 (1975), 203–16; id., *A History of Niger, 1850–1960* (Cambridge, 1983), in particular 128–31; Samuel Decalo, *Historical Dictionary of Niger* (2nd edn., London, 1989), 114–15; Paul Stoller, *Embodying Colonial Memories: Spirit Possession, Power, and the Hauka in West Africa* (New York, 1995).

[8] Delafosse, 'Note relative à la condition des métis', 84.

[9] See the article 'A l'Institut Colonial', *La Presse Coloniale*, 17 Nov. 1926.

were responding. If one métis treated a black African with contempt on racial grounds, how can one say with any certainty that the latter would not have reacted at least with suspicion to the next métis he or she encountered? How far did the widespread belief that métis received preferential treatment from the French alter perceptions? How far did the informal policy of segregation represented by the *orphelinats de métis* affect indigenous social relations?

The evidence does support the idea that the *orphelinats de métis* were pointed to as examples of racial favouritism by certain sections of African society, particularly with the growing assertiveness of those black Africans referred to as 'évolués'. A good example of this tendency comes from the Congo, in French Equatorial Africa. Black African delegates at the Conseil Représentatif du Moyen Congo in 1948 expressed hostility towards special institutions for métis when they debated a motion to suppress funds for the métis orphanage in Boko. One delegate complained that the French had been trying to form métis into 'a superior race', adding that 'we do not want to let this race into our territory.' The chair of the council felt that such institutions favoured métis 'to the benefit of racism', and that the children should be returned to their 'milieu of origin'. Another delegate expressed displeasure that 'We privilege a foreign race whereas black orphans do not receive assistance'. The motion was narrowly passed.[10]

One of the delegates, a Monsieur Tchitchelle, added that: 'The métis is a European or he is an African. If he is a European, he only has to live with Europeans, or if, despite his skin colour, he considers himself an African, he only has to continue to live with us.'[11] Métis were therefore presented with a choice, albeit a less straightforward choice than that presented by Tchitchelle: were they, despite their skin colour, Africans; or were they, despite their skin colour, Europeans?

Tchitchelle's remarks were representative of the time, for in certain quarters métis were increasingly challenged to assert their 'Africanness' as political activity and pan-African ideas spread in West Africa, particularly from the 1940s.[12] Léopold Sédar Senghor, one of the originators of the concept of *négritude*, himself invited métis to see themselves first and foremost as Africans in an article in *Réveil*, the newspaper of the inter-territorial political organization, the Rassemblement Démocratique

---

[10] CAOM, AP 1194, Conseil Représentatif du Moyen-Congo, meetings of 10 Sept. and 17 Nov. 1948.

[11] Ibid.

[12] For background to these developments, see J. Ayodele Langley, *Pan-Africanism and Nationalism in West Africa 1900–1945* (Oxford, 1973).

Africain. Senghor denied that there was a 'métis problem' in West Africa, on the grounds that the problems facing métis were no different to those which faced any other minority in Africa. In any case, he argued, all Africans were of mixed race to some degree. He saw no future in the 'racial' particularism of the recently founded métis group, the Association Philanthropique des Métis Français en AOF, concluding that: 'What métis are hungering and thirsting for is justice, not philanthropy.' As such, he argued that the association would best serve the cause of métis by shutting itself down. 'What are we waiting for to be a united people?' challenged Senghor.[13]

Senghor's call for pan-African unity was a contribution to a debate which had been taking place in the pages of *Réveil* for several months. This debate was initiated by a métis veterinary surgeon named Maurice Camara. Camara pleaded that métis should not be judged according to the behaviour of those who denied their African roots. 'If some métis disown the black man', he wrote, 'that is not a reason to repudiate the métis on principle.'[14] Taking up the argument, another writer blamed the colonial power for alienating métis from African society:

It is the European who taught the métis that his personal dignity as a *mulâtre* forbade him from assimilating to black society, or marrying a black woman if she was more cultivated than him. In this way . . . the white man, not content merely to have turned his back on his paternal duties, seeks by his insinuations to detach the métis from the sole milieu in which it is possible for him to find a suspicion of happiness, from those who, far from turning their backs on him, have unconditionally adopted him as their own.[15]

This argument did not, however, place métis themselves beyond criticism, and those who continued to deny their African heritage were liable to be identified more or less as representatives of the colonial power. As one Senegalese phrased it as French rule in West Africa neared its end: 'Métis who believe themselves to be natives of Bordeaux or Marseilles can now start packing their bags along with their compatriots, because no one is asking them to remain in black Africa for ever.'[16]

Abdoulaye Sadji's novel *Nini, mulâtresse du Sénégal* provides a more subtle and suggestive example of black African reaction to those métis who

---

[13] Senghor, 'Il n'y a pas de problème du métis', *Réveil*, 8 May 1947. Senghor was not in fact a member of the RDA. On Senghor's theory of 'le métissage culturel', see Vaillant, *Black, French, and African*, 176, 241.

[14] 'Un essai d'étude sur le problème des métis', *Réveil*, 28 Nov. 1946.

[15] 'Quelques observations sur "l'essai d'étude sur le problème des métis"', *Réveil*, 13 Jan. 1947.

[16] Danfakha Makhan, 'Combattre le mariage mixte pour conserver la grande race noire', *Paris-Dakar*, 19 July 1957; see also *L'Eurafricain*, 24 (1957), 38.

chose to play down their African ancestry. Though the novel undoubtedly merits detailed analysis, the problems involved in using it as a historical source should not be ignored. Some background details are therefore necessary before considering the ideas contained in the book.

Abdoulaye Sadji was born in Rufisque in Senegal in 1910. Qualifying as a teacher in 1929, he wrote *Nini, mulâtresse du Sénégal* in 1935, while teaching in Saint-Louis. The novel did not appear until 1947, however, in instalments across the first four issues of the literary journal *Présence Africaine*, a forum for African cultural and political concerns.[17]

The eponymous central character of *Nini* is a 22-year-old métisse from Saint-Louis, around whose life and loves the plot revolves. Briefly, Nini—whose full name is Virginie Maerle—thinks of herself as white. She prefers not to acknowledge her blackness and disparages 'les indigènes', one of whom has the effrontery to propose marriage to her. This proposal is rejected with the utmost cruelty by Nini, who is involved with a Frenchman named Martineau. At one stage Martineau promises to marry her, but this promise goes unfulfilled: he returns to France, and we learn later that he was married all along. Nini resigns from her post as a typist in the colonial administration when she discovers that she owes the position to the intervention of a relation from the African side of her family. All her friendships and family relationships disintegrate, and the novel ends with Nini boarding an aeroplane bound for France.

As a psychological portrait, the possible implications of the novel were soon recognized; indeed, Frantz Fanon's pioneering ethnopsychological study *Black Skin, White Masks*, first published in 1952, quotes extensively from *Nini* in the chapter entitled 'The Woman of Colour and the White Man'.[18] But Fanon's analysis of the novel now seems flawed. The problem lies less in the fact that Fanon misrepresents the text at certain points than in his apparently unquestioning acceptance of Sadji's novel as a form of documentary evidence. In fact, the complexion of the novel is altered by the knowledge that Sadji himself had been in love with a métisse named Nini Dodds, who came from a long-established mixed-race family in Saint-Louis. Sadji's affections, however, were rejected, apparently on the basis

[17] For biographical details, see Amadou Booker Washington Sadji, *Abdoulaye Sadji. Biographie, 1910–1961* (Paris, 1997). Hans-Jürgen Lüsebrink produces convincing evidence to suggest that *Nini* was written in 1935 in his *Schrift, Buch und Lektüre in der französischsprachigen literatur Afrikas* (Tübingen, 1990), 59–60, though Sadji's biographer (his eldest son) maintains that it was composed while he was teaching in Louga in Senegal in the 1940s (A. B. W. Sadji, *Abdoulaye Sadji*, 70, 85). See also Dorothy S. Blair, *African Literature in French* (Cambridge, 1976), 189–90.

[18] Frantz Fanon, *Black Skin, White Masks* (London, 1993), 53–62.

that he was black; Dodds preferred instead the attentions of an unscrupulous white man.[19]

Even if one makes due allowance for the concept of the authorial voice, the similarities between the text and the author's own life are too strong to be overlooked. As a result, the systematic demolition of the fictional Nini's character is rendered even more discomfiting than it would have been anyway, and Fanon's argument that the character symbolizes a behavioural type prevalent among mixed-race women loses some of its potency. Sadji, for his part, attempted to deflect such criticisms in his preface to the novel:

*Nini* is not, as some believe, a bill of indictment which can be explained by an amorous disappointment in the author's life. *Nini* is the eternal moral portrait of the *mulâtresse*, be she from Senegal, the Caribbean, or the two Americas. It is the portrait of the physical and moral hybrid who, in the thoughtless spontaneity of her reactions, seek always to raise herself above her given condition in life, that is to say above a humanity which she consider to be inferior but to which an inescapable destiny links her.

One could plead on behalf of this group of people or blame them. I believe it to be more charitable neither to plead nor blame, but to offer them, as in a mirror, the reality of what they are. This is not to act as a moralist or an executioner, but as a philanthropist.[20]

Sadji's own terms deserve analysis. The first point to be emphasized is that the novel is avowedly concerned with mixed-race women, rather than men. Indeed, one of the most striking features of the text is that it contains no mixed-race male characters. Nini lives with her aunt and grandmother, themselves both of mixed race. The métis community of Saint-Louis as portrayed in the novel seems to be almost entirely populated by young women with names like Nana, Riri, and Dédée. Though Sadji writes that mixed-race men have their own internal hierarchy, based primarily on skin colour and family line, 'the will to segregation is most noticeable among *mulâtresses*'.[21] The subject is thus established as the *mulâtresse*, while mixed-race men are effectively exempted from what follows.

This gender-based division makes it difficult at times to say whether Sadji's criticisms are reserved for mixed-race women or directed at women

[19] Reyss, 'Saint-Louis du Sénégal', 63, 264. Sadji's biographer sheds no light on this point, but does reveal that his first wife, whom he married in 1931, was a métisse from Ziguinchor; indeed, of the six women he married in the course of his life, three were métisses. The last of these was Simone Carrère, from an old Saint-Louisian family; she was the only of Sadji's wives to marry him according to the *état civil*. This makes Sadji's 'eternal portrait' of the *mulâtresse* all the more peculiar. See A. B. W. Sadji, *Sadji*, 44–9.
[20] Preface to Abdoulaye Sadji, *Nini, mulâtresse du Sénégal* (3rd edn., Paris, 1988), 7–8.
[21] Ibid. 42.

in general. This suspicion arises, for example, when he speaks of: 'Their need for gesticulation, their love of ridiculous display, their calculated, histrionic, sickening attitudes . . .'[22] The tone is spiteful, arguably misogynistic, and his claim to be holding up a mirror to the behaviour of mixed-race women seems disingenuous. But this disgust is mixed with attraction. 'The charms of a *mulâtresse* are powerful', we learn. These charms derive from their dual heredity. Their African heredity gives them a lithe, languorous sensuality. Onto this their Western heredity grafts 'a received or imitated French education'. Their vocabulary is 'richer . . . than the most resonant African dialects', they carry themselves well, their clothes flatter their 'restless figures', and they use cosmetics to make themselves all the more alluring.[23]

In practice, Sadji portrays mixed-race women as voluptuous and lascivious—a stereotype which was common among French writers.[24] Indeed, the character of Nini echoes in certain respects that of Cora, the spahi's mixed-race lover from Saint-Louis in Pierre Loti's *Le Roman d'un spahi*. At one point the spahi remarks that he is slightly disgusted by Cora's 'shamelessness'.[25] Similarly, in Sadji's novel Nini and her peers use their 'charms' to seduce white men. White men are excused of blame for being tempted by 'trim and fresh-looking' *mulâtresses* who 'ask only to give themselves away'.[26] We are told that 'There is no dancer more lascivious and clinging than a *mulâtresse*'.[27] As for Nini herself, from the moment she left the convent at the age of 15 she has collected lovers 'as one collects stamps'.[28] This image is sustained as we see Nini looking through her private photograph album, which contains pictures of a succession of lovers, some of whom remained for 'a few weeks of tropical ennui', some for one night only. The album also contains erotic pictures of herself, in one of which she is smiling with 'the diabolical air of the fallen woman'.[29]

Sadji paints a portrait of Nini in which implications of decadence coexist with a strong element of sexual fantasy. But Nini's sexual habits are representative of something more: they constitute an example of 'the instability of her fickle character',[30] which, in the language of Sadji as in that of so many of the French writers discussed elsewhere, was regarded as the natural condition of the 'hybrid'. For the character of Nini, therefore, Sadji relies heavily on a series of pre-existing stereotypes of race and gender.

---

[22] Ibid. 95.    [23] Ibid. 154.
[24] See e.g. Dr Jacobus, *L'Art d'aimer aux colonies*, 243, and 150: '*Mulâtresses*, whose nervous system is more developed . . . are more lascivious than their black mothers.'
[25] Loti, *Le Roman d'un spahi*, 41.    [26] Abdoulaye Sadji, *Nini*, 49.
[27] Ibid. 58.    [28] Ibid. 34, 70.    [29] Ibid. 92.    [30] Ibid. 215.

The most challenging aspect of Sadji's work lies instead in the questions it raises about ethnic identity among métis. First, it should be pointed out that Sadji undermines his own claim to be describing all *mulâtresses* and their alleged tendency to raise themselves above what they consider to be inferior African society. At two points in the text he notes that some métisses live 'à l'indigène'. These 'nonconformists' have received an education in Wolof, style their hair in the same fashion as other Senegalese women, and notwithstanding their skin colour live in the heart of indigenous society.[31] Neither Sadji's preface nor Fanon's analysis makes due allowance for this option.

Nini and her contemporaries are seen as a 'new generation', with different social attitudes to those of Nini's aunt, Hortense, and her grandmother, Hélène. Nini appears not to hold strong religious beliefs, but both Hortense and Hélène attend mass regularly. Hélène in particular, however, also remains in contact with African society and its traditional culture. Indeed, she seeks out the services of a marabout in an attempt to divine whether Martineau will marry Nini. On her deathbed towards the end of the novel Hélène rejects a French doctor's medicine, requesting instead that the marabout come and rescue her from the demons which she believes to be afflicting her. 'No more white men here!' she exclaims. 'They have lied to us, violated us, abandoned us. They have filled our black parents and our guardian spirits with jealousy and spite.'[32] The marabout's prescription for Hélène's ailment involves the ritual sacrifice of a bull to appease the spirits of her maternal ancestors. Hortense, though defending 'black science' to Nini, feels unable to follow through such a public form of treatment.[33] Even so, Hortense harbours no delusions about her genealogy; it is she who turns to an influential black African relation to secure Nini a post in the colonial administration.

Nini, on the other hand, denies or attempts to conceal every vestige of 'blackness' and rejects traditional sources of African identity. She whitens her skin with powder and refuses to speak Wolof. Unlike Hortense, she makes a virtue out of not being able to cook, leaving the work to African servants; in this, the text suggests, she is imitating European women in Senegal. Convinced of her whiteness, she proclaims that black people will never be able to assimilate completely; at one point, in the company of two French men, she even defends slavery. She opposes marriages between blacks and whites, seeing no contradiction between this belief and her ultimate aspiration, which is to marry a French man. She has a

---

[31] Abdoulaye Sadji, *Nini*, 20, 43–4.     [32] Ibid. 182.     [33] Ibid. 185–8.

nightmare in which Africans carrying knives surround her in a dark forest. She dislikes any form of contact with blacks and is habitually discourteous to them.[34] In attempting to be recognized as white, Nini exhibits what Fanon describes as 'overcompensating behaviour'.[35] Other sources suggest that such behaviour was not uncommon among French West African métis. This will be dealt with at length later in this chapter.

In differentiating between the behaviour of Hélène, Hortense, and Nini, Sadji locates Nini as a child of a particular time. The economic influence of the métis community of Saint-Louis has been progressively on the wane since the mid-nineteenth century, and black Africans have increasingly come to dominate local politics.[36] Nini deeply resents the power of the class of educated black Africans to which Sadji himself belonged. Her hostility to the black Africans she encounters in positions of responsibility in the office where she works barely conceals her unease at the changes taking place in Saint-Louisian society.

Sadji states that the *mulâtresses* of Saint-Louis are 'victims, without being aware of it, of humiliating treatment at the hands of the Europeans to whom they cling'.[37] But when Nini is unwittingly teased by Martineau for her intellectual pretensions, Sadji is inviting the reader to participate in a private joke at her expense:

—Have you read Dante and Machiavelli?
—Oh yes, Dante, the revolutionary of the Girondin party. What eloquence!
—Machiavelli?
—He's great too, he has a style all of his own.[38]

In many ways this exchange encapsulates the tone of the novel as a whole. There is a pervasive atmosphere of *Schadenfreude* as Nini's life is dismantled before our eyes. Ultimately, Sadji's self-proclaimed 'philanthropy' proves to be less than disinterested, but his novel does provide a valuable insight into the way members of the French-educated African elite in Senegal regarded the métis community.[39]

This section has suggested that black Africans, while associating métis in some way with the colonial power, tended also to see them as constitutive

---

[34] Ibid. 14, 16, 40–1, 46, 135–6, 142–3. Nini's dream could have been lifted straight from the pages of O. Mannoni, *Prospero and Caliban: The Psychology of Colonization* (New York, 1964: first published 1950), in particular 89–92.
[35] Fanon, *Black Skin, White Masks*, 58.
[36] This process is best described in Johnson, *The Emergence of Black Politics in Senegal*.
[37] Abdoulaye Sadji, *Nini*, 46.     [38] Ibid. 36.
[39] For a much gentler portrait of a métisse in a West African novel, see ch. 10 of the Guinean novelist Camara Laye's *L'Enfant noir* (Paris, 1953).

of a separate (if somewhat fragmented) social group. Nini is shown reflecting bitterly at one point on 'the lie of her existence' between black and white, a 'hybrid', 'belonging to no normal society'.[40] Similar comments were made by the black African teachers who helped to compile the response from Cotonou in Dahomey to the enquiries of the Commission Guernut in 1938. Métis, they claimed, attempted to resemble whites while disdaining the African side of their family; their goal, in the words of the report, was 'an inaccessible ideal'. The report alleged that as a result they not only became jealous of whites, but also aroused suspicion from black Africans; their only remaining options were to live among themselves or to leave the country of their birth.[41] The following section will assess the validity of these claims.

### THE INTERNAL EXILE?

One of the problems involved in studying the lives of French West African métis lies in the fact that while much was written about them as a group, individually their lives tend to remain hidden from view in the sources available. Few métis held positions of prominence, and in any case the experiences of the likes of Gabriel d'Arboussier, a founder and one-time general secretary of the Rassemblement Démocratique Africain, did not mirror those of the majority.[42] Nevertheless, certain names do reappear sufficiently often in a variety of sources to allow the reconstruction of the life histories, however sketchy and incomplete, of a handful of métis.

An entry point is afforded by a list providing details of the eighty métis who, between 1931 and 1934, benefited from the legislation passed in September 1930 enabling *métis non reconnus* to seek recognition of their French citizen status, as discussed in the previous chapter.[43] This list reveals that the majority of métis recognized as French citizens between 1931

---

[40]  Abdoulaye Sadji, *Nini*, 177–8.        [41]  CAOM, Commission Guernut 101.

[42]  Perhaps the most significant difference was that d'Arboussier's parents, a colonial administrator and a Fulani woman from a notable family, were legally married under French law. Educated in France, he joined the colonial administration before embracing Marxism and rising to prominence in the RDA. For biographical details, see Raph Uwechue (ed.), *Makers of Modern Africa* (2nd edn., London, 1991), 63; Edward Mortimer, *France and the Africans, 1944–1960: A Political History* (London, 1969), 73–4; Cohen, 'The French Governors', 44.

[43]  ANS, FM: 23G 23. Twenty-three of the successful applicants had been born in the French Soudan, seventeen in the Ivory Coast, fifteen in Dahomey, fifteen in Guinea, six in Senegal, two in Niger, two in Upper Volta, and none in Mauritania.

and 1934 were aged between 20 and 30. It has been calculated that the percentage of métis aged 15 or over in the Ivory Coast rose from 41.8 per cent to 53.7 per cent between 1926 and 1936.[44] The proportion was higher in the French Soudan, perhaps because French expansion had taken place somewhat earlier there.[45] Growing numbers of métis were therefore reaching maturity in the early 1930s. It is no coincidence that the earliest of the *mutualités de métis*, which will be discussed later in this chapter, were founded at this time. This was also the first generation of métis to have been raised in the secular, French-run *orphelinats de métis*. The high proportion of successful applications from the French Soudan—about a third—testifies to the continuity of the assistance given by that colony to métis children. (The relatively low figure from Senegal, on the other hand, can be explained more by the fact that métis born in the Four Communes already held French citizenship, and therefore had no need for the decree of September 1930.)

The list offers some interesting insights into the degree of mobility of métis. Thirteen of the eighty métis recognized as French citizens between 1931 and 1934 lived in a colony other than that in which they were born. That this was a common phenomenon is supported by another list, drawn up by administrators in the French Soudan in 1937. This gave the names of 144 adult métis: 107 who had been born in the French Soudan and continued to live there; eleven who lived in the colony but had been born in another part of French West Africa; and twenty-six who had been born in the Soudan but now lived elsewhere. Of this latter category, seventeen were living in a different colony in the federation, five were in France, and one in Indochina.[46]

More striking yet is the degree of mobility within each colony. On the 1931 to 1934 list, only ten of the eighty métis named were living in their town or village of birth at the time of their application to be recognized as French citizens. To take Guinean métis as an example, of the fifteen successful applicants all but one, Michel Georges *dit* Demaison from Conakry, had moved from their place of birth. Conakry, the administrative capital and most cosmopolitan town in the colony, was unsurprisingly the most common destination; five métis from other parts of Guinea and two from other colonies applied to be recognized as French citizens while

---

[44] Tirefort, 'Européens et assimilés en Basse Côte d'Ivoire', 644.

[45] For statistics, see CAOM, Commission Guernut 101.

[46] ANS, FM: O 685. This list further revealed that these 144 métis had produced 131 children among them. Employment statistics for these people (unfortunately not matched to names) can be found in ANS, FM: 2H 17, Lt.-G. Rougier to GG, 9 Apr. 1937.

living there. Three Guinean métis left the colony, for Bamako, Ziguinchor (in southern Senegal), and Dakar.[47]

One should be wary of reading too much into these statistics. It should first be remembered that to be recognized as a French citizen, each métis had to provide evidence of an upbringing that was observably 'French' in style; in practice, as suggested in the previous chapter, most tended to occupy 'respectable' positions in society. To some extent, therefore, the list analysed above represents a self-selecting sample. It is not surprising to find that these métis seem to have gravitated towards towns, because the 'civilized' person likely to be recognized as a French citizen was almost by definition urbanized.

Several other factors may have helped to determine the movements of these métis. It may have been that the mother's degree of mobility played as much of a role as that of the métis themselves. On the other hand, it seems likely that a large proportion of these métis had spent time in an orphanage; the location of this institution (most of which were based in urban areas) may have played a part in where they came to live. Most importantly, however, it is often difficult to say how far an apparent tendency to itinerancy was connected to the type of work performed by these people. Teachers and medical workers, for example, had little control over where they were to be posted. On the list mentioned earlier of adult métis in the French Soudan in 1937, ten of the twenty-six who had moved to a different colony were midwives. Did the métis born in Allada in Dahomey who was recognized as a French citizen in 1933 go to Dakar for personal reasons, or because he had a government posting there?[48]

The sources rarely allow a full response to such questions. Moreover, the sources which do exist tend to concern métis who had received some assistance from the French administration. Many, of course, 'slipped through the net' and lived in varying degrees of poverty, as Denise Savineau found when venturing into the African quarter of Cotonou in Dahomey when compiling her report on women and the family in French West Africa in 1937–8.[49] It is difficult to draw conclusions about such individuals. The following brief case studies do, however, suggest certain similarities in the lives led by a particular kind of métis.

[47] ANS, FM: 23G 23.        [48] ANS, FM: 2H 17; FM: 23G 23.

[49] ANS, FM: 17G 381, Savineau report 6: Dahomey, 26–30. Tales of métis living in penury can also be found scattered through the pages of *L'Eurafricain*, the journal of the Union des Eurafricains de l'AOF, throughout the 1950s.

CASE STUDY ONE: PIERRE, ÉMILE, AND
GERMAINE KAMARA *DIT* DELASSUS

Pierre Kamara *dit* Delassus was born in 1897 or 1898 in Kita, about a hundred miles west of Bamako. His mother was a Bambara from Ségou named Makoura Kamara, while his father, Monsieur Delassus, was a colonial doctor. His parents' relationship lasted at least five years. Pierre's brother, Émile, was born in 1900, and a sister, Germaine, followed two years later. All three were said to be healthy children in 1910 when they featured in the survey on *métissage* conducted by the Société d'Anthropologie de Paris. Émile had the lightest skin of the three, with 'the finest features', though all were said to resemble their father to a significant degree.[50] Their father did not formally recognize them as his own children.

By 1910 Makoura Kamara had married an African man in Toukoto, near Kita. All three children were now boarders at the orphanage in Ségou and day-pupils at the local *école régionale*. Germaine started school in January 1910. Pierre was said to be above average in French, arithmetic, and geography. Émile, on the other hand, displayed little enthusiasm or aptitude for his studies. The children described themselves as Catholics; Pierre had received some religious education from the Pères Blancs in Kita.[51]

In November 1911 Pierre was transferred to the *école des fils de chefs* in Kayes. In April 1912 he wrote to Madame Pion-Roux, the former head of the orphanage in Ségou. He explained that he was one of a group of children known as the 'Élèves Moniteurs', who hoped to train as teachers at the *école normale* in Saint-Louis.[52] Pierre had already been able to acquire some teaching experience with a class of younger children. He was unhappy in Kayes and confided to Mme Pion-Roux that he wished he could talk with his brother, 'le bon diable' Émile. This wish was granted a few months later when the orphanage in Ségou closed and its boarders, Émile among them, were moved to Kayes.[53]

By 1918 Pierre Kamara *dit* Delassus was teaching at the École Professionnelle de Bamako. In February of that year he was one of the signatories to a letter (reproduced in full in the previous chapter) in which a group

[50] 'Enquête sur les croisements ethniques', 390–1.     [51] Ibid.

[52] This section became known as the École William Ponty when it was relocated to Gorée in 1913.

[53] IF, 5940 vol. 2. This file also contains a letter from Émile Kamara to Mme Pion-Roux dated 1 July 1912. Germaine would in theory have been sent to the new mixed orphanage in Kayes, although there are no records to support this.

of *métis non reconnus* expressed their desire to perform military service on the same basis as French citizens.[54] In March he made an independent request to the same effect. 'Despite my lack of education,' he wrote, 'I consider myself better than a *tirailleur*.' With his 'French tendencies', he continued, 'I wish, as a son of France, to be at the service of the mother country'. He signed a declaration stating his desire to be governed by French civil law and renouncing his local legal status, a necessary preliminary to becoming a French citizen. His lobbying of the authorities, while sympathetically received, was unsuccessful. Nevertheless, his belief in his 'Frenchness' comes through clearly. His renunciation of his local legal status appears superficially to symbolize a desire to distance himself from those he taught.[55]

Both Pierre and Émile Kamara *dit* Delassus were still resident in the French Soudan in the 1930s. Émile was living in Koulikoro, near Bamako, when he was recognized as a French citizen in September 1932. A list from 1937 further reveals that he married a métisse, one of nineteen recorded 'ménages métis' in the French Soudan at that time.[56]

### CASE STUDY TWO: ALEXANDRE DIALLO *DIT* GAUTHIER

Alexandre Diallo *dit* Gauthier was born in Ouagadougou in 1898. His father was an official in the postal service in French West Africa, but he died in the village of Kouri, then part of the French Soudan, when Alexandre was still a child.[57] Alexandre's mother was a Fulani named Pinda Diallo; she had herself been born in Ouagadougou, and was still living there at the time of the survey by the Société d'Anthropologie de Paris. The survey described her as very intelligent, and noted that she spoke French well. Alexandre was said to resemble his mother, who in common with many Fulani was fair-skinned. (In 1902 Dr Barot placed the Fulani at the top of a list of West African women preferred by European men; he also singled them out as being 'relatively faithful'.[58])

By 1910 Alexandre, like the subjects of the previous case study, was living in the orphanage in Ségou, over 300 miles from his place of birth.

[54] ANS, H 25. [55] Ibid.
[56] ANS, FM: 23G 23; FM: O 685, 'Renseignements concernant les métis'.
[57] Both Kouri and Ouagadougou were in the territory which was to become Upper Volta. These family details can be found in 'Enquête sur les croisements ethniques', 395–6. M Gauthier's date of death is not provided.
[58] Barot, *Guide pratique*, 329–30.

Like Pierre and Émile Kamara *dit* Delassus, he does not appear to have travelled to stay with his mother during the summer holidays. Madame Pion-Roux described him as 'the most intelligent of our métis, but the laziest'. Alexandre recounted in a letter to one of Mme Pion-Roux's daughters how Monsieur Pion-Roux had punished him and made him cry for not paying attention in class. In another letter, he spoke of how M Pion-Roux (described by Mme Pion-Roux as 'his papa') had temporarily prevented him from taking his summer holiday as a punishment for tearing four pages out of his exercise book.[59]

Despite these difficulties, he was accepted by the École Pinet-Laprade on the island of Gorée, near Dakar, which trained manual workers to an advanced level. In 1917, however, he was expelled for disciplinary reasons.[60] In 1918 he was working as a trainee clerk in the Department of Public Works in Koulouba, a suburb of Bamako and the administrative capital of the French Soudan (Upper Senegal and Niger as it was then). At this time he, too, wrote to the Governor of Upper Senegal and Niger expressing his desire to be a naturalized French citizen, requesting in the meantime that he be allowed to sign up for service in a French military corps.[61]

His job in the colonial administration does not appear to have lasted long, and at some point between 1918 and 1922 he went to France, working as an attendant on the sailing-ship *Joinville*. In 1922, by which time he was living in Paris, his application for French citizenship was rejected.[62] He was still living in France in 1937, but this last reference does not reveal what sort of life he led there.[63]

CASE STUDY THREE: ALBERT LARBAT

Albert Larbat was born in 1900 in Pama, near Fada N'Gourma in what was to become Upper Volta. As in the two previous case studies, he spent time in Ségou in what he later described as the 'anonymity' of the orphan-ages of the French Soudan, although there is little information on his life during this period.[64] Between 1916 and 1919 he was trained as a teacher at the École William Ponty on the island of Gorée. His wife was a métisse who had herself been raised in the orphanages of the French Soudan. In

[59] IF, 5940 vol. 2.
[60] ANS, FM: 23G 46. On the École Pinet-Laprade, see Bouche, *L'Enseignement*, 525–45.
[61] ANS, H 25.        [62] ANS, FM: 23G 46.        [63] ANS, FM: O 685.
[64] Larbat is referred to in one of the letters written by the children in the Ségou orphan-age (IF, 5940 vol. 2), though there are no surviving letters by Larbat himself from this period.

1918 she was in the first class to take the course in midwifery at the new medical school in Dakar.

Larbat and his wife then embarked on a series of jobs in a variety of locations, recalled by Larbat in a somewhat rambling letter written in 1949.[65] In 1927, he stated, 'I was described as a "bastard" by an administrator who nonetheless had five métis children, of whom two attended my school. In my exasperation I saw red . . . but I preferred to hand in my resignation.' He found an accounting job in Ouagadougou instead. In 1929 his wife— now a mother of four—was posted to another town. Married civil servants lived in fear of this occurrence. Larbat claimed that her posting was the result of 'connivance' between the Inspector of Education and the Head Doctor. 'Never having known the joys of family life in our childhood,' he wrote, 'we could not accept a separation which broke up our young household.' A group of Soudanese métis made a similar complaint in 1937; Governor-General de Coppet replied, however, that such separations were rare, and that the administration endeavoured always to post married civil servants to the same area.[66]

In October 1934 Larbat was recognized as a French citizen. When he made his application he was living in Mopti in the French Soudan, but by 1937—at which time he and his wife had seven children—he had moved again, this time to the Ivory Coast.[67] Under the Vichy administration in French West Africa, his was one of the few 'métis families' to receive a family allowance on the same terms as Europeans. This came to an end (wrote Larbat) 'with de Gaulle', when 'a European bachelor' stopped his benefit on the basis that only French people whose mother and father were both of European origin were eligible. This was clearly a matter of some importance to Larbat, who by 1949 had ten children.

In 1945 Larbat was, in his own words, chosen by his compatriots to be president of the Union Voltaïque, which campaigned for the re-establishment of the colony of Upper Volta. When this event took place in 1947, Larbat claimed that those who had elected him then abandoned him. 'A métis cannot represent the Mossi people', he commented wryly.[68]

---

[65] See ANS, FM: 2H 22.

[66] ANS, FM: O 685, 'Un groupe de métis' to Ministre des Colonies, Bamako, 15 Apr. 1937; CAOM, Commission Guernut 101, GG to Gvr. du Soudan français (circulated to 'les métis de Bamako'), 18 Sept. 1937. See also ANS, FM: 17G 381, Savineau report 1: Bamako, 14.

[67] ANS, FM: 23G 23; FM: O 685.

[68] Larbat may have been exaggerating the importance of his role in the Union Voltaïque; Morgenthau gives the name of the group's leader as Zébango Pohi (in *Political Parties*, 419). For more on the Union Voltaïque see Elliott P. Skinner, *The Mossi of the Upper Volta: The Political Development of a Sudanese People* (Stanford, 1964), 179–85.

Larbat felt that he had been treated in bad faith by 'selfish Europeans' who forgot France's humanitarian ideals. The main purpose of his lengthy apologia, however, seems to have been to press his case to be allowed to teach again. In this he was unlikely to succeed, as Governor Mouragues of Upper Volta explicitly opposed such a suggestion in a letter to the Governor-General in April 1949. Mouragues pointed out that Larbat had not taught for eleven years. More importantly, however, he described Larbat as being 'of a difficult character, unstable and bitter', with a penchant for impetuous political activity. As such, Mouragues concluded that a resumption of teaching duties would do no good either to Larbat himself or to the education service as a whole.[69]

These three case studies resemble each other in several key details. Each métis had had minimal contact with his parents; spent his childhood in an orphanage; received some form of advanced training in one of the federal schools in Senegal, leading to employment by the colonial administration; and had sought to acquire French citizenship. Many other métis could have told similar stories, and although it was not possible here to write a satisfactory individual study of any métisses, the case of Albert Larbat's wife suggests that the experiences of mixed-race women were often in many respects not markedly different to those of the men.

These life stories are characterized by a general sense of rootlessness and alienation, both from indigenous society and from the sources of real power in the colonial regime. Admittedly, we cannot know what lay behind Alexandre Diallo *dit* Gauthier's decision to leave Africa and attempt to create a new life for himself in France. However, the search for a sense of belonging and self-worth seems to have been acutely important to métis.

Albert Larbat is a particularly interesting case in this respect. His desire to be recognized as a French citizen does not have to be interpreted as a process of distancing from African society; it might equally be seen as an attempt to remove some of the stigma of illegitimacy which led a French man to call him a 'bastard'. Larbat saw no shame in working with his black African 'compatriots', as he put it, but seems to have decided that he could never truly be 'one of them' any more than the average white colonial official was likely to accept him as French. Governor Mouragues appears to have regarded Larbat as the stereotyped 'unstable' and embittered métis. Here, however, he should be seen as an individual whose upbringing and available options influenced an ongoing series of choices as he tried to assert a measure of control over his life and establish some form of social identity.

A further example of the ambiguities and complexities of individual métis identity is provided by a passage from *Africa Dances*, the English anthropologist Geoffrey Gorer's account of his travels in French West Africa in the early 1930s. In Bamako, Gorer encountered three métis. The first had a Madagascan mother and a Corsican father. Gorer describes him as 'a limpet with a grievance', whose 'pretentiousness and . . . flashy appearance made him intolerable to the Europeans'. The other two métis came from Saint-Louis. One of them, according to Gorer, was 'completely negroid in appearance', and 'identified himself with the negroes'. Gorer reserved his most extensive observations, however, for the second of the two Saint-Louisians:

The younger mulatto, R., seemed physically like a South American with sharp features, wavy hair and café-au-lait skin. He was far too elegant, with a wasp-like waist, and was always dressed in riding clothes with a crop in his hand, as if he had just returned from an (imaginary) polo field. He spoke French with a preciosity of accent which is usually only heard in parodies of the Comédie Française, and took great care to insinuate into the conversation the names of the great and good whose houses he had managed to enter. He had spent several years in Paris in the unavailing attempt to make a good marriage, and had but recently returned to Africa; he had first taken a position in a lawyer's office, for he had wanted to go into politics, but had then transferred to the administration as more stable; he was working in the customs. Before we left he presented us with copies of a pamphlet he had edited about colonial policy; even from the viewpoint of the Action Française it was reactionary, with its repetition of ragged clichés about security, 'la mission civilisatrice française', the A.O.F. as a 'réservoir d'hommes', and panicky about the menace of Bolshevism and Islamism. . . . The mulatto who denies his negro blood fills me with the same kind of disgust as the loyal Jews who protest to Hitler their solidarity with the Nazis.[70]

Gorer's description of 'R.' carries strong echoes of Fanon's portrait of the French West Indian who returns from a journey to France speaking French in an overtly literary or bombastic style. This, writes Fanon, 'is evidence of a dislocation, a separation'. In many respects, 'R.' embodies what Fanon terms the 'massive psychoexistential complex' brought about by 'the juxtaposition of the white and black races'.[71] In his desire to 'turn white', 'R.' has overcompensated to a point where he risks ridicule or abuse.

---

[70] Geoffrey Gorer, *Africa Dances* (2nd edn., London, 1949: first published 1935), 81–2.
[71] See Fanon, *Black Skin, White Masks*, in particular 12–14, 23–5.

On a superficial level, 'R.' appears to be engaging in an exaggerated form of imitation, and, rather like the fictional character of Nini, aspires to the 'inaccessible ideal' of resembling the French. Yet this interpretation misrepresents the reality. 'R.''s choice of clothing and style of speech were not designed to facilitate his entry into French society. Instead, in magnifying certain aspects of French (or European) dress and speech, 'R.' was in the process of creating something new, which went beyond mere 'imitation'. The *hauka* movement, with its ritualized representations of colonial society, has been interpreted as a 'defence mechanism', devised as a response to the crisis posed by colonial rule.[72] A similar interpretation should be possible in the case presented here. This is not to suggest that 'R.' was likely to have done any more than confirm his marginal position in West African society. However, it seems more fruitful to look on the character of 'R.' as emblematic of an unsuccessful attempt to find a satisfactory strategy for survival in colonial society.

The case of 'R.' should not, however, imply that métis were most likely to act as individuals in their search for a viable identity in colonial society. From the 1930s, French West African métis increasingly sought to create a mutually protective space which would enable them to emerge as a social group with shared interests, mediating the ambiguities of social identity through collective action. The most conspicuous examples of this tendency are provided by the *mutualités de métis*. The following section will focus on these organizations.

### THE QUEST FOR A COLLECTIVE IDENTITY

Voluntary associations set up by Africans played an important role in colonial French West Africa. On one level, these associations served a valuable integrative function for migrants to the rapidly expanding urban centres of the federation, particularly after the First World War.[73] More importantly, Michael Crowder has observed that in such associations can be found 'the origins of modern political organisations in French West Africa'. Strict controls imposed by the colonial authorities ensured, however, that until March 1937, when the Popular Front government introduced

---

[72] Fuglestad, 'Les Hauka', 216.
[73] See Michael Crowder, *West Africa under Colonial Rule* (London, 1968), 336–42. The best analysis of the social role of such associations in West Africa is Kenneth Little, *West African Urbanization. A Study of Voluntary Associations in Social Change* (Cambridge, 1965). Also of interest is Claude Meillassoux, *Urbanization of an African Community: Voluntary Associations in Bamako* (Seattle, 1968).

limited freedom of association, such organizations had to avoid any suspicion of political activity to survive. Before 1937, therefore, most were cultural or sporting associations, or represented the interests of a particular ethnic group.[74]

In such a climate, the colonial government in Guinea authorized in 1933 the foundation of the Société de Secours Mutuels des Métis de la Guinée Française.[75] By the end of the decade similar societies had been officially authorized in the Ivory Coast, the French Soudan, Niger, and Togo, the security services having first checked up on those involved.

These associations were at once social groups, charities, pressure groups, and insurance societies. The statutes of the Guinean society illustrate some of the functions served by these organizations. From 1944, when the fees in the founding statutes were revised, it cost 100 francs to join the society, followed by a monthly payment of twenty-five francs. Each member was then entitled to a range of benefits. Members who were unemployed or hospitalized could call upon the society to help pay their upkeep for a period of three or four months respectively. If a member died, the society would contribute to the cost of the funeral; a smaller sum of money was payable on the death of a member's child, 'ascendant', or wife—which suggests that the Guinean *mutualité* at least consisted mainly of men.[76]

In addition to these benefits, the society promised to meet the burial costs when an indigent métis who was not a member of the society died. As such, all métis, whether rich or poor, were deemed to be 'deserving'. In this way, the society was formalizing an inclusive definition of the métis community in Guinea. The philanthropic aspect of the society's work further enabled its members to feel a greater sense of control over their own destinies.[77]

Philanthropy was similarly to the fore in the activities of the Mutualité des Métis du Soudan Français. From the time it was founded in 1937 the society took a special interest in the métis orphanages of the French Soudan. Having been brought up in such institutions themselves—the society's first president, Paul Leroux, had attended the orphanage in Ségou—members knew that boredom was one of the worst aspects of life there. In an effort to tackle the problem of idleness, thought to be a factor in the pregnancies

---

[74] Crowder, *West Africa under Colonial Rule*, 441–3.
[75] *Journal Officiel de la Guinée Française*, 15 July 1933, 414.
[76] Ibid. 15 Dec. 1943, 219; also ANS, FM: 21G 79.
[77] These observations on the significance of charity among métis are partly inspired by Lionel Caplan, 'Poverty and the Culture of Charity Among Anglo-Indians in Madras, S. India', paper presented at the Institute of Social and Cultural Anthropology, Oxford, 24 Nov. 1995.

which caused problems from time to time, the society supplied the orphan-age for métis girls in Bamako with skipping-ropes, balls, and various other games, along with a grant for the creation of a small library. This would enable the replacement of such books as *La Fillette bien élevée*, written in 1902 and described by a school inspector as 'lifeless moralizing' and 'of practically no interest'.[78]

These small-scale charitable acts helped to create new opportunities for the emergent métis community in the French Soudan. By behaving in a manner which visibly conformed to norms of social responsibility valorized by the French, the Mutualité des Métis du Soudan Français was quickly able to forge links with the colonial authorities, the beneficial effects of which almost as rapidly became apparent. In November 1937, for example, Governor Rougier of the French Soudan praised the assistance of the society in finding an acceptable solution to the scandal caused when two métisses became pregnant in the girls' orphanage in Bamako.[79] That same month, as a result of the society's lobbying, the allowance due to the mother of each infant métis too young to be admitted to an orphanage was approximately doubled, from between fifteen and thirty francs per month to fifty francs. In addition, the president of the society was placed on a par with district administrators in being able to recommend people for this allowance.[80]

The Soudanese government, indeed, was sufficiently impressed with the conduct of the society that when the Commission Guernut sent out its survey on the 'métis problem', the Mutualité des Métis du Soudan was given the task of completing the colony's response to the commission's questionnaire. In February 1938, moreover, a delegation from the society (whose membership had risen to eighty-six by 1939) met with Governor-General de Coppet to discuss matters relating to the treatment of métis. There, they were able to express their desire to be able to reach levels of the civil service normally reserved for Europeans.[81] Philanthropy, therefore, can be seen both as an expression and a further cause of the growing social auto-nomy and sense of empowerment of the métis community in French West Africa.

While the *mutualités de métis* cultivated good relations with the French authorities from the outset, their position in relation to black Africans was

[78] ANS, FM: O 685, report on the Orphelinat des Métisses de Bamako, 17 Nov. 1937.
[79] ANS, FM: 2H 1, Gvr. du Soudan français to GG, 16 Nov. 1937, and above, Ch. 3.
[80] CAOM, Commission Guernut 101; ANS, FM: 2H 22, Gvr. Louveau to GG, 19 Aug. 1947.
[81] CAOM, Commission Guernut 101; ANS, FM: 2H 13, Gvr. du Soudan français to GG, 23 Jan. 1940.

less well defined. In 1937, for example, the *mutualité des métis* in the Ivory Coast was campaigning for the re-establishment of an institution for métis boys in that colony. The boys' orphanage in Bingerville had been closed in 1931, since when the children had been living 'à l'indigène'. At this time, the president of the local *mutualité* was none other than Jean Delafosse, the younger of Maurice Delafosse's two sons by his union with Amoïn Kré.[82] In August 1937 Delafosse wrote to the Colonial Ministry, complaining that 'the suppression of the Bingerville orphanage for métis is a real disaster for the future of the race'.[83]

This statement implies that Jean Delafosse, representing the interests of the métis community of the Ivory Coast, thought of métis as a separate 'race', and believed they should be removed in some way from indigenous society to preserve this separateness. His subsequent career suggests that at some point he ceased to make this distinction, as he became increasingly involved in West African politics, eventually becoming the first Minister of Finance when the Ivory Coast gained independence.[84] In the 1930s, however, he was expressing an unease about social relations between métis and other Africans which seems to have been common throughout the early years of the *mutualités de métis*. An example of a similar tendency is provided by the statutes of the Guinean *mutualité*, which offered a grant of 200 francs to any member who contracted a marriage under the French Civil Code with 'a person of the white race or of European ancestry'. Marriages to black Africans were not susceptible to the same rewards; they do not even appear to have been countenanced.[85]

Similar attitudes, albeit with a slightly different cultural origin, existed in the first organization which purported to speak for métis across the whole of French West Africa. The Association Philanthropique des Métis Français en AOF, based in Dakar, was officially recognized in July 1944, taking advantage of a decree of 1943 which restored the freedom of association suppressed under the rule of the Vichy administration in French West Africa.

In November 1946 the association's president, Louis Patterson, a métis from an old Saint-Louisian family, wrote to the Colonial Minister with a

[82] See Ch. 1.

[83] CAOM, Direction du Contrôle 962 dossier 81. A 'Foyer des Métis' was eventually created in 1939, where métis children could be taught, in the words of one inspector, to be 'good and useful citizens'.

[84] For more on the careers of both Jean Delafosse and his brother Henri, see Louise Delafosse, *Maurice Delafosse*, 164.

[85] *Journal Officiel de la Guinée Française*, 15 Dec. 1943, 219.

number of requests. Patterson expressed his unease, for example, at the extension of political representation in Africa, fearing that the 'natives' elected to local assemblies would not approve grants to special homes for métis: 'Are we to cast the métis into the mass of the population after forty years of just and unremitting effort to make of him the self-conscious son of a European?'[86] Nor did Patterson approve of Félix Eboué's influential plan to group métis and black African 'orphans' together;[87] this, he felt, failed to respect the 'human dignity' of métis, who were 'Frenchmen born in Africa'. In short, Patterson played down his 'Africanness' in a manner which recalls the attitudes of the fictional character of Nini. Most of all, he concluded: 'We do not want the fact that we were born in Africa with more or less distant black ancestry to force us to drag around a ball and chain labelled "African".'[88]

In many respects, Patterson exhibits what Cruise O'Brien describes as the 'kind of stilted French chauvinism' of the old mixed-race families of Saint-Louis, an attitude she found still to be prevalent when conducting research there in the late 1960s.[89] Patterson's goals did not reflect those of the majority of métis, who were attempting to develop a new social identity which was more in tune with the realities of post-war West Africa, where Africans were playing an increasingly active political and social role. As such, it is not surprising that Patterson's association soon slipped into inactivity.

In 1949, however, the organization was revived under a new name, the Union des Eurafricains de l'AOF, and with a new mission. The driving force behind this development was Nicolas Rigonaux, a métis in his mid-thirties who had moved to Dakar from Cotonou in Dahomey.[90] The Union des Eurafricains was representative of a much greater number of West African métis.[91] Serving in many ways as an umbrella organization for the local *mutualités*, the Union des Eurafricains created regional sections across French West Africa, and cultivated (with the assistance of the French authorities) links with similar organizations in French Equatorial Africa, Indochina, and Madagascar.[92]

---

[86] CAOM, AP 1194, Patterson to Ministre des Colonies, 6 Nov. 1946; also see ANS, FM: 21G 79, Patterson to GG, 7 Feb. 1946.
[87] See Ch. 3 above.      [88] CAOM, AP 1194.
[89] Cruise O'Brien, *White Society in Black Africa*, 264–5.
[90] See ANS, FM: 23G 23, Lt.-G. du Dahomey to GG, 1 Mar. 1937.
[91] In fact, Rigonaux once complained that 'There are as few bourgeois métis among our number as our membership has honourable fathers'; by 'bourgeois métis', it seems probable that he was referring to the likes of Patterson. See *L'Eurafricain*, 10 (1951), 46; 9 (1950), 12.
[92] See e.g. ANS, FM: 2H 22, Rigonaux to GG, 27 June 1949.

Examples given above suggested that the sense of métis identity vis-à-vis black Africans in the 1930s and early 1940s was characterized by a certain unease. By the time of the foundation of the Union des Eurafricains, however, some of these tensions were beginning to be resolved. Similarly, the burgeoning social identity among the urbanized, comparatively well-educated métis who typically joined the association was more fully developed. Most obviously, the society's decision to refer to métis as 'Eurafricans',[93] a term appearing for the first time, is significant, suggesting a conjoining of identities, and, in the process, the creation of something new. Moreover, while those involved in the society tended to emphasize the primacy of French civilization and culture, this did not in itself involve a denial of 'Africanness'. In a letter sent in May 1949 to all members of the new society, Rigonaux wrote that 'Our case will be that of any assimilable African', thereby identifying métis primarily with the aspirations of other educated Africans; in any event, as he observed in the same letter, as a scattered minority, métis could not hope to separate their fate from the fate of what he called the 'native populations'.[94]

Later that year Rigonaux wrote that: 'A human being cannot belong simultaneously to two races and two civilizations; he must opt for one or the other or sink into the anonymous despair of an individual without social ties.'[95] Rigonaux was admitting, therefore, that there was a choice to be made; the choice, however, was as much between social alienation and some viable form of social identity as it was between 'two civilizations'. Elsewhere, he insisted that 'The métis . . . is not in the least embarrassed by the lack of sophistication of his native kin'. Unlike Patterson, who regarded his African heritage as a 'ball and chain', Rigonaux felt that, if anything, métis were hampered more by 'the ball and chain of illegitimacy'.[96]

One of the statutes of the Union des Eurafricains stated that the society would combat all forms of racial prejudice. The remaining statutes, however, suggest that this was understood in a particular way. The society aimed to ensure that 'French Eurafricans' were treated on equal terms with French people from the *métropole*. It would counsel the African mothers of métis children, to help them to raise and educate their children 'à la française'. Moreover, it would work to maintain among West African métis 'the

[93] The term 'Eurafrican' is not to be confused with the concept of 'Eurafrique' described by John Chipman in *French Power in Africa* (Oxford, 1989), 61–84, though in some respects the parallels may not be inappropriate.
[94] ANS, FM: 2H 22, letter to members of the Union des Eurafricains, 15 May 1949.
[95] ANS, FM: 2H 22.
[96] Ibid., Rigonaux to Haut-Commissaire Béchard, 12 Jan. 1950.

secular feelings of loyalty to France which they have always held'.[97] For Rigonaux, métis were the 'avant-garde of France's civilizing influence'.[98]

In effect, Rigonaux was asking the members of his association to abide by the 'civilizing' ideals of French colonialism more faithfully than had the French themselves. The conduct of métis should, he felt, be 'above all criticism, the more so because we are claiming to act as links between two races'.[99] As suggested earlier in discussing the charitable works of the *mutualités de métis*, the demonstration of social virtues idealized by the French helped to create links to the real sources of power in French West Africa, legitimizing the claims of métis to an identity in elite society.

Rigonaux envisaged métis moving towards 'complete Gallicization',[100] but in saying this he was not denying the possibility that black Africans could do likewise. Nor did this mean that the French were beyond criticism: French men were regularly condemned for their failings (especially as fathers) in the pages of *L'Eurafricain*, the society's journal. In 1957 *L'Eurafricain* reported a complaint from the Mutualité des Eurafricains de la Côte d'Ivoire that 'French Africa is overflowing with *petits blancs* [poor whites] who tarnish the true civilizing face of France'.[101] This was typical of the kind of criticism made by educated Africans of the influx of European workers to post-war French West Africa,[102] but it was the principles by which the French claimed to operate that continued to matter most of all; these principles had been taught in the schools and orphanages attended by métis, and were now taken up as a set of values which helped to structure their lives.

The association functioned with considerable vigour during the early 1950s. Its campaign for the full application of the Civil Code relating to paternity suits in French West Africa met with success, part of one of the society's more general aims to clarify the legal status of métis. Full details were supplied in *L'Eurafricain* of all the pieces of legislation from which métis could benefit. The association helped métis to find work, and through its intervention placed several children in orphanages.[103] It also offered financial assistance to métis for a number of different reasons. In 1951, for example, *L'Eurafricain* provided details of forty-four grants. These were most commonly paid to abandoned métis children or the mothers of métis; there were also several grants for the unemployed and students.

[97] Ibid.     [98] Ibid., Rigonaux to GG, 27 June 1949.
[99] *L'Eurafricain*, 8 (1950), 44.     [100] Ibid. 9 (1950), 12.     [101] Ibid. 24 (1957), 21.
[102] For more on the so-called 'petits blancs' and race relations in post-war French West Africa, see Cruise O'Brien, *White Society in Black Africa*, 66–87.
[103] ANS, FM: 2H 22.

The association met the cost of three burials; made a payment of 15,000 francs CFA 'to the orphanages of the federation', along with 5,000 francs CFA to buy toys for the children in these institutions; and sent a further 5,000 francs CFA to three métis who were receiving treatment in a leprosarium in Bamako.[104] Marriages were celebrated at the headquarters of the association, which was also represented at baptisms and funerals. In short: 'Everything which touches the Eurafrican community becomes a family affair.'[105]

This principle was at work in 1952, when the society created a small home for abandoned children in Dakar. This development was a powerful symbol of the ability of the métis community to take care of itself. In the home, a dozen or so métis boys aged between 5 and 14 benefited from 'the concern of the whole métis family'. Rigonaux and his wife (who themselves had five children) played an active part in the institution, which had many more applicants than available places. Most of the children attended the cathedral school in Dakar. On Sunday, the Catholics among them went to mass. In 1953 the boys celebrated Christmas with métisses from the local home run by the Soeurs de Saint-Joseph de Cluny.[106]

This information, especially in the light of its relation to what could be seen as an attempt to create a model home for métis, would seem to confirm a statement made in an article in *Réveil* in 1947, that 'most métis include the religious component in their conception of the perfect *mulâtre*'.[107] Yet religion barely featured in the pages of *L'Eurafricain*. In fact, the Union des Eurafricains, as proclaimed in its statutes, was a secular organization; its identity did not in any way depend on religious belief. There were, of course, individual métis for whom the Catholic faith especially was important, but in the Union des Eurafricains the French programme of secularization which was so influential in the creation of the first orphanages for métis children appears to have triumphed. The message the society spread to métis across the federation was inclusive and non-sectarian.

The campaigning spirit which pervades the early issues of *L'Eurafricain* dissipated somewhat as the 1950s progressed. Financial difficulties may have been one reason for this; a lack of funds delayed the publication of one issue of the journal in 1957. It was at this time, however, that métis

---

[104] *L'Eurafricain*, 12 (1951), 26–7.    [105] Ibid., no number (Dec. 1949), 5.
[106] Ibid. 16 (1953), 23–5; 17 (1954), 48–50. The orphanage of the Union des Eurafricains was still functioning in 1959, albeit under a new name and in new buildings in a suburb of Dakar (26, 1959).
[107] 'Quelques observations sur "l'essai d'étude sur le problème des métis"', *Réveil*, 13 Jan. 1947.

organizations gained a new dimension, as a 'Congrès International des Métis' was held in Brazzaville in April 1957. Rigonaux was one of twenty-nine delegates to attend this congress, at which there were also represent-atives from the Belgian Congo, Vietnam, and Angola. In August 1957 the Ministry of the Interior authorized a Paris-based organization called the Union Internationale des Métis.[108]

The cover of the final issue of *L'Eurafricain* before independence in 1960 featured a photograph of Mademoiselle Marie Céline, a métisse from Niger who had just been crowned 'Miss Eurafrique'.[109] Her title suggests in many ways a resolution to Nini's dilemma, with standards of beauty now being defined by métis on their own terms, rather than by reference to the European standards to which the character of Nini so desperately wished to conform. As such, Marie Céline might be said to embody the new form of social identity which West African métis had struggled so hard to define.

### CONCLUSION: LE BAL DES EURAFRICAINS

This chapter has shown that a coherent sense of identity among métis in colonial society took time to emerge; moreover, as the case studies pre-sented here suggest, the search for social identity was beset with problems. The case of Albert Larbat, for example, illustrates that it was all too easy for métis to feel socially marginal or even persecuted. The reactionary defence of colonialism offered by 'R.', along with his denial of his 'African-ness', might further be taken to represent what Fanon described as the 'internalization . . . or epidermalization of inferiority'.[110] 'R.''s identity was founded on the desire that his colour might be forgotten in a society where 'whiteness' was (or, at best, seemed to be) an index of power.

At times, métis despaired of ever finding the sense of identity they desired. In 1937, for example, a group of métis from the French Soudan offered, in a letter to the journal *Le Monde Colonial Illustré*, the following 'solution' to their predicament as they saw it:

It is pointless . . . to continue to delude ourselves any longer. Therefore, to sat-isfy the wishes and desires of métis, since all the evidence suggests that nothing of value can be done for them, a decree should be passed formally prohibiting any amorous or conjugal relations between the two races.[111]

---

[108] *L'Eurafricain*, 25 (1958).    [109] Ibid. 27 (1960).
[110] Fanon, *Black Skin, White Masks*, 13.
[111] Letter to *Le Monde Colonial Illustré*, Aug. 1937, 205, from 'Un groupe de métis soudanais' from Bamako.

Other métis, however, did not accept that marginality was their unavoid-
able destiny. By acting collectively in voluntary associations, they were able
to mediate some of the problems of métis identity. Indeed, Paul Leroux,
first president of the Mutualité des Métis du Soudan, strongly criticized
the authors of the letter cited above in a later issue of *Le Monde Colonial
Illustré*, making it clear that they were not members of his organization.[112]

Significantly, Leroux also made a point of contradicting their suggestion
that métis were poorly treated by 'the natives'. The relationship between
métis and other Africans perhaps held the key to the development by métis
of a more satisfactory social identity. The racial 'intermediacy' of métis
had been all but pathologized, the mixture of races thought by the French
and even, apparently, by Africans such as Abdoulaye Sadji, to create unstable 'hybrids'. Gradually, however, métis began to see this mixture as a
positive strength, as symbolized, for example, in the growing use of the
term 'Eurafrican'.

The *mutualités de métis* did more than define the boundaries of the métis
community. Through their charitable activities, they began to appropriate the ideals which the French themselves had used to legitimize their
presence in Africa. This enabled them to create links with the colonial
authorities which proved to be advantageous, allowing métis to claim a role
in elite society.

The success of this strategy can perhaps be seen most clearly in the
account given in *L'Eurafricain* of the ball held by the Union des Eurafricains de l'AOF in Dakar in April 1950. At this function, the president of
the society, Nicolas Rigonaux, spoke proudly of 'our humanitarian and
eminently French activity' before an assembly of dignitaries, both French
and African. High Commissioner Béchard was unable to attend, but a
number of high-ranking colonial officials were present, along with several
other important people, including the American consul in Dakar and Seydou
Nourou Tall, Grand Marabout of the Tijaniyya, the largest Muslim brother-
hood in Senegal.[113] One society member wrote of the evening in *L'Eurafricain* that those who attended the ball 'were not whites, blacks and métis;
they were simply friends from every part of black Africa and France. For
in the Union des Eurafricains, there is one word the meaning of which
we will never understand. That word is "RACISM".'[114]

[112] *Le Monde Colonial Illustré*, Oct. 1937, 248.
[113] Seydou Nourou Tall was a descendant of al-Hajj Umar Tall; he was publicly linked
with Senghor's Bloc Démocratique Sénégalais, having previously backed the Vichy regime
(Morgenthau, *Political Parties*, 147). Another of the guests at the ball was a Mademoiselle
Senghor. High Commissioner Béchard did manage to attend the society's ball in 1951.
[114] *L'Eurafricain*, 8 (1950), 1–8.

The ball of 1950 symbolized the kind of social relations desired by métis in colonial society. Though West African métis were still as likely to be in need of charity as in a position to supply it, and while the members of the Union des Eurafricains could in no way be said to have held any true power in French West Africa, on this evening, to members of the association, it seemed that métis had made their debut in society.

# Conclusion

At the beginning of this book I noted that the amount of attention paid by the French to métis seemed, to some observers, to be out of proportion to the numbers involved. In concluding, we must return to the problem of explaining why this was so.

One of the common strands of this study has been the apparently fluid and ambivalent nature of métis identity throughout the colonial period. This is true both in terms of how the French perceived métis and, as discussed in Chapter 6, in the way métis perceived themselves. Yet this identity—or rather, these identities—were not entirely free-floating.

In her analysis of the links between the psychiatric profession and the legal system in *fin-de-siècle* France, Ruth Harris notes that psychiatric concepts were founded on a number of dichotomies, such as normal and pathological, mind and body, equilibrium and destabilization, and so on. 'These polarities', argues Harris, 'provided the boundaries of scientific debate, containing within them deeper cultural tensions.'[1]

French colonial discourse was constituted on a similar roll-call of Cartesian dualities: the colonizer and the colonized, the civilized and the savage, the modern and the primitive, black and white—the list seems endless. These fixed points circumscribed a less well-defined continuum, where the 'cultural tensions' identified by Harris challenged the dualistic certainties upon which the colonial power sought to base its authority. It is my argument here that métis, the children of empire, embodied the tensions within these dichotomies, providing living proof of the impossibility of sustaining the very basis of colonial domination. It was for this reason that a committed colonialist such as Auguste Terrier should have written, during a visit to the orphanage in Ségou in 1911: 'One feels uneasy watching them.'[2]

The métis population resulted from the first unsustainable separation, that of European men and West African women. In the *métropole*, miscegenation was commonly portrayed as unnatural, and was associated with social destabilization. Particularly in the latter half of the nineteenth century, as argued in Chapter 4, the condemnation of miscegenation often served to conceal a critique of Republicanism, or crystallized French fears

[1] Harris, *Murders and Madness*, 19.
[2] IF, 5940 vol. 1, *carnet de voyage*, entry from 28 Jan. 1911.

of cultural and 'racial' decline. The products of interracial unions were pathologized as unstable, degenerate hybrids. The parallels with the psychiatric dichotomies identified by Harris are not accidental. With their alleged lack of vigour and partial or total infertility, métis were stigmatized as the antithesis of the healthy, productive, fertile citizen. These stereotyped métis characteristics entered the realms of public discourse and proved remarkably resilient, even in times when the fears which had helped to shape them were less acute.

As seen in Chapter 1, however, condemnation of miscegenation was never enough to prevent it from taking place in the colonies. There, the image of the degenerate hybrid threatened at points to unravel the progressive ideology of the 'civilizing mission'. This ideology seemed to be under even greater threat from the reality of the abandonment of large numbers of métis children by their French fathers. The administrator François de Coutouly, for example, warned in 1918 that métis risked becoming 'the palpable and unflattering proof of the hollowness of our great principles, the falseness of our fine theories, the hypocrisy of our so-called civilizing mission'.[3]

The French administration attempted to counteract this threat by placing métis children in so-called 'orphanages'. As was seen in Chapter 3, policy towards the *orphelinats de métis* was in a constant state of flux in the different colonies of French West Africa. These institutions were supposed to remove métis from the milieu of their mothers into a more 'civilized' environment. In practice, however, administrators would sometimes defend poor living conditions in such institutions on the basis that these were the conditions the child would experience later on in life.

The inconstancy of administrative policy towards métis children stemmed partly from a sense of confusion as to their racial identity, and partly under the influence of another dualistic tension, that between the potential auxiliary and the potential *déclassé*. Some French observers regarded the 'intermediacy' of métis as a strength, in the sense that they were thought able to provide a link between French and indigenous society. Others contended that 'intermediacy' in practice meant social isolation, or saw the links between métis and indigenous society as worthy of mistrust. While at certain times métis were encouraged to meet the labour needs of the colonial administration—for example, in the medical profession after the First World War—at other times the authorities in some areas were concerned to avoid over-training métis as these needs contracted. These tensions concealed

---

[3] François de Coutouly, 'Note sur les Métis en A.O.F.', 9.

the unease felt by the French at administering a territory in which they were outnumbered (according to the 1938 census) by approximately 750 to 1.[4]

The eligibility of métis for French citizenship, as discussed in Chapter 5, brought other fears to the surface. The possibility for Africans to acquire French citizenship was a central element in the legitimizing concept of 'assimilation', which itself suggested a break with the traditional dichotomies of colonial rule. In the words of Albert Memmi, indeed, assimilation is 'the opposite of colonization', as it 'tends to eliminate the distinctions between the colonizers and the colonized, and thereby eliminates the colonial relationship'.[5] In practice, however, even the proof of French paternity did not guarantee accession to French citizenship. Métis identity seemed to the French too fluid and ill-defined to justify automatic entry to 'the French City', and threw into relief the limits of the notion of 'assimilation'.

West African métis, therefore, appeared in the interstices of a series of dualistic oppositions. Where the characteristics ascribed to them by the French had varied considerably, métis themselves found it no easy task to define a coherent identity in colonial society. Some métis gravitated to one or other pole, rejecting either the African or the European part of their heritage. As suggested in Chapter 6, however, a section of the métis population began to assert an identity which did not depend on this either/or strategy, and which saw their 'intermediacy', so often stigmatized, as a strength. In doing this, they sought to free themselves from the dualistic shackles of colonizer and colonized, of black and white; to arrive, indeed, almost without knowing it, at a position where the colonial relationship had ceased to exist.

---

[4] See *Le Monde Colonial Illustré*, 184 (Oct. 1938), p. xxix.
[5] Albert Memmi, *The Colonizer and the Colonized* (2nd edn., New York, 1974: first published 1957), 149–50.

# BIBLIOGRAPHY

PRIMARY SOURCES

*(i) Archival Sources*

*Archives Nationales de la République du Sénégal (ANS), Building administratif, avenue Roume, Dakar*
Archives du gouvernement général de l'AOF
  Series G—Politique et administration générale
    Subseries  1G—Études générales
                5G—Côte d'Ivoire
                7G—Guinée
                8G—Dahomey
                9G—Mauretanie
                10G—Haute-Volta
                11G—Niger
                13G—Sénégal
                15G—Soudan
                17G—Affaires politiques
                21G—Police et sûreté
                23G—Etat-civil
  Series  H—Santé et affaires sociales
        J—Enseignement jusqu'en 1920
        M—Justice
        O—Enseignement après 1920

The archives of the federal government of French West Africa are classified in two series. Documents relating to the period before 1920 are indexed in C. Faure and J. Charpy, *Répertoire des archives*, 7 vols. (Rufisque, 1954–5); these documents are also available on microfilm in the Centre des Archives d'Outre-Mer in Aix-en-Provence and at the Centre d'Accueil et de Recherche des Archives Nationales in Paris. Most of series G for the post-1920 period is also now available on microfilm in Aix and Paris, although when the research for this book was conducted the newer material had not been properly organized. I have indicated the post-1920 material in the footnotes with the letters FM (Fonds Moderne).

*Centre des Archives d'Outre-Mer (CAOM), 29 chemin du Moulin Detesta, 13090 Aix-en-Provence*
  Series: Affaires Politiques (AP)
        Commission Guernut

186     *Bibliography*

Conseil Supérieur des Colonies (CSC)
Direction du Contrôle
Série géographique (SG):  Dahomey
Sénégal
Soudan

*Institut de France (IF), 23 quai de Conti, Paris 75006*
Fonds Terrier

*(ii) Printed Primary Sources*

ABOR, R., *Des reconnaissances frauduleuses d'enfants naturels en Indochine* (Hanoi, 1917).
ANFREVILLE DE LA SALLE, Dr D', *Notre vieux Sénégal. Son histoire, son état actuel, ce qu'il peut devenir* (Paris, 1909).
BAROT, L. J., *Guide pratique de l'européen dans l'Afrique occidentale* (Paris, 1902).
BÉRENGER-FÉRAUD, L.-J.-B., *Les Peuplades de la Sénégambie* (Paris, 1879).
—— 'Note sur la fécondité des mulâtres du Sénégal', *Revue d'Anthropologie* (1879), 580–5.
BLACHE, J., *Vrais noirs et vrais blancs d'Afrique au vingtième siècle* (Orleans, 1922).
BLANCHARD, Dr, 'L'École de Médecine de l'A.O.F., de sa fondation à l'année 1934', *Annales de Médecine et de Pharmacie Coloniales* (1935), 90–111.
BONIFACY, Lt.-Col., 'Les Métis franco-tonkinois', *Revue Anthropologique* (1911), 259–66.
BORDEAUX, H., *Nos Indes noires. Voyage en Afrique occidentale* (Paris, 1936).
BROCA, P., 'Recherches sur l'ethnologie de la France', *Mémoires de la Société d'Anthropologie de Paris* (1860–1), 1–56.
—— *On the Phenomena of Hybridity in the Genus Homo*, ed. C. C. Blake (London, 1864).
CARRÈRE, F. and P. HOLLE, *De la Sénégambie Française* (Paris, 1855).
CHIVAS-BARON, C., *La Femme française aux colonies* (Paris, 1929).
—— *Côte d'Ivoire* (Paris, 1939).
CORNEVIN, R., 'Les Métis dans la colonisation française. L'hésitation métisse', college thesis (École Nationale de la France d'Outre-Mer, 1941–2).
CORRE, A., *L'Ethnographie criminelle* (Paris, 1894).
COUTOULY, F. DE, 'La Question des métis en Afrique occidentale française', *La Revue Indigène* (1912), 545–9.
—— 'Note sur les métis en A.O.F.', *Bulletin de la Société des Anciens Élèves de l'École Coloniale* (May 1918), 4–12.
CZAPSKI, Comte DE HUTTEN, Dr HUBRECHT, and Dr DRYEPONDT, 'Rapport sur la question de l'acclimatement des populations de race blanche en pays tropicaux', in Institut Colonial International, *Compte rendu de la session tenue à Brunswick les 20, 21 et 22 avril 1911*, i (Brussels, 1911), 341–436.
DARESTE, P., *Traité de droit colonial* (2 vols., Paris, 1931).

DELAFOSSE M., 'Note relative à la condition des métis en Afrique Occidentale Française', in Institut Colonial International, *Rapports préliminaires* (Brussels, 1923), 78–94.

DELAVIGNETTE, R., *Freedom and Authority in French West Africa* (London, 1950).

DESBIEFS, M., *Le Vice en Algérie* (Paris, 1900).

DESCHAMPS, H., *Roi de la brousse. Mémoires d'autres mondes* (Nancy, 1975).

DUBOIS, F., *Notre beau Niger* (Paris, 1911).

*Enquête coloniale dans l'Afrique française occidentale et équatoriale sur l'organisation de la famille indigène, les fiançailles, le mariage avec une esquisse générale des langues de l'Afrique et une esquisse ethnologique des principales populations de l'Afrique française équatoriale par le Dr. Poutrin* (Paris, 1930).

FAURE, J.-L. (ed.), *La Vie aux colonies. Préparation de la femme à la vie coloniale* (Paris, 1938).

FERRY, E., *La France en Afrique* (Paris, 1905).

FOUILLÉE, A., 'Le Caractère des races humaines et l'avenir de la race blanche', *Revue des Deux Mondes* (July 1894), 76–107.

GIRAULT, A., *Principes de colonisation et de législation coloniale*, 3 vols. (Paris, 1921–30).

GOBINEAU, J.-A. DE, *Essai sur l'inégalité des races humaines*, 4 vols. (Paris, 1853–5).

GORER, G., *Africa Dances* (2nd edn., London, 1949).

GOSSARD, P., *Études sur le métissage, principalement en A.O.F.* (Paris, 1934).

HARDY, G., *Une Conquête morale. L'Enseignement en A.O.F.* (Paris, 1917).

—— *L'Enseignement au Sénégal de 1817 à 1854* (Paris, 1920).

—— *Ergaste, ou la vocation coloniale* (Paris, 1929).

—— 'L'enseignement aux indigènes: possessions françaises d'Afrique', in Bibliothèque Coloniale Internationale, *Rapports préliminaires* (Brussels, 1931), 239–471.

HERVÉ, G., 'Noirs et blancs. Le croisement des races aux États-Unis et la théorie de la "Miscégénation"', *Revue Anthropologique* (1906), 337–58.

—— 'Enquête sur les croisements ethniques', *Revue Anthropologique* (1912), 337–96.

INSTITUT COLONIAL INTERNATIONAL, 'Discussion de la question de l'acclimatement de la race blanche dans les colonies tropicales', in *Compte rendu de la session tenue à La Haye le 2 juin 1909* (Brussels, 1909), 138–87.

JACOBUS X . . . , Dr (pseudonym), *L'Art d'aimer aux colonies* (Paris, 1927).

KEITA, A., *Femme d'Afrique. La Vie d'Aoua Keita racontée par elle-même* (Paris, 1975).

LAYE, C., *L'Enfant noir* (Paris, 1953).

LE BARBIER, L., *La Côte d'Ivoire* (Paris, 1916).

LEVARÉ, A., *Le Confort aux colonies* (Paris, 1929).

LONDRES, A., *Terre d'ébène* (Paris, 1929).

LOTI, P., *Le Roman d'un spahi* (Paris, 1974).

MAIR, L. P., *Native Policies in Africa* (London, 1936).

—— 'African Marriage and Social Change', in A. Phillips (ed.), *Survey of African Marriage and Family Life* (London, 1953), 1–171.

MAIROT, L., 'Les Écoles du Haut-Sénégal et Niger', *Revue de l'Enseignement Colonial* (1905), 129–36.

MARTIAL, R., *Les Métis* (Paris, 1942).

MAZET, J., *La Condition juridique des métis dans les possessions françaises* (Paris, 1932).

MOREAU, P., *Les Indigènes d'A.O.F. Leur condition politique et économique* (Paris, 1938).

MUMFORD, W. B. and G. S. ORDE-BROWN, *Africans Learn To Be French* (London, 1937).

NOGUE, M., 'Les Sages-femmes auxiliaires en Afrique Occidentale Française', *Bulletins du Comité d'Études Historiques et Scientifiques de l'Afrique Occidentale Française*, 2 (1923), 315–51.

PAUCHET, C., 'Le Problème des métis en Afrique', college thesis (École Nationale de la France d'Outre-Mer, 1947–8).

PÉRIER, J.-A.-N., 'Essai sur les croisements ethniques', *Mémoires de la Société d'Anthropologie de Paris*, 2 (1863–5), 261–374.

PHILLIPS, A. (ed.), *Survey of African Marriage and Family Life* (London, 1953).

POIRIER, C., *Manuel-formulaire théorique et pratique sur l'état civil et la nationalité*, 2 vols. (Tananarive, 1936).

POUCHET, G., *The Plurality of the Human Race*, ed. H. J. C. Beavan (London, 1864).

RENAN, E., *La Réforme intellectuale et morale de la France* (Paris, 1871).

ROYER, L. C., *La Maîtresse noire* (Paris, 1928).

SADJI, A., *Nini, mulâtresse du Sénégal* (3rd edn., Paris, 1988).

SARRAUT, A., *La Mise en valeur des colonies françaises* (Paris, 1923).

SAUSSURE, L. DE, *La Psychologie de la colonisation française dans ses rapports avec les sociétés indigènes* (Paris, 1899).

SEABROOK, W., *The White Monk of Timbuctoo* (London, 1934).

SOCÉ, O., *Mirages de Paris* (Paris, 1937).

*Statuts de l'Oeuvre des Enfants Métis Abandonnés* (Saint-Louis, 1932).

THIELLEMENT, A., *Azawar* (Saint-Vaast-la-Hougue, 1949).

VACHER DE LAPOUGE, G., 'La Dépopulation de la France', *Revue d'anthropologie* (1887), 69–80.

VALRIANT, J., *Si blanche sous le grand soleil* (Paris, 1951).

VIGNON, L., *Un Programme de politique coloniale. Les Questions indigènes* (Paris, 1919).


OTHER PRIMARY JOURNALS AND NEWSPAPERS CITED

*Azione Coloniale.*
*Bulletin d'Information et de Renseignements Coloniaux de l'A.O.F.*
*Journal Officiel de la Côte d'Ivoire.*
*Journal Officiel de l'Afrique Française Libre et de l'Afrique Équatoriale Française.*
*Journal Officiel de l'Afrique Occidentale Française.*
*Journal Officiel de la Guinée Française.*

*Journal Officiel du Soudan Français.*
*La Dépêche Coloniale.*
*La Française.*
*La Presse Coloniale.*
*L'Eurafricain.*
*Le Journal des Coloniaux et l'Armée Coloniale Réunis.*
*Le Monde Colonial Illustré.*
*Le Petit Parisien.*
*Les Annales Coloniales.*
*Paris-Dakar.*
*Réveil.*
*Revue des Questions Coloniales et Maritimes.*

SECONDARY SOURCES

ADAS, M., 'Scientific Standards and Colonial Education in British India and French Senegal', in T. Meade and M. Walker (eds.), *Science, Medicine and Cultural Imperialism* (Basingstoke, 1991), 4–35.
AFIGBO, A. E., 'Men of Two Continents: An African Interpretation', in L. H. Gann and P. Duignan (eds.), *African Proconsuls: European Governors in Africa* (New York, 1978), 523–34.
AJAYI, J. F. A. and M. CROWDER (eds.), *History of West Africa*, ii (2nd edn., Harlow, 1987).
—— 'West Africa 1919–1939: The Colonial Situation', in ibid. 578–607.
AJAYI, J. F. A. and J. D. Y. PEEL (eds.), *People and Empires in African History* (Harlow, 1992).
ALBER, J.-L., C. BAVOUX, and M. WATIN (eds.), *Métissages*, ii (Saint-Denis de la Réunion, 1991).
ALBERTAN-COPPOLA, S., 'La Notion de métissage à travers les dictionnaires du XVIIIᵉᵐᵉ siècle', in J.-C. C. Marimoutou and J.-M. Racault (eds.), *Métissages*, i (Saint-Denis de la Réunion, 1992), 35–50.
ANDREW, C. M. and A. S. KANYA-FORSTNER, *France Overseas: The Great War and the Climax of French Imperial Expansion* (London, 1981).
ASSOULINE, P., *Albert Londres. Vie et mort d'un grand reporter, 1884–1932* (Paris, 1989).
BÂ, A. H., *L'étrange destin de Wangrin* (Paris, 1973).
—— *Amkoullel, l'enfant peul* (Arles, 1991).
—— *Oui, mon commandant!* (Arles, 1994).
BALIBAR, E. and I. WALLERSTEIN, *Race, Nation, Class: Ambiguous Identities* (London, 1991).
BALLHATCHET, K., *Race, Sex and Class under the Raj: Imperial Attitudes and their Critics, 1793–1905* (London, 1980).

BARROWS, L. C., 'Louis Léon César Faidherbe (1818–1889)', in L. H. Gann and P. Duignan (eds.), *African Proconsuls. European Governors in Africa* (New York, 1978), 51–79.

BARROWS, S., *Distorting Mirrors: Visions of the Crowd in Late Nineteenth-Century France* (New Haven, 1981).

BENOIST, J.-R. DE, *Église et pouvoir colonial au Soudan français* (Paris, 1987).

BETTS, R. F., *Assimilation and Association in French Colonial Theory, 1890–1914* (New York, 1961).

BIDDISS, M. D., *Father of Racist Ideology: The Social and Political Thought of Count Gobineau* (London, 1970).

BIONDI, J.-P., *Saint-Louis du Sénégal* (Paris, 1987).

BLAIR, D. S., *African Literature in French* (Cambridge, 1976).

BLANCKAERT, C. (ed.), *Des sciences contre l'homme*, 2 vols. (Paris, 1993).

—— (ed.), *Le Terrain des sciences humaines. Instructions et enquêtes (XVIIIᵉ–XXᵉ siècle)* (Paris, 1997).

BLEY, H., *South-West Africa under German Rule 1894–1914* (Evanston, Ill., 1971).

BOUCHE, D., *L'Enseignement dans les territoires français de l'Afrique occidentale de 1817 à 1920. Mission civilisatrice ou formation d'une élite?*, 2 vols. (Paris, 1975).

BOWLER, P. J., *Evolution: The History of an Idea* (Berkeley, 1984).

*Brazzaville. Janvier-février 1944. Aux sources de la décolonisation. Colloque organisé par l'Institut Charles-de-Gaulle et l'Institut d'Histoire du Temps Présent les 22 et 23 mai 1987* (Paris, 1988).

BROOKS, G. E., 'The Signares of Saint-Louis and Gorée: Women Entrepreneurs in Eighteenth-Century Senegal', in N. J. Hafkin and E. G. Bay (eds.), *Women in Africa: Studies in Social and Economic Change* (Stanford, 1976), 19–44.

BRUNSCHWIG, H., 'Louis Gustave Binger (1856–1936)', in L. H. Gann and P. Duignan (eds.), *African Proconsuls: European Governors in Africa* (New York, 1978), 109–26.

BUELL, R. L., *The Native Problem in Africa*, 2 vols. (New York, 1928).

BUSIA, A. P. A., 'Miscegenation and Metonymy: Sexuality and Power in the Colonial Novel', *Ethnic and Racial Studies*, 9 (1986), 360–72.

CALLAWAY, H., *Gender, Culture and Empire: European Women in Colonial Nigeria* (Basingstoke, 1987).

CHAMBERLIN, J. E. and S. L. GILMAN (eds.), *Degeneration: The Dark Side of Progress* (New York, 1985).

CHIPMAN, J., *French Power in Africa* (Oxford, 1989).

CLARK, L. L., *Social Darwinism in France* (Birmingham, Ala., 1984).

COHEN, W. B., *Rulers of Empire: The French Colonial Service in Africa* (Stanford, 1971).

—— 'Literature and Race: Nineteenth-Century French Fiction, Blacks and Africa, 1800–1880', *Race and Class*, 16 (1974), 181–205.

—— 'The French Governors', in L. H. Gann and P. Duignan (eds.), *African Proconsuls: European Governors in Africa* (New York, 1978), 19–50.

—— *The French Encounter With Africans: White Responses to Blacks, 1530–1880* (Bloomington, Ind., 1980).

CONKLIN, A., *A Mission to Civilize: The Republican Idea of Empire in France and West Africa, 1895–1930* (Stanford, 1997).

COOPER, F. and A. L. STOLER, 'Tensions of Empire: Colonial Control and Visions of Rule', *American Ethnologist*, 16 (1989), 609–21.

COQUERY-VIDROVITCH, C. (ed.), *L'Afrique occidentale au temps des français* (Paris, 1992).

COURSIER, A., *Faidherbe 1818–1889. Du Sénégal à l'armée du nord* (Paris, 1989).

CROWDER, M., *Senegal: A Study of French Assimilation Policy* (London, 1962).

—— *West Africa under Colonial Rule* (London, 1968).

CURTIN, P., S. FEIERMAN, L. THOMPSON, and J. VANSINA, *African History* (London, 1988).

DECALO, S., *Historical Dictionary of Niger* (2nd edn., London, 1989).

DELAFOSSE, L., *Maurice Delafosse. Le berrichon conquis par l'Afrique* (Paris, 1976).

DENG, F. M. and M. W. DALY, *'Bonds of Silk': The Human Factor in the British Administration of the Sudan* (East Lansing, Mich., 1989).

DENZER, L., 'Gender and Decolonization: A Study of Three Women in West African Public Life', in J. F. A. Ajayi and J. D. Y. Peel (eds.), *People and Empires in African History* (Harlow, 1992), 217–36.

DEROO, E., G. DEROO, and M.-C. DE TAILLAC, *Aux colonies* (Paris, 1992).

DÉSALMAND, P., *Histoire de l'éducation en Côte d'Ivoire*, 2 vols. (Abidjan, 1983).

DIGEON, C., *La Crise allemande de la pensée française, 1870–1914* (Paris, 1959).

DUMAS, J.-P., 'Effets de la décolonisation sur la nationalité française des métis', *Revue Juridique et Politique, Indépendance et Coopération* (1970), 35–50.

ECHENBERG, M., *Colonial Conscripts: The Tirailleurs Sénégalais in French West Africa, 1857–1960* (Portsmouth, NH, 1991).

EDDY, J. H., 'Buffon's *Histoire Naturelle*: History? A Critique of Recent Interpretations', *Isis*, 85 (1994), 644–61.

FANON, F., *Black Skin, White Masks* (London, 1993).

FUGLESTAD, F., 'Les Hauka: une interprétation historique', *Cahiers d'Études Africaines*, 15 (1975), 203–16.

—— *A History of Niger, 1850–1960* (Cambridge, 1983).

GANN, L. H. and P. DUIGNAN (eds.), *African Proconsuls: European Governors in Africa* (New York, 1978).

GARDINIER, D. E., 'The French Impact on Education in Africa, 1817–1960,' in G. W. Johnson (ed.), *Double Impact: France and Africa in the Age of Imperialism* (Westport, Conn., 1985), 333–44.

GAUCHER, J., *Les Débuts de l'enseignement en Afrique francophone. Jean Dard et l'école mutuelle de Saint-Louis du Sénégal* (Paris, 1968).

GIFFORD, P. and T. C. WEISKEL, 'African Education in a Colonial Context: French and British Styles', in P. Gifford and W. R. Louis (eds.), *France and Britain in Africa* (New Haven, 1971), 663–711.

GOLDIN, I., *Making Race: The Politics and Economics of Coloured Identity in South Africa* (London, 1987).

HAFKIN, N. J. and E. G. BAY (eds.), *Women in Africa: Studies in Social and Economic Change* (Stanford, 1976).

HAILEY, Lord, *An African Survey* (2nd edn., London, 1956).

HARDING, L., 'Les Écoles des Pères Blancs au Soudan français, 1895–1920', *Cahiers d'Études Africaines*, 11 (1971), 101–28.

HARGREAVES, A. G., *The Colonial Experience in French Fiction: A Study of Pierre Loti, Ernest Psichari and Pierre Mille* (London, 1981).

HARGREAVES, J. D., 'Assimilation in Eighteenth-Century Senegal', *Journal of African History*, 6 (1965), 177–84.

—— *France and West Africa: An Anthology of Historical Documents* (London, 1969).

—— 'The European Partition of West Africa', in J. F. A. Ajayi and M. Crowder (eds.), *History of West Africa*, ii (2nd edn., Harlow, 1987), 403–28.

—— *Decolonization in Africa* (Harlow, 1988).

HARRIS, R., *Murders and Madness: Medicine, Law, and Society in the Fin de Siècle* (Oxford, 1989).

HARRISON, C., *France and Islam in West Africa, 1860–1960* (Cambridge, 1988).

—— T. B. INGAWA, and S. M. MARTIN, 'The Establishment of Colonial Rule in West Africa, *c.*1900–1914', in J. F. A. Ajayi and M. Crowder (eds.), *History of West Africa*, ii (2nd edn., Harlow, 1987), 485–545.

HENRIQUES, F., *Children of Caliban: Miscegenation* (London, 1974).

HODEIR, C. and M. PIERRE, *L'Exposition coloniale* (Paris, 1991).

HYAM, R., 'Concubinage and the Colonial Service: The Crewe Circular (1909)', *Journal of Imperial and Commonwealth History*, 14 (1986), 170–86.

—— *Empire and Sexuality: The British Experience* (Manchester, 1990).

JOHNSON, G. W., *The Emergence of Black Politics in Senegal: The Struggle for Power in the Four Communes, 1900–1920* (Stanford, 1971).

—— 'William Ponty and Republican Paternalism in French West Africa (1866–1915)', in L. H. Gann and P. Duignan (eds.), *African Proconsuls: European Governors in Africa* (New York, 1978), 127–56.

—— (ed.), *Double Impact: France and Africa in the Age of Imperialism* (Westport, Conn., 1985).

JONES, S., *The Language of the Genes* (London, 1993).

KAMBOU-FERRAND, J.-M., 'Souffre, gémis, mais marche! Regard d'une paysanne lobi sur sa vie au temps colonial', in G. Massa and Y. G. Madiéga (eds.), *La Haute-Volta coloniale. Temoignages, recherches, regards* (Paris, 1995), 147–56.

KLEJMAN, L. and F. ROCHEFORT, *L'Égalité en marche. Le Féminisme sous la Troisième République* (Paris, 1989).

KNIBIEHLER, Y. and R. GOUTALIER, *La Femme au temps des colonies* (Paris, 1985).

LANGLEY, J. A., *Pan-Africanism and Nationalism in West Africa 1900–1945* (Oxford, 1973).

LARKIN, M., *Church and State after the Dreyfus Affair: The Separation Issue in France* (London, 1974).

LEONARDO, M. DI (ed.), *Gender at the Crossroads of Knowledge: Feminist Anthropology in the Postmodern Era* (Berkeley, 1991).

LITTLE, K., *West African Urbanization: A Study of Voluntary Associations in Social Change* (Cambridge, 1965).

LÜSEBRINK, H.-J., *Schrift, Buch und Lektüre in der französischsprachigen literatur Afrikas* (Tübingen, 1990).

LY-TALL, M. and D. ROBINSON, 'The Western Sudan and the coming of the French', in J. F. A. Ajayi and M. Crowder (eds.), *History of West Africa*, ii (2nd edn., Harlow, 1987), 340–78.

McCLELLAND, J. S., *The Crowd and the Mob: From Plato to Canetti* (London, 1989).

McMILLAN, J. F., *Dreyfus to de Gaulle: Politics and Society in France 1898–1969* (London, 1985).

MANCHUELLE, F., 'Métis et colons: la famille Devès et l'émergence politique des Africains au Sénégal, 1881–1897', *Cahiers d'Études Africaines*, 24 (1984), 477–504.

MANNONI, O., *Prospero and Caliban: The Psychology of Colonization* (New York, 1964).

MARIMOUTOU, J.-C. C. and J.-M. RACAULT (eds.), *Métissages*, i (Saint-Denis de la Réunion, 1992).

MARTINKUS-ZEMP, A., *Le Blanc et le Noir. Essai d'une déscription de la vision du Noir par le Blanc dans la littérature française de l'entre-deux-guerres* (Paris, 1975).

MASSA, G. and Y. G. MADIÉGA (eds.), *La Haute-Volta coloniale. Témoignages, recherches, regards* (Paris, 1995).

MASSIN, B., 'Lutte des classes, lutte des races', in C. Blanckaert (ed.), *Des sciences contre l'homme*, i (Paris, 1993), 127–43.

MAYEUR, J.-M. and M. REBÉRIOUX, *The Third Republic from its Origins to the Great War, 1871–1914* (Cambridge, 1984).

MEADE, T. and M. WALKER (eds.), *Science, Medicine and Cultural Imperialism* (Basingstoke, 1991).

MEILLASSOUX, C., *Urbanization of an African Community: Voluntary Associations in Bamako* (Seattle, 1968).

MEMMI, A., *The Colonizer and the Colonized* (2nd edn., New York, 1974).

MORGENTHAU, R. S., *Political Parties in French-Speaking West Africa* (Oxford, 1964).

MORTIMER, E., *France and the Africans, 1944–1960: A Political History* (London, 1969).

NEMO, G. L., 'Mission et colonisation. Saint-Joseph de Cluny, la première congrégation de femmes au Sénégal de 1819 à 1904', MA thesis (Univ. of Paris I, 1985).

—— 'Les Effectifs des écoles et des orphelinats des Soeurs de Saint-Joseph de Cluny au Sénégal', MA thesis (Univ. of Paris I, 1986).

NEWBURY, C. W., 'The Formation of the Government General of French West Africa', *Journal of African History*, 1 (1960), 111–28.

NEWITT, M., *Portugal in Africa: The Last Hundred Years* (London, 1981).

NYE, R. A., *The Origins of Crowd Psychology: Gustave Le Bon and the Crisis of Mass Democracy in the Third Republic* (London, 1975).

—— 'Degeneration and the Medical Model of Cultural Crisis in the French Belle Epoque', in S. Drescher, D. Sabean, and A. Sharlin (eds.), *Political Symbolism in Modern Europe* (New Brunswick, NJ, 1982), 19–41.

—— *Crime, Madness and Politics in Modern France: The Medical Concept of National Decline* (Princeton, NJ, 1984).

—— *Masculinity and Male Codes of Honour in Modern France* (Oxford, 1993).

O'BRIEN, R. C., *White Society in Black Africa: The French of Senegal* (London, 1972).

OSBORNE, M. A., *Nature, the Exotic, and the Science of French Colonialism* (Bloomington, Ind., 1994).

PAKENHAM, T., *The Scramble for Africa* (London, 1991).

PARTIN, M. O., *Waldeck-Rousseau, Combes, and the Church: The Politics of Anticlericalism, 1899–1905* (Durham, NC, 1969).

PICK, D., *Faces of Degeneration: A European Disorder, c.1848–c.1918* (Cambridge, 1989).

POLÉNYK, M., 'Race pure et "bâtardisation": l'exemple du sud-ouest Africain Allemand. Contexte idéologique et esquisse d'un aspect de la colonisation allemande', in J.-L. Alber, C. Bavoux, and M. Watin (eds.), *Métissages*, ii (Saint-Denis de la Réunion, 1991), 241–52.

PROVINE, W. B., 'Geneticists and the Biology of Race Crossing', *Science*, 182 (1973), 790–6.

RENUCCI, F., *Souvenirs de femmes au temps des colonies* (Paris, 1988).

REYSS, N., 'Saint-Louis du Sénégal à l'époque précoloniale. L'Emergence d'une société métisse originale, 1658–1854', Ph.D. thesis (Univ. of Paris I, 1983).

ROSANVALLON, P., *Le Sacré du citoyen. Histoire du suffrage universel en France* (Paris, 1992).

SABATIER, P., 'Did Africans Really Learn To Be French? The Francophone Elite of the École William Ponty', in G. W. Johnson (ed.), *Double Impact: France and Africa in the Age of Imperialism* (Westport, Conn., 1985), 179–87.

SACKUR, A., 'The French Revolution and Race Relations in Senegal, 1780–1810', in J. F. A. Ajayi and J. D. Y. Peel, *People and Empires in African History* (Harlow, 1992), 69–87.

SADJI, A. B. W., *Abdoulaye Sadji. Biographie, 1910–1961* (Paris, 1997).

SBACCHI, A., *Ethiopia under Mussolini: Fascism and the Colonial Experience* (London, 1985).

SCHAFER, S., *Children in Moral Danger and the Problem of Government in Third Republic France* (Princeton, NJ, 1997).

SCHILLER, F., *Paul Broca: Founder of French Anthropology, Explorer of the Brain* (Berkeley, 1979).

SCHNAPPER, D., *La France de l'intégration. Sociologie de la nation en 1990* (Paris, 1991).

SCHNEIDER, W. H., *Quality and Quantity: The Quest for Biological Regeneration in Twentieth-Century France* (Cambridge, 1990).

SEARING, J. F., *West African Slavery and Atlantic Commerce: The Senegal River Valley, 1700–1860* (Cambridge, 1993).

SIBEUD, E., 'Du questionnaire à la pratique: l'enquête de la Société Antiesclava-giste de France sur la famille africaine en 1910', in C. Blanckaert (ed.), *Le Terrain des sciences humaines. Instructions et enquêtes (XVIIIᵉ–XXᵉ siècle)* (Paris, 1997), 329–55.

SIEDENTOP, L., *Tocqueville* (Oxford, 1994).

SKINNER, E. P., *The Mossi of the Upper Volta: The Political Development of a Sudanese People* (Stanford, 1964).

SPENGLER, J. J., *France Faces Depopulation: Postlude Edition, 1936–1976* (Durham, NC, 1979).

SPITZER, L., *The Creoles of Sierra Leone: Responses to Colonialism, 1870–1945* (Madison, Wis., 1974).

STEPAN, N. L., 'Biological Degeneration: Races and Proper Places', in J. E. Chamberlin and S. L. Gilman (eds.), *Degeneration: The Dark Side of Progress* (New York, 1985), 97–120.

STOCKING, G. W., *Race, Culture and Evolution: Essays in the History of Anthropology* (New York, 1968).

STOLER, A., 'Carnal Knowledge and Imperial Power: Gender, Race, and Morality in Colonial Asia', in Micaela di Leonardo (ed.), *Gender at the Crossroads of Knowledge: Feminist Anthropology in the Postmodern Era* (Berkeley, 1991), 51–101.

—— 'Sexual Affronts and Racial Frontiers: European Identities and the Cultural Politics of Exclusion in Colonial Southeast Asia', *Comparative Studies in Society and History*, 34 (1992), 514–51.

STOLLER, P., *Embodying Colonial Memories: Spirit Possession, Power, and the Hauka in West Africa* (New York, 1995).

TAGUIEFF, P.-A., 'Doctrines de la race et hantise du métissage. Fragments d'une histoire de la mixophobie savante', *Nouvelle revue d'ethnopsychiatrie*, 17 (1991), 53–100.

—— 'La Bataille des sangs', in C. Blanckaert (ed.), *Des sciences contre l'homme*, i (Paris, 1993), 144–67.

THOBIE, J., G. MEYNIER, C. COQUERY-VIDROVITCH, and C.-R. AGERON, *Histoire de la France coloniale*, ii (Paris, 1990).

TIREFORT, A., 'Européens et assimilés en Basse Côte d'Ivoire 1893–1960. Mythes et réalités d'une société coloniale', Ph.D. thesis (Univ. of Bordeaux III, 1989).

TODOROV, T., *On Human Diversity* (Cambridge, Mass., 1993).

TUDESCO, J. P., 'Missionaries and French Imperialism: The Role of Catholic Missionaries in French Colonial Expansion, 1880–1905', Ph.D. thesis (Univ. of Connecticut, 1980).

UWECHUE, R. (ed.), *Makers of Modern Africa: Profiles in History* (2nd edn., London, 1991).

VAILLANT, J. G., *Black, French, and African: A Life of Léopold Sédar Senghor* (Cambridge, Mass., 1990).

WEBSTER, J. B. and A. A. BOAHEN, *West Africa Since 1800* (2nd edn., Harlow, 1980).

WEINSTEIN, B., *Éboué* (New York, 1972).

WHITE, O., 'Miscegenation and Colonial Society in French West Africa, c.1900–1960', D.Phil. thesis (Univ. of Oxford, 1996).

ZELDIN, T., *France 1848–1945*, 2 vols. (Oxford, 1973–7).

# INDEX